CLIMATIC MEDIA

ELEMENTS   *A series edited
by Stacy Alaimo and Nicole Starosielski*

CLIMATIC MEDIA

TRANSPACIFIC EXPERIMENTS IN ATMOSPHERIC CONTROL

YURIKO FURUHATA

DUKE UNIVERSITY PRESS   DURHAM AND LONDON   2022

Library of Congress Cataloging-in-Publication Data
Names: Furuhata, Yuriko, [date] author.
Title: Climatic media : transpacific experiments in atmospheric control /
Yuriko Furuhata.
Other titles: Elements (Duke University Press)
Description: Durham : Duke University Press, 2022. |
Series: Elements | Includes bibliographical references and index.
Identifiers: LCCN 2021022481 (print)
LCCN 2021022482 (ebook)
ISBN 9781478015192 (hardcover)
ISBN 9781478017806 (paperback)
ISBN 9781478022435 (ebook)
Subjects: LCSH: Weather control—Social aspects—Japan. |
Weather control—Technological innovations—Environmental
aspects—Japan. | Digital media—Environmental aspects—Japan. |
City planning—Environmental aspects—Japan. | Weather control—
Social aspects—United States. | Weather control—Technological
innovations—Environmental aspects—United States. | Digital
media—Environmental aspects—United States. | City planning—
Environmental aspects—United States. | BISAC: SOCIAL SCIENCE /
Media Studies | HISTORY / Asia / Japan
Classification: LCC QC928 .F878 2022 (print) | LCC QC928 (ebook) |
DDC 304.2/5—dc23
LC record available at https://lccn.loc.gov/2021022481
LC ebook record available at https://lccn.loc.gov/2021022482

Cover art: Clouds. Courtesy Enrique Estrada/EyeEm and Getty Images.

Duke University Press gratefully acknowledges the William Dawson
Scholar Fund at McGill University, which provided funds toward the
publication of this book.

It is a small wonder that this book is finally complete. Writing this book was at turns delightful and difficult, as the project kept expanding. I waded through an ever-expanding sea of documents, chasing clouds of enchanting thoughts one after the other. Over the past decade, many people have helped me navigate through this path that led to the book's current form.

I want to begin by expressing my sincere gratitude to Yatsuka Hajime, whose pathbreaking research on the imperial roots of Tange Lab and Metabolism and their interests in future planning inspired me to develop my own analysis of these architects. I also extend my gratitude to Arata Isozaki and Associates and Tange Associates and Kawasumi Akio Office for their generous permission to reproduce images.

I had the fortune of working with my wonderful editor Courtney Berger and Elements book series coeditors Nicole Starosielski and Stacy Alaimo. I owe special thanks to Nicole, whose enthusiastic support for this project helped me reshape this book at the final stages of writing. I am also grateful to the two generous reviewers of the manuscript who offered incisive comments and suggestions that undoubtedly helped broaden the book's potential readership.

I also want to add my special thanks to Weihong Bao and Orit Halpern, two friends whose intellectual generosity and shared excitement in thinking about media and the environment provided constant inspiration over the course of writing this book. I was lucky to find a vibrant community of kindred spirits among the members of various reading groups that I participated in over the years, and I thank Thomas Pringle and Derek Woods in particular. I am also incredibly fortunate to have so many brilliant and supportive colleagues at McGill University in the Departments of East Asian Studies and Art History and Communication Studies, and I want to especially thank Darin Barney, Carrie Rentschler, and Jonathan Sterne for reading drafts of several chapters at different stages of their developments. Thanks also go to the generous mentors and friends who offered encouragement, advice, and support along the way: Rey Chow, Wendy Hui Kyong Chun, Mary Ann Doane, Bishnupriya Ghosh, Lynne Joyrich, Akira Mizuta Lippit, Karen Redrobe, and Bhaskar Sarkar.

Huge thanks go to all my delightful friends with whom I often shared my quirky research interests and other fun aspects of life in Montreal and beyond: Clemens Apprich, David Baumflek, Luca Caminati, Michelle Cho, Kimberly Chung, Kay Dickinson, Megan Fernandes, Gal Gvili, Tomoko Komatsuzaki, the late Christine Lamarre, Thomas Lamarre, Rahul Mukherjee, Joshua Neves, Ara Osterweil, Nelly Pinkrah, Masha Salazkina, Will Straw, Jeremy Tai, Alanna Thain, Teresa Villa-Ignacio, Mike Zryd, and my dear "Brown gang" friends, including David Bering-Porter, Roxanne Carter, Melissa DiFilippi, Joshua Guilford, Ani Maitra, Pooja Rangan, Julie Levin Russo, Tess Takahashi, Michael Siegel, and Braxton Soderman.

Thank you also to colleagues and friends who kindly invited me to give talks, to participate in workshops and other collaborative occasions over the years, offering generative feedback and warm encouragement at these events: Lisa Åkervall, Peter Bloom, Craig Buckley, James Leo Cahill, Rüdiger Campe, Francesco Casetti, Nadine Chan, Alenda Chang, Aleena Chia, Steve Choe, Hyunjung Cho, Steven Chung, Zeynep Çelik Alexander, Heather Davis, Noam Elcott, Victor Fan, Jennifer Fay, Michael Fisch, William Gardner, Bernard Dionysius Geoghegan, Thomas Gaubatz, Aaron Gerow, Shūzō Azuchi Gulliver, Lisa Han, Gō Hirasawa, Mél Hogan, Hikari Hori, Erkki Huhtamo, Tung-Hui Hu, Erin Huang, Mayumo Inoue, Brian Jacobson, Kajri Jain, Melody Jue, Ayako Kano, Kara Keeling, Brian Larkin, Lawrence Lek, Jie Li, Reinhold Martin, Shigeru Matsui, Debashree Mukherjee, Livia Monnet, Patrick Noonan, Dan O'Neill, Jeremy Packer, Weixian Pan, Anne Pasek, Lisa Parks, Jussi Parikka, Raffaele Pernice, John Durham Peters, Franz Prichard, Ying Qian, Paul Roquet, Julian Ross, Rafico Ruiz, Miryam Sas, Jeff Scheible, Pooja Sen, Sarah Sharma, Ayesha Vemuri, Janet Walker, Haidee Wasson, Kenneth White, Soyoung Yoon, Tomiko Yoda, and Alexander Zahlten.

I also want to thank Susan Albury, William Page, and Sandra Korn for their assistance through the production process; Celia Braves for crafting the index; and all the wonderful copyeditors who have read this manuscript at various stages: Colin Crawford, Nicolas Holt, Brent Lin, and

Jacqueline Ristola. I also have been fortunate to have had the chance to share my research interests with brilliant graduate and undergraduate students who took various iterations of my "Media and Environment" seminars offered at McGill. Thank you for thinking outside the box with me.

This book was made possible with the support of my families on both sides of the Pacific. Heartfelt thanks go to my mother, whose unshakable curiosity about the wonders of the world I share; to my sister, whose tenderness and strength I admire; to my nephews, who I hope will one day read my work; to my in-laws, whose kindness keeps me warm even in Montreal winters; and to my father, who passed away at the early stage of this project. It was my father's utter silence about his childhood spent during and after the war on the Japanese-occupied and then Soviet Union–occupied Sakhalin Island that nudged me to consider more closely Japan's settler colonial projects in cold climate regions. Last but not least, this book would not have been finished, or even started without the day-to-day care, constant encouragement, and astute feedback of my amazing partner Marc Steinberg, who may have been secretly worried about the meandering directions that my research took over the years, but always kept a bright smile on his face and cheered me on.

The pandemic that hit toward the end of writing this book revealed another layer of the ongoing explication of the atmosphere through technology. Although this event is not directly reflected in the book's analysis of air-conditioning, ventilation, indoor weather, or the tracking and monitoring of populations, its contemporary resonance will hopefully be palpable to its readers. I am grateful to have received and witnessed much kindness, solidarity, mutual aid, and empathy during these uncertain times.

The research conducted for this book was supported by the William Dawson Scholar Fund at McGill University and a SSHRC Insight Grant from the Canadian government.

An earlier version of chapter 1 appeared as "The Fog Medium: Visualizing and Engineering the Atmosphere" in *Screening Genealogies: From Optical Device to Environmental Medium*, edited by Craig Buckley, Rüdiger Campe, and Francesco Casetti (Amsterdam: Amsterdam University Press, 2019), and sections of chapters 3 and 5 have appeared in my chapter "Tange Lab and Biopolitics: From Geopolitics of the Sphere to the Nervous System of the Nation" in *Beyond Imperial Aesthetics: Theories of*

Art and Politics in Japan, edited by Steve Choe and Mayumo Inoue (Hong Kong: University of Hong Kong Press, 2019); my chapter "Architecture as Atmospheric Media: Tange Lab and Cybernetics" in *Media Theory in Japan*, edited by Marc Steinberg and Alexander Zahlten (Durham, NC: Duke University Press, 2017); and my article "Multimedia Environments and Security Operations: Expo '70 as a Laboratory of Governance" in *Grey Room* 54 (winter 2014): 56–79.

All translations from Japanese sources are mine unless otherwise noted.

Summer in Asia can be unbearably hot and humid. The rising air temperature in metropolitan cities like Tokyo in the middle of summer makes you duck into shopping malls and underground metro stations, and grasp for handheld miniature fans. A wearable air conditioner that you can slip into the back pocket of a customized T-shirt, which you control with a virtual thermostat on your smartphone app, is apparently the next big thing.[1] As the planet keeps heating up and extreme weather wreaks havoc on our cities, we crave more portable air-conditioned bubbles to carry with us and more climate-controlled shelters to inhabit.

Albeit at an immensely larger scale and by different mechanisms, the desire to cool down the atmospheric bubble in which we inhabit animates the discourse on planetary climate engineering. While we breathe mechanically filtered air and keep our bodies cooled inside air-conditioned houses and offices with the help of computational media such as smartphone apps, the use of solar radiation management to enhance the reflective capacities of clouds to block incoming sunlight and thus cool down the planet is gaining traction among scientists, engineers, and investors. The same thermostatic desire to build microclimates around us and to regulate Earth's macroclimate through geoengineering is increasingly defining the relationship between media and climate that we encounter in our daily life.

This desire for atmospheric bubbles controlled by a virtual thermostat has historical and geopolitical roots. The aim of this book is to trace these roots by offering a media studies perspective on a transpacific genealogy of atmospheric control with emphasis on the legacies of Japan's imperial expansionism and its Cold War alliance with the United States.[2] Central to this story are the crucial roles played by Japanese scientists, architects, and artists in developing and shaping the technologies and media infrastructures used today to monitor and modify both local weather and planetary climate. Climate engineering is interpreted broadly in this book to mean not only planetary-scale geoengineering but also the modification of microclimates within controlled and enclosed environments, such as a laboratory, a greenhouse, or an air-conditioned building.

Some of these technologies of engineering indoor climates are simple cooling devices, such as fog-based air conditioners, which are now part of the infrastructure of cloud computing. Others involve more complex simulation models and chemical reactions as in the case of numerical weather prediction, cloud seeding, and tear gas. These technologies directly "condition" and alter Earth's atmosphere, albeit at different scales. Conditioning the atmosphere by means of these technologies targets the physicochemical composition of the air, which in turn creates microclimates that affect the behavior or "conduct" of people and things. Conditioning air and conditioning people are two sides of the same operation. As Daniel Barber aptly writes in his analysis of modernist architecture's use of the façade and shades, "Air conditioning is people conditioning."[3] Additional technologies of atmospheric control discussed in this book work through signals in the air and on the ground, as in the case of networked systems of computing and surveillance designed for the purpose of the social conditioning of urban populations. All of these are forms of atmospheric control that operate through the mediation of what I will call, in this book, *climatic media.*

The genealogy of climatic media offered in this book thus covers a range of experiments, from the modification of natural weather in the sky and the production of artificial weather inside built environments to the transformation of urban infrastructures filled with systems of ambient intelligence, smart sensors, cameras, and sometimes clouds of tear gas. By connecting dots and nodes across seemingly distant histories of architecture, atmospheric science, digital computing, and environmental art on both sides of the Pacific, I analyze how media became articulated with climates, and trace climatic operations of media through various technologies and techniques of atmospheric control. Emerging at different historical moments, these media aim to manipulate the atmosphere and exert (or at least aspire to exert) a calculated control over both the environment and the lives within it. Together, they express what I call *thermostatic desire*, a technophilic desire to posit atmosphere itself as an object of calibration, control, and engineering.

This thermostatic desire manifests in both geopolitical and biopolitical motives to secure a livable future environment, either through engineering the atmosphere itself, or engineering built structures to protect certain populations from (and threaten others with) an increasingly inhospitable atmosphere. Engineering of the atmosphere often operates as a means of geopolitical and biopolitical governance. More broadly, the atmosphere and its elements incorporated into climatic media also speak to modern anxieties not only about nature itself—limited resources, increasingly extreme natural weather events, rising sea levels, and warming temperatures—but also about the technologies used to mediate, control, or secure a habitable environment.

To follow Peter Sloterdijk's well-known provocation, the twentieth century is marked by a paradoxical process of "explicating" and instrumentalizing the taken-for-granted background givenness of the atmosphere.[4] First with aviation and the use of poison gas, and later with the weaponization of weather and radioactive fallout from atomic bombs during both World War II and the Cold War, technology made explicit (and thus explicated) the question of security as the central focus of territorial control over the atmosphere. With the rise of greenhouse effects and anthropogenic climate change, this territorial understanding of the atmosphere has also yielded to the planetary awareness of Earth's atmosphere as the limits of the habitable environment. The deepening climate crisis poses an existential threat for the future. By way of response, scientists, engineers, policy makers, and others fall back on a reframing of Earth's gaseous envelope via a territorial logic of governance, which began in the mid-twentieth century.

To analyze this process of atmospheric explication from the perspective of media studies, I highlight different ways in which technological conditioning and engineering of indoor and outdoor atmospheres operate as climatic media. My use of the term *climatic media* is in part inspired by the discussion of making climate change legible through the mediation of thermal imaging, photographs, charts, diagrams, and other instruments of data visualization in the field of architecture.[5] In addition to technical images, which make climatic fluctuations legible, I suggest that we need to expand the referential scope of climatic media more broadly, in the following two senses.

First, we can expand the definition of media to include the materiality of elements that condition our milieu. These include natural elements such as fog, snow, and rain as well as chemical elements and compounds such as silver iodide, nitrogen, and phosphorus. My rationale for this comes in the wake of recent turns to environmental studies, infrastructure studies, media ecology, media archaeology, and so-called German media theory within North American media studies.[6] These reorientations of media studies to move beyond conventional media objects (e.g., film, radio, television, telephone, the internet, and social media) push us to rethink our assumptions about media primarily as tools, channels, and platforms of recording, storage, broadcasting, telecommunicating, and data processing. As John Durham Peters suggests, the natural elements of weather can also be considered "sky media," as the sky has been historically aligned with timekeeping technologies such as the clock and the calendar.[7] Building on these recent elemental approaches in media studies (about which I will say more shortly), I pay close attention to the materiality of natural and chemical elements in my genealogical exploration of climatic media.

Second, I suggest that we expand the definition of media to include the architectural, scientific, and artistic techniques and technologies of producing climate-controlled bubbles and modifying weather. These techniques and technologies work as media that actively mediate and shape what counts as a habitable environment and for whom it appears livable. But habitability is only one part of the story that the following chapters tell. This story of climatic media also includes meteorological experiments such as site-specific modifications of weather by scientists, architects, artists, and militaries. My argument is that intertwined experiments in indoor climate engineering, weather modification, and networked computing in Japan and the United States during World War II and the Cold War played a key role in the later development of the techniques and technologies of building air-conditioned bubbles, which have become an integral part of the critical infrastructures of our contemporary cities.

As David Gissen and others have suggested, the conception of architecture as "a conditioned space" is quite modern.[8] Studying architecture from the standpoint of producing comfort through air-conditioning is also well established. Reyner Banham, for instance, analyzed modernist architecture through its mechanisms of ventilation, air-conditioning, and illumination in his classic work *The Architecture of the Well-Tempered Environment* (1969).[9] More recent studies of air-conditioned spaces further explore the political, environmental, and economic consequences of designing "well-tempered" environments that ostensibly increase the comfort and productivity of those inside them. From British colonial houses in the tropics to gentrification in American cities (the latter intensified by the air-conditioned interiors of commercial buildings), these studies collectively suggest that climate design has been central to the history of modern architecture.[10]

This book addresses a similar set of concerns but does so with different takeaways in mind. I foreground the imperial roots of Japanese architecture through the work of Tange Lab architects, including those associated with the internationally renowned postwar architectural movement of Metabolism. In particular, I examine their experiments with architectural techniques and technologies of climate engineering in the form of capsule houses and shelters, some of which were designed to withstand extreme weather conditions in Antarctica and the Arctic.

I also read these architectural experiments in relation to meteorological experiments with fog, snow, and rain undertaken by Japanese scientists and artists. The work of the physicist Nakaya Ukichirō—known as the inventor of the world's first artificial snow crystal as well as being an expert on ice, snow, and frost formations—offers one point of scientific anchorage for my inquiry. The Low Temperature Science Laboratory and the Institute of Low Temperature Science at Hokkaidō University, which he established in the 1930s, helped advance research on cryospheric and atmospheric science. Japanese researchers at the laboratory observed and studied the impacts of fog, snow, frost, and ice on farmlands, railroads, housing, and military aircraft. Some of their studies were meant to directly aid Japanese colonial settlements in Manchuria in the 1940s and were later consulted by architects who designed capsule housing for Antarctic expeditions in the 1950s.

The cryospheric and atmospheric research conducted by scientists at the Institute of Low Temperature Science also aided Nakaya Fujiko, Nakaya Ukichirō's daughter and environmental artist known for her exquisite fog sculptures. Moreover, these scientific, architectural, and artistic experiments with weather and climate had institutional and personal ties to North American counterparts as well. These transpacific affiliations and connections span across diverse groups and institutions in the United States, including Experiments in Art and Technology and the Snow, Ice, and Permafrost Research Establishment. Tracing these interdisciplinary arcs, which traverse the Pacific, is like following winds and storms that blow across state borders. It is this spirit of the atmospheric circulations of air that inspires my transpacific approach in this book.

Just as climate design matters to architecture, temperature matters to media. As Nicole Starosielski argues, precise control over temperature at the elemental level of manipulating minerals and metals is crucial for the construction and maintenance of analog and digital media. These minerals and metals are mined, cooked, refined, and homogenized in order to ensure the consistent performance and smooth operation of such media. From the mining of coltan used for smartphones to the purification of copper and silica used for cable networks, thermal manipulations of minerals and metals are integral to our contemporary media conditions.[11]

The elemental conditions of media can also affect the atmospheric bubbles we create and carry around with us. To take a banal example, think of our portable sonic milieu. On extremely cold days, the tiny connector between my iPhone and earphones often stops working as I walk through snowy streets listening to music, bursting the ambient sonic bubble that I had created around me. Such a technological breakdown is a subtle reminder that elemental conditions materially affect the performance of digital media objects. Their optimal performance also relies on other material conditions, such as the extraction and processing of rare earth minerals and metals, which generate toxic by-products and contribute to polluting water, air, and soil. These chemical elements, too, operate as media in their capacity to serve as an intermediary agent of action and as a milieu that surrounds us.

Recently, scholars across disciplines in the humanities and social sciences have turned their eyes to the capacious concept of *element* and developed new materialist, post-phenomenological, and ecocritical approaches to studying relations between human and more-than-human actors. These elemental modes of thinking cover a diverse body of research, some of which treat elements along the lines of the classic primary matter in Greek philosophy (air, water, fire, and earth), while others turn to the molecular compositions of fossils, plastics, and chemical pollutants.[12]

Within the field of media studies, scholars such as Nicole Starosielski, John Durham Peters, Jussi Parikka, and Jennifer Gabrys have called attention to the material and infrastructural reliance of our media objects on the technological manipulation of elements—from laptops to fiber-optic cables. They urge us to rethink the production, distribution, and operation of technical media in relation to various elements, such as natural weather, metals, minerals, and chemical compounds.[13] My approach to climatic media similarly foregrounds the mediating functions and affordances of natural and synthetic elements, which form the material basis of architectural enclosures and air-conditioning systems that operate as climatic media.

The elemental approach to media that takes material relations and performances of matter seriously is echoed in the study of atmosphere and atmospherics in the fields of cultural and human geography. For instance, Peter Adey draws on the Greek philosophy of classic elements, in particular the element of air and the alchemic metaphor of elemental affinities, to propose an interdisciplinary method of studying "an elemental geography of air." For him, air is as much a primary matter as an affective relation. In dialogue with the works of Ben Anderson and Derek McCormack among others who approach atmosphere relationally, Adey proposes thinking of elements as preindividual tendencies toward structures of feeling, shaped by the geopolitical, economic, and philosophical interests of the time.[14] Other scholars, such as Andreas Philippopoulos-Mihalopoulos and Mark Whitehead, have approached the question of atmosphere in relation to the juridical and governmental practices of partitioning space and instituting laws and civic norms.[15]

A contrasting discourse on atmosphere is found in the field of marketing, where atmospherics is discussed as a retail design practice that aims to manipulate consumers' emotional states and encourage them to purchase products through the use of ambient effects, such as sound, smell, and lighting.[16] Within the field of Japanese media studies, Paul Roquet has taken up this marketing practice of atmospherics to analyze how an ambient factor, such as the background music of Muzak, functions as "a tool of atmospheric mood regulation" and an instrument of neoliberal subjectivization. The simple act of listening to a personally curated playlist in order to motivate oneself to get through the day, for instance, works as a somatic technique of the self.[17]

The growing body of literature on atmosphere and atmospherics explores the affective and sensorial dimensions of atmosphere and their attendant techniques of the self. My approach, by contrast, puts less emphasis on the affective and sensorial processes of subjectivization and focuses instead on the intersections of scientific, architectural, and artistic deployments of the physical atmosphere. I do so in order to analyze the transpacific context of climatic media in the twentieth century with an eye toward the lingering legacies of Japanese imperialism and the Cold War.

While my approach to atmospheric control takes a different path than the body of literature that foregrounds the affective, subjective, and sensorial understanding of atmosphere and atmospherics, it shares an understanding of atmosphere as both meteorological and social, as well as geophysical and political. Indeed, this duality of atmosphere is why I present atmospheric control as a double process of conditioning: *air-conditioning* and *social conditioning*.[18] Both forms of atmospheric control require climatic media as their conduits and means of governing, managing, regulating, and optimizing the movements of elements and lives.

The meaning of atmospheric control is hence twofold. On the one hand, it is about controlling atmospheric phenomena in order to create site-specific microclimates, such as the aesthetic use of artificial fog to create a responsive environment, the weaponization of hurricanes, and the use of artificial fog to cool down data centers. On the other hand, I use the term *atmospheric control* to mean the instrumentalization of built environments and ambient factors such as light, sound, temperature, and humidity for the purpose of policing and managing the circulations of bodies that move through these environments.[19]

A banal example of atmospheric control as an instrument of social conditioning is the deployment of infrasound to keep people and mosquitoes away. Infrasound is allegedly being used by convenience stores in order to deter teenagers from loitering at their storefronts. This experimental use of infrasound for the purpose of deterrence targets the demographic group of youth; a certain range of high frequencies are only audible by young people, and as we grow older we lose our hearing capacity for these frequencies.[20] Such preventive uses of ambient elements like infrasound on humans and insects has increased along with the proliferation of sensors, meters, and surveillance cameras that track down and monitor the movements of the urban population, a situation that has become pervasive in recent smart city initiatives.

More relevant to this book is the example of McDonald's strategic use of hard, uncomfortable seats and overly cold air-conditioning inside their restaurants to discourage customers from remaining too long. Air temperature here works as an atmospheric means of social conditioning, ensuring the continual and fast-paced circulation of customers in and out of the building.[21] An even more obtrusive case of atmospheric control for the explicit purpose of regulating the conduct of people occurs with the use of tear gas for urban policing. Tear gas is a much more harmful form of outdoor air-conditioning that is also a means of social conditioning. Conditioning of the atmosphere is thus part of what Michel Foucault calls the modern regime of governmentality, which operates through the "conduct of conduct," governing people and things by nudging, guiding, leading, and controlling the manner in which they behave.[22] Accordingly, I use the term *conditioning* to mean modifying, habituating, training, acclimatizing, and altering states of being. The processes of atmospheric control that operate at the levels of physical air and social conduct, I argue, are enabled and mediated by a variety of technologies that I heuristically call climatic media. The operations of atmospheric control mediated by climatic media target both the physical air as well as the conducts and behaviors of those who inhale or inhabit such an altered atmosphere.

CULTURAL TECHNIQUES AND ELEMENTAL PHILOSOPHIES

One way to analyze how atmospheric control works through the double process of air-conditioning and social conditioning is to look at specific technologies as they mediate, demarcate, and articulate different actors, objects, and milieus. Here, it is important to keep in mind that these technologies as well as the cultural techniques associated with them are both culturally and historically situated.

The work of the German media scholar Bernhard Siegert provides a useful framework for examining how the nonmechanical techniques as well as technologies of atmospheric control can operate as forms of climatic media. The methodological approach of studying media through the lens of "cultural techniques" (*Kulturtechniken*) often goes by the label German media theory. Like elemental philosophy, this German school of media studies, with its orientation toward archaeology and anthropology, affords a methodological opening to expand the conceptual scope of media.

Media broadly understood as cultural techniques—in addition to machine-based technologies—can encompass humble mediating devices, such as the door and the wall, as Siegert has noted. The built interface of the house provides the technical conditions of possibility for the operation of the symbolic separation between nature and culture, inside and outside, sacred and profane, and other binary distinctions that structure our daily lives.[23] In a predictably post-structuralist manner,

Siegert argues that these binary symbolic distinctions are constantly undone through the intermediary cultural techniques of media themselves. His reliance on structural binaries notwithstanding, a useful takeaway from Siegert's account of cultural techniques is that the technical operation of media is both material and symbolic. The door-as-media, for instance, physically lets something or someone pass through it, as much as it symbolically demarcates the inside from the outside.[24]

Siegert's media archaeological theory of cultural techniques has some methodological limitations, however. As Weihong Bao persuasively argues, Siegert's theory of media reproduces certain colonial assumptions of early cultural anthropology and archaeology about non-Western cultures.[25] With such critique in mind, this book traces the transpacific context of specific techniques and technologies of atmospheric control. I adopt this media archaeological approach to cultural techniques with caution, in no small part because my investigation of climatic media is concerned with the imperial and colonial ambitions that use architecture and science as a means of expanding geopolitical spheres of influence by certain states and empires, including the former Japanese Empire.

As I elaborate more in later chapters, the architectural techniques and technologies of building walls and roofs to construct greenhouses, domed cities, and spaceship-like capsule houses, in fact, have much in common with the modern imperial projects of biopolitically managing habitats and the human populations within them. Like crops and plants grown inside greenhouses, humans have been managed and fostered inside climate-controlled environments. Seemingly innocuous agricultural metaphors that dominate the contemporary vocabulary of geoengineering (e.g., *seeding* clouds with silver iodide particles) also suggest how agricultural techniques for cultivating crops have inspired geoengineering technologies for cultivating rain. Like the plants on the land, the clouds in the sky are seen as cultivable, as if the weather can be tended, fertilized, and harvested like terrestrial vegetation. These agricultural analogies of cultivation point to underlying epistemic assumptions and cultural expectations that accompany the operations of atmospheric control. To read such operations through the media theoretical lens of cultural techniques thus means to attend to the assumptions behind these analogies.

With the advent of digital computers used for weather forecasting and other future-oriented predictions, techniques and technologies for cultivating weather have advanced and converged with techniques and technologies for designing and constructing air-conditioned computer rooms and data centers. Read alongside earlier colonial practices of building shelters and greenhouses, these climate-controlled "houses" for computers present a variation of the same thermostatic desire. Computers, like humans and plants, need to be sheltered (and cultivated if we follow this analogy) inside architectural bubbles that offer temperate climates. German media theory's take on cultural techniques, in short, enables me to take this methodological move to explore architectural techniques of air-conditioning and geoengineering technologies of weather modification as genealogically linked yet divergent forms of climatic media.

To explain this methodological move, let me turn to another anecdote of air-conditioning in Asia. This anecdote illustrates how the element of wind and its technical manipulation may be analyzed from the perspective of media studies. In my visit to Hong Kong one summer, I was struck by what appeared to be an odd sight. Many of the city's highrise apartment complexes and skyscrapers showed fairly large holes in their middle sections. What I heard was that in accordance with local lore and the feng shui (literally, "wind and water") principle of not cutting off good energy flows, these holes let mythical dragons fly through the buildings. It turns out that these stunning architectural features have the more pragmatic effect of ventilating air in an otherwise densely built urban environment. Combined with engineering knowledge, these dragon holes help air-condition the island by creating breezeways to let the tropical air circulate.[26]

For Peters, rethinking techniques of controlling natural elements like air and wind requires a philosophy of elements such as the Greek philosophy of primary matter (earth, water, air, and fire).[27] But these mythical dragons slip through the epistemological grid of Greek elemental philosophy, as they follow the Chinese philosophy of five elements, or more precisely, five elemental phases: wood, fire, earth, metal, and water. To commit to fully philosophizing elemental media within media studies requires accounting for different cosmological and epistemological lineages of understanding what we mean by the term *element*, while paying particular attention to the conditions in which such elements are manipulated in attempts to control them. Historically and culturally situated studies of elemental media invite us to think about elemental philosophies in a more comparative framework and to probe the epistemological basis of elements themselves.[28]

This is not, however, a simple call to think elemental philosophies comparatively beyond the Western cosmological paradigm of Greek philosophy. Nor do I suggest that we need an Eastern cosmology of elemental media based on the philosophy of five phases. After all, there are myriad local interpretative differences, historical transformations, and political appropriations of feng shui (a geomantic art that developed as an imperial practice in ancient China). Unlike Hong Kong and Singapore, where it still exerts some influence on urban design, the Communist government in mainland China banned it as superstition. In Japan, feng shui found its popular application in designing the interior spaces of domestic architecture, rather than locating auspicious sites for ancestral graves or designing harmonious cities as it was originally intended.[29]

More importantly, to analyze the so-called dragon holes in Hong Kong buildings solely through the cosmological or philosophical framework of elements and primary matter is to overlook the important fact that they are not simply built for the cosmological movement of mythical creatures or, more precisely, the auspicious energy that they represent. They are also designed for ventilating the tropical air. In this case the philosophy of elements (be it Greek or Chinese) alone cannot offer a full picture of the architectural technique for ventilating air by creating breezeways in the middle of high-rise buildings. Analyzing this cultural technique of controlling atmospheric phenomena within urban space as a problem of engineering the air, in short, prompts us to pivot away from the philosophical understanding of elemental control and toward a historically situated set of skills, technologies, and knowledges.

Furthermore, neither Greek nor Chinese philosophy can explain the epistemic basis of cloud seeding, a chemically induced technology of controlling weather. Operationalized in the 1950s, the modification of weather by seeding clouds with chemical compounds such as silver iodide theoretically allowed one to artificially induce rain. Geoengineering through chemistry, mediated by the scientific knowledge of modern meteorology, has supplanted ritualized forms of rainmaking. With the rise of cloud seeding, *chemical* elements have become the direct medium of controlling the *natural* elements of weather.

Meteorology became the modern science of weather only after its object of study moved away from a wide range of "meteors" in the classic sense. It henceforth became the science of weather devoid of rituals and omens wherein the atmosphere was an object of laboratory experiments and scientific measurements. Before the rise of modern meteorology, technical attempts to modify weather were closely aligned with cosmological and religious interpretations of atmospheric and celestial phenomena. In Europe, for instance, various phenomena in the sky—not just weather but also comets, eclipses, and even earthquakes—were generally called meteors. Such meteors were interpreted as prophetic omens and messages from the gods and divine entities.[30] In Japan, like other parts of East Asia, folk rituals for rainmaking similarly called upon dragon gods and other divine figures. Weather modification was the domain of rituals, and its operation was not yet technologized.

Crucial to the epistemological shift in emphasis from extraordinary meteor to ordinary weather "was a removal of phenomena from a *spatially* defined region to a *physico-chemically* defined body of air" in the late eighteenth and early nineteenth centuries.[31] Ordinary weather became a scientific object of prediction only after the epistemological reorientation of the atmosphere took place. Meteorological phenomena were no longer explained by mystical interactions between the indivisible elements of air and water in the celestial and sublunary regions, but by Earth's gravity, barometric pressure, and molecular interactions among chemical elements such as oxygen and hydrogen in the atmosphere.

The chemical wonder of cloud seeding to bring artificial rain, unlike rainmaking rituals, presupposed a different cosmological outlook on meteorological conditions, as it aimed to technologically control and modify weather.[32] Since the mid-twentieth century, chemically induced rainmaking has been popular in many parts of East Asia and Southeast Asia where the lore of dragon gods associated with rainmaking rituals and the philosophy of five elemental phases once explained meteorological wonders. Like the United States and Japan, China was one of the early experimenters of cloud seeding.[33] Today, China continues to carry out localized weather modification projects and invests heavily in geoengineering research.[34]

Similarly, Japanese hydroelectric companies have financed a number of weather-modification experiments to increase rainfall since the 1950s. Armed with dry ice and airplanes that spray clouds with silver iodide particles, these modern-day rainmakers have conjured chemically seeded clouds in the sky instead of offering supplication to the dragon gods. Japanese scientists have also long contemplated the possibilities of climate engineering. Take, for instance, a proposal to barricade the Drake Passage by the Japanese physicist and futurologist Higuchi Keiji (who unsurprisingly was also a student of Nakaya Ukichirō). Higuchi proposed a speculative project of engineering the planetary climate by building a gigantic dam made of ice near Antarctica to alter the direction of ocean currents. Higuchi, an expert on snow and ice science, presented his vision of this "iceberg dam" at the International Conference on Future Research in 1970. His aim was to develop computational models for long-term climate change by thinking through this hypothetical use of icebergs as building materials to create a dam to alter the cold ocean currents flowing from Antarctica to the Japanese archipelago.[35]

At the basis of such a proposal to geoengineer the planet was the cybernetic vision of controlling the planet's imaginary thermostat through feedback loops. This demonstrates a crucial shift from the merely chemical understanding of weather modification to a cybernetic model of geoengineering. Arguably, the epistemological parameters of controlling weather shifted once again: from chemistry to cybernetics.

The discourse of cybernetics hence played a significant role in bridging scientific, architectural, and artistic experiments with artificial weather. Along with systems theory, it not only influenced the futurological vision of climate engineering but also urban planning and design practices in Japan, much as it did in the United States.[36] Dreams of modifying the weather and rerouting ocean currents were fostered in relation to cybernetics. The cybernetic logic of feedback also found its application in architecture and urban design in the mid-twentieth century. While national defense experts associated with think tanks such as the RAND Corporation introduced the view of the city as a cybernetic system to the field of urban planning in the United States, it was Tange Lab and Metabolist architects (some of whom were ardent "futurologists") who helped bring cybernetics and systems theory into urban design in Japan. The connections across futurology, cybernetics, and systems theory that led to proto-smart city experiments, including little-discussed visits by Norbert Wiener to Japan, will be explored in later chapters.

These futuristic dreams of geoengineering the planet and regulating cities as cybernetic systems were in large part prompted by the exponential increase in access to digital computers, which made it easier to simulate climate change and urban developments.[37] Since the 1950s and 1960s, both meteorology and urban design have been mediated by computers. With the increased reliance on numerical computational models and global networks of satellites, sensors, and supercomputers supported by enormous communication and energy infrastructures (not the least of which are air-conditioned data centers), weather prediction has moved far away from reading the sky for signs and interpreting weather charts. Architects and urban planners have also changed their outlook on cities. One of the goals of this book is to explore how digital computers and cybernetics brought together the seemingly distant fields of atmospheric science and architecture.

TRANSPACIFIC GEOPOLITICS OF CLIMATE

If the planetary scale of climate geoengineering is put into practice, the results will be unevenly distributed; some countries and regions will benefit more while others will suffer more severe droughts, floods, and heatwaves. Engineering of the planetary climate is increasingly seen as "the 'whose-hand-on-the-thermostat' problem."[38] Given there will be no evenly distributed climate across the planet, the question of who gets to program and moderate this geoengineering thermostat remains deeply problematic and is a source of geopolitical tensions as well.

To think about climate is therefore to think about geopolitics. In fact, modern geopolitical thinking was always already climate dependent. That is to say, climate is geopolitical not only because of pragmatic concerns of international regulations over carbon emissions, geoengineering, and climate refugees (though these are certainly important). Climate is also geopolitical because of the historicity of the notion of *climate* and how it has been mobilized in direct support of imperial and settler colonial projects.

In its basic sense climate means the average weather conditions of a particular geographical zone; it has always been integral to the modern discipline of geography. And modern geography started as an imperial science, which shared a climatically determinist view of culture with philosophy and meteorology.[39] Studies of settler colonialism and imperialism have shown that the challenges posed by harsh and unfamiliar climate conditions prompted European settlers, explorers, geographers, architects, and engineers to develop various techniques and technologies of acclimatization. These strategies of acclimatization, including air-conditioning, were often discussed and framed in the climatically determinist discourse of culture and race.[40]

In the nineteenth century, as Japan was developing as a fledgling empire, the climatic determinism that informed Euro-American settler colonial practices also found its home there. From the northern islands of Sakhalin and Hokkaidō, the homeland of the Indigenous Ainu people, to Taiwan, Manchuria, and the Pacific Islands, Japanese colonial administrators, along with scientists and architects, sought a means of acclimatizing settlers and transforming the climatic conditions of the occupied territories of the Japanese Empire.[41]

For one salient example of Japanese climatic determinism, which was in tune with the state project of empire building, let me briefly turn to the work of the Kyoto School philosopher Watsuji Tetsurō. His well-known analysis of the existential connection between climatic zones and ethnonational characters in *Climate and Culture* (*Fūdo*, 1935) draws heavily on and echoes the language of Euro-American discourses on climatic determinism. As Roquet notes, Watsuji viewed the self-understanding of one's existence as always mediated through one's "affective relationship with the larger climate." A nation's climate also forms the basis of a shared sense of belonging: "Because everyone is shaped by the weather together, Watsuji argues, and (he implies) all shaped *in the same way*, atmosphere can be understood as the original force that ties a nation together."[42] It is this affective process of subjectivization that Roquet links to neoliberal technologies of mood regulation.

In the context of this book, what interests me most about *Climate and Culture*, however, is not Watsuji's theorization of subjectivity, but his turn to a set of texts written by German and Swedish geopoliticians. Starting with the late eighteenth-century German philosopher Johann Gottfried von Herder's coinage of the term *Klimatologie* (climatology), Watsuji reviews the work of the founding figures of German geography including Friedrich Ratzel and Rudolf Kjellén, the latter of whom coined the term *Geopolitik* (geopolitics). Watsuji discusses their geopolitical theory of the state "as a living organism" that naturally propels itself toward expanding its living space (*Lebensraum*) at length.[43] Given the fact that some of the texts he discusses were published just a few years before Watsuji's own work, it is not surprising that, as a philosopher who positioned himself as an interlocutor and critic of Martin Heidegger, Watsuji actively engaged with the latest German scholarship in the late 1920s and early 1930s. The intellectual exchange between the two fascist states—Germany and Japan—is indeed central to the analysis of Japan's wartime discourse on geopolitics that I develop in later chapters.

Watsuji's work also demonstrates that the modern conception of geopolitics is inseparable from climate determinism. This geopolitical view of the state as a living organism heavily influenced the Japanese architectural experiments to expand the living sphere. Architectural experiments with climate-controlled buildings and their views of cities as living organisms, undertaken by renowned architects associated with Tange Lab (including the Metabolist group) before and during the Cold War, exemplify this geopolitical undertone of atmospheric control as expressed in the field of architecture.

In the 1950s and 1960s, thinking about climate became geopolitical in another sense. It was then that the studies of radioactive fallout caused by nuclear weapons testing reshaped the field of atmospheric science. Global wind patterns were mapped, and ecological and biomedical data of the devastating effects of radiation were collected at testing sites. The United States deliberately chose the Marshall Islands in the Pacific, inhabited by the Indigenous people of the islands, as its nuclear weapons testing site (among other locations) for their presumably insular ecosystem. Atmospheric research on radiation and ecosystem theory then led to the new vision of an integrated planetary biosphere.[44]

It was also during the Cold War that the weaponization of weather control was operationalized (before it was subsequently banned), and the fear of a nuclear winter informed the work of atmospheric chemists such as Paul Crutzen, who later popularized the notion of the Anthropocene and proposed geoengineering as a technological solution to the anthropogenic climate crisis in the 2000s. As Jairus Victor Grove suggests, the concept of the Anthropocene developed by Crutzen and others involved in the debates on nuclear winter during the Cold War is geopolitical through and through.[45] For this reason, I contend that we need to conceive geopolitics broadly in order to account for the ecological dimensions of the *geo-* (literally, "earth"), while keeping in mind that the interests of states have shaped scientific knowledge production in the fields of ecology and atmospheric science.

These broader trends in scientific knowledge production concerning climate and atmosphere are tied to Japan's geopolitical reorientation over the course of the twentieth century. The early decades of the twentieth century witnessed Japan's imperial and colonial project of expanding its living sphere into Northeast Asia, Southeast Asia, and the Southern Pacific. This project relied on various techniques and technologies of infrastructure building such as telecommunications and railroad networks, enlisting myriad collaborations among architects, scientists, and engineers. After the end of World War II, Japan lost its overseas colonies but forged a close geopolitical alliance with the United States. The transpacific geopolitics of the region in the mid-twentieth century is heavily marked by the Cold War period. My exploration of climatic media therefore foregrounds technologies of engineering the atmosphere, including fog dispersal, computerized weather forecasting, and geoengineering in the form of weaponized hurricanes. Technologies of inventing artificial weather phenomena such as artificial snow, fog, and storms were often developed in direct service to expanding human habitats in otherwise inhospitable environments as well as maneuvering in battlefields during the Cold War. This was an era when modifying natural elements such as weather and climate became the direct object of national security, territorial expansion, and military science.

In sum, the genealogical analysis of climatic media in this book is oriented around Japan and its geopolitical relationship to the United States. I embrace this position in order to counter the often default assumption that Europe and North America are the global center of media history. By insisting on the transpacific dimension of climatic media, I also depart from the more nation-centric approach to media that is still dominant in area studies.[46] As Lisa Yoneyama reminds us, "Conjunctive critique of the transwar, transpacific connections not only helps us see that the US Cold War Empire cannot be effectively framed as a critical analytic unless the midcentury relationship with Japan is simultaneously scrutinized. It also necessitates a critique of knowledge production about Japan's colonial empire and what its imperializing practices meant varyingly to modernity, race, and visions for the new world."[47]

Highlighting the significance of the transpacific traffic between Japan and the United States also means that we look at geopolitics as relational dynamics of power played out between nation-states bent on expanding their spheres of influence, territories, and securing their national borders while struggling to control the weather and other atmospheric phenomena that elude these borders. Yet, unlike the geopolitical concept of territory, tropical cyclones, heatwaves, the polar vortex, and snowstorms are borderless like the ocean currents that circulate around the globe. A similarly mobile analysis is therefore needed to track these weather phenomena and the technological attempts to contain and cultivate them.

CHAPTER OUTLINES

To unpack this transpacific geopolitical context that gave rise to various technologies of atmospheric control, the first two chapters of the book focus on the artistic and scientific productions of artificial weather, tracing the inventions and developments of artificial snowflakes, cloud seeding, digital computing, and numerical weather prediction in Japan and the United States. The next two chapters are organized around the architectural experiments of designing climate-controlled and air-conditioned bubbles such as capsule housing and domed cities, and how these experiments are mediated by biopolitical and cybernetic conceptions of organisms and their environments. The final chapter brings together the geopolitical context of the Cold War and the cybernetic approaches to atmospheric control by analyzing tear gas and networked surveillance as intertwined technologies of air-conditioning and social conditioning. Expo '70, Japan's first World's Fair in 1970, offers a connecting thread through the chapters, since many of the engineers, artists, and architects analyzed in this book participated in this fair, which functioned as a social laboratory where various technological experiments with air-conditioning, climate engineering, networked computing, ambient surveillance, and crowd control were executed.

Focusing on the nexus between environmental art, atmospheric science, and cloud computing, chapter 1 traces a genealogy of what I call *site-specific weather control*. Urban infrastructures such as energy grids, fiber-optic cables, air ducts, water pipes, thermostats, and computer systems are all affected by and anticipate the effects of outdoor weather. The recent attempts to use fog and snow as cooling elements for data centers' air-conditioning systems offers an entry point to rethink how weather became articulated with cloud computing. The institutional and technological conditions that connected environmental art to atmospheric science and cloud computing in the 1950s and 1960s offer a useful lens through which to understand how atmospheric control over weather phenomena became integrated into the geopolitical alliance between Japan and the United States during the Cold War.

In order to trace this genealogy of site-specific weather control, I turn to an exquisite work of fog sculpture by Nakaya Fujiko. Foregrounding the institutional nexus between her invention of fog sculpture and the work of her father, Nakaya Ukichirō, who invented artificial snowflakes, this chapter unfolds the artwork's lineage back to the earlier practice of visualizing atmospheric phenomena such as air currents on the one hand, and to the later practice of engineering the atmosphere, including the weaponization of weather, on the other. In so doing, this chapter grounds the book's inquiry into climatic media, analyzing how artificial weather became part of the infrastructure of cloud computing.

Following this connection between artificial weather and digital computing, chapter 2 examines the transpacific context of numerical weather prediction and futurology. Central to my analysis is the material reliance of future forecasting and weather forecasting on the infrastructure of air-conditioning. The argument of this chapter is that the computational prediction of the future relies on artificial climatization. The operationalization of numerical weather prediction was contingent upon cooling down computer rooms at the research institutes where these early experiments of computerized weather forecasting took place. The production of indoor artificial weather by mechanical air-conditioning systems was hence integral to the prediction of outdoor natural weather.

By unpacking the epistemological claims behind futurology and its utopian embrace of digital computing, this chapter also situates thermostatic desire in relation to the territorial understanding of atmospheric futurity. This way of imagining the atmospheric future, moreover, is what drives the ongoing acceleration and intensification of hyperlocalized weather forecasting and smart air-conditioning today. Thus, I end this chapter with an examination of the territorializing impulse that undergirds atmospheric control.

After mapping how weather forecasting, weather control, and air-conditioning work together to posit the atmospheric future as an object of computing and engineering, in chapter 3 I turn to architecture as climatic media. My argument is that architectural techniques and technologies of building walls and roofs, including those for computer rooms and data centers, function as media of atmospheric control. To ground this investigation of architectural techniques and technologies of atmospheric control, I trace the imperial roots of Tange Lab, the internationally celebrated center of Japanese architectural experimentation in the mid-twentieth century. The goal of this chapter is to situate architecture as climatic media within the transpacific geopolitics of Japan's colonial history and its subsequent Cold War alliance with the United States. With this context established, this chapter narrates the desire to colonize and territorialize hitherto inhospitable environments through architectural techniques and technologies of creating atmospheric bubbles. These architectural bubbles, I argue, operate as greenhouses for human inhabitants.

More specifically, chapter 3 delves into the geopolitical discourse of expanding the empire's living sphere toward cold climate regions. In so doing, this chapter tracks the same territorializing impulse—running from Tange Lab architects' proposals to build capsule housing and domed cities in Antarctica and the Arctic to contemporary examples of similarly domed bubbles such as Amazon's Spheres, the tech company's signature headquarters building in Seattle. Paying close attention to the wartime geopolitical understanding of organisms and their living spheres—the view of territoriality that informed architectural design—I analyze how thermostatic desire works across differently scaled and imagined territorial "spheres."

Chapter 4 turns to Tange Lab affiliated Metabolist architects' use of petrochemical products, in particular plastics, as their building materials. I take their design of prefabricated "capsules" as a point of departure to analyze how capsule architecture as climatic media elucidates current debates on the petro-economy, climate change, and planetary geoengineering. My argument is that atmospheric control through climatic media is often imagined as scalable, and thus applicable to the smaller units of capsule houses and space capsules, as well as to the larger units of cities and even the entire planet. To unpack this fantasy of scalability at the core of Metabolist capsule architecture exemplified by the work of Kurokawa Kishō, I focus on the ecosystem analogy of Earth as a spaceship (i.e., "Spaceship Earth") that gained traction among architects, economists, and scientists in the late 1960s. Once it was imagined as a gigantic space capsule covered with its atmospheric shell, Earth emerged as an object of technological intervention, namely, geoengineering. This imagination of the planetary capsule has recently returned with vigor amid contemporary debates on the Anthropocene.

In order to clarify the relevance of Metabolist architecture to the current discourse on geoengineering, this chapter zooms in on the central metaphor of *metabolism* that Metabolist architects used as their group's namesake, a metaphor they borrowed from the work of Marx and Engels in order to highlight their ecological vision of capsules and megastructures as living organisms. Read alongside the more recent Marxist ecological theory of the "metabolic rift" and debates on the Anthropocene, the ecological undertones of Metabolist architecture present an ecological dilemma of sustainability: they aspire to produce sustainable architecture, and yet their reliance on plastics and their petro-economic financing undermine their aspiration at the material level. I suggest that current debates around geoengineering, such as the seeding of the stratosphere with sulfur dioxide particles to bring down the temperature of Earth's atmosphere, exemplify similar ecological and ideological dilemmas.

After unfolding these transpacific genealogical affinities among the developments of computing, architecture, and climate engineering in earlier sections of the book, chapter 5 turns our attention to the (geo) political stakes of atmospheric control from the confluence of two types of climatic media used to condition and govern urban populations: tear gas and networked surveillance. Tear gas and networked surveillance emerged as twin strategies of urban policing in the mid-twentieth century on both sides of the Pacific as street-based protests against state-sanctioned racism, the Vietnam War, and the Japan-US Security Treaty unfolded in urban spaces. Here, I trace the intersecting lineages of these policing tactics, as tear gas descended directly from earlier military uses of poison gas, and networked surveillance anticipated the proliferation of ambient sensors in the urban environment. Analyzing how these two forms of climatic media developed simultaneously to police, monitor, and manage the movements of urban populations, this chapter also brings us back to atmospheric control's reliance on computation.

Tear gas and networked surveillance work together to condition air and people. The genealogical development of air-conditioning and social conditioning performed by these media, I suggest, comes into view when read through what I call "the cybernetic turn" of architecture and urban design. Put differently, the genealogical threads of digital computing and future forecasting established in earlier chapters return here through the lens of cybernetics. More specifically, this chapter traces crucial connections between the American cybernetician Norbert Wiener and Japan. Following this transpacific nexus between Japanese and American cybernetic discourses, I then explore how the logics of cybernetics became part of networked surveillance, which then paved the ground for later experiments with smart urbanism.

In the conclusion, I offer a reflection on my own genealogical method of analyzing climatic media by considering the similarity between the critical act of explication and the failure of infrastructure. I also briefly discuss the historicity of ecological metaphors in relation to the methodological approach known as "media ecology."

Together, these chapters track the parallel and intertwined historical developments of digital computers, atmospheric science, and architectural and artistic experiments. In doing so, this book moves genealogically across multiple fields of inquiry, unearthing hidden affinities among different actors and institutions. Connecting the dots from the past to the present thus assists us in making sense of the ongoing—and intensifying—investment in techniques and technologies of manipulating the atmosphere to suit human needs.

From the transformation of artificial fog from an artistic medium that shapes a responsive environment to an infrastructural means of cooling data centers (chapter 1); from the birth of numerical weather prediction and regional air-conditioning to the rise of hyperlocalized weather prediction using artificial intelligence and smart air-conditioning that individually curate air flows (chapter 2); from the imperial project of expanding the living sphere of the Japanese Empire as a living organism to the Silicon Valley dream of space settlements (chapter 3); from the early application of plastics to make Metabolist capsules to the current proposal to geoengineer the stratosphere to cool down Earth's atmosphere (chapter 4); and from the earlier use of tear gas and networked surveillance to police urban populations to the contemporary use of microsensors, trackers, and other data collecting devices that form our increasingly smart urban infrastructures (chapter 5); each of these chapters reads the past as the historical a priori of the present we live in.

This present we inhabit is marked by both intensifying climate instability and media connectivity. We are living through the time of climate crisis and the option of geoengineering is now back on the table or at least debated earnestly as a supposedly viable means of mitigating the impact of global warming. If engineering a personally curated atmospheric bubble by a wearable air conditioner is one response to current climate conditions, the other pole is the planetary cooling of the atmosphere through technologies of geoengineering. Both are technophilic responses to the rising temperature of our lived environment. In the meantime, we continue to feed data to and live with a proliferating number of smart media devices that operate in the predictive mode of anticipating our moves and desires in a constant feedback loop. This is the mode of atmospheric futurity whose genealogies this book tracks.

In sum, to analyze atmospheric control through the lens of climatic media means to follow and unpack these elemental, material, infrastructural, and geopolitical loops that bind media to climate. It is to this task of tracing such loops that I now turn.

Fogs, as the Japanese environmental artist Nakaya Fujiko once noted, are clouds that descend onto Earth.[1] These earthly clouds, or at least their artificial counterpart, have become an infrastructural element of contemporary air-conditioning facilities, including those inside data centers. When we walk around the city of Tokyo on hot summer days, we also find tiny nozzles spouting misty water vapors to cool down storefronts and train stations. Similar air-conditioning devices that generate artificial fogs are installed inside hidden pipes of data centers to cool down computers, quietly safeguarding our daily use of cloud computing.

Operating these data centers that support the metaphorical "cloud" of data is quite energy intensive. As Jennifer Holt and Patrick Vonderau put it, "If the cloud were a country, it would have the fifth largest electricity demand in the world."[2] The regulation of temperature, humidity, and circulation of air is integral to the operation of this metaphorical cloud. Data centers in search of sustainable and low-cost electricity are hence relocating to cold climate regions, such as Norway, Iceland, and

Canada, to use the naturally cool temperature outside to cut down on their air-conditioning costs inside.[3] Several venture capitalists and tech companies in Japan are also exploring the potential of recycling summer snow in northern cities such as Bibai and Ishikari in Hokkaidō to cool down data centers. The idea is to cover a mountain of leftover snow from the winter with insulating materials to keep it from melting and use it to refrigerate the water that runs through cooling pipes buried below the mountain before it circulates inside these data centers.[4]

Unpacking a transpacific geopolitical context of site-specific weather control, this chapter explores how technological manipulations of atmospheric phenomena such as snow and fog became articulated with the material infrastructure of cloud computing, including the air-conditioning of data centers. Instead of focusing on energy grids, fiber-optic cables, air ducts, water pipes, thermostats, and computer systems that make up various components of this infrastructure, however, I focus on a genealogical connection between weather control and environmental art. My argument is that understanding this connection allows us to read the geopolitics of cloud computing in a new light.

In order to trace this genealogy of site-specific weather control, I first turn to the dual functions of fog as both a screening device and as an atmospheric phenomenon in its own right. A focal point of this genealogical investigation is Nakaya Fujiko's fog sculptures. Nayaka's work was first presented as an integral component of the Pepsi Pavilion at Expo '70, an event designed by the artist and engineer collective Experiments in Art and Technology (E.A.T.) to which she belonged. This exquisite artwork stands out as both a pioneering work of Japanese environmental art and a salient example of climatic media.

Consisting of water-based artificial fog, softly concealing the outer shell of the dome-shaped pavilion, this delicate sculpture bridges artistic and scientific lineages of controlling atmospheric phenomena such as fog, clouds, mist, smoke, and rain. In what follows, I argue that an environmental artwork such as Nakaya's fog sculpture not only participates in what Peter Sloterdijk has called the process of "atmospheric-explication"—a process that transforms the taken-for-granted givenness of the environment into an explicit object of manipulation—but also links the history of art to the history of science and technology.[5] Read through this framework of atmospheric explication, the fog sculpture appears as more than a mere device for visual obfuscation, and serves as a means of calling attention to the larger historical processes of studying and controlling atmospheric phenomena. An exploration of this work also allows us to trace the genealogical background of artificial fog and its entanglements with warfare, cloud seeding, and geoengineering.[6]

The work of fog sculpture, I suggest, serves as a unique point of convergence between two heterogeneous lines of descent: the practice of *visualizing* atmospheric phenomena such as air currents, in which fog serves as a projection and camouflage screen, on the one hand; and the practice of *engineering* the atmosphere, including weather control that artificially produces fog, rain, and snow, on the other. The aim of this chapter is to investigate how and why these lines of descent intersected at a specific moment through an interdisciplinary group of artists, scientists, and engineers coming from Japan and the United States, whose political alliance was cemented during the Cold War. Seen from this geopolitical perspective, the historical timing of the fog sculpture matters a great deal. For the invention of artificial fog as an artistic medium is inseparable from the geopolitical conditions of the twentieth century in which the atmosphere was articulated with and as technical media.

VISUALIZING THE ATMOSPHERE: ART

Before turning to the fog sculpture at the Pepsi Pavilion, I want to briefly summarize the ways in which fog, and cloud-like substances in general, have long functioned as screening and visualizing devices. With the invention of electric light, clouds in the night sky became a medium of telecommunication. The nineteenth century witnessed an increased desire to reach the sky and turn clouds into a surface for projection. Clouds thus became a medium of "celestial projection," a surface for projections that ranged from flashing Morse code for military communication, to illuminated letters and pictures for commercial advertisements. In one such experiment with "cloud telegraphy," a large mirror was used to bounce electric light as projected signals onto clouds. Some inventors such as Amos Dolbear even imagined that weather forecasts could one day be "given by a series of flashes" reflected onto clouds.[7] The idea of using clouds as a screen was also behind the 1893 Chicago World's Fair's "electric cloud projector" used to "project the daily number of visitors in the daytime, and to beam texts and pictures in the clouds after dark."[8]

The idea of projecting images onto clouds, however, was not limited to marketing and military strategists. Magicians, artists, and scientists also saw the potential in combining electric-light projections and gaseous screens. In the early nineteenth century, the Belgian physicist and magician Étienne-Gaspard Robertson made use of smoke to enhance the ghostly spectacles of his phantasmagoria.[9] A similar desire to use the visual effect of smoke, fog, and clouds pervaded visual artists in the twentieth century. One salient example is László Moholy-Nagy's whimsical proposal to use "clouds or artificial fog banks" for light-projection work.[10] His dream came true with the artistic use of dry ice and fog machines in theatrical performances, projection-based light art, and expanded cinema that flourished from the 1960s onward. The most well-known work in this context is Anthony McCall's "solid light film," *Line Describing a Cone* (1973), a work that combines the sculpting force of the light beam emitted by a film projector with the ambient effect produced by a smoke machine (or, in its early exhibition, cigarette smoke).[11]

A number of other artists and filmmakers have made similar attempts to incorporate cigarette smoke, dry-ice fumes, and other gaseous substances as projection surfaces in their filmic and installation works. The Japanese experimental filmmaker Matsumoto Toshio, for instance, initially planned to use smoke grenades and dry ice to create a three-dimensional ambient screen for his expanded cinema piece, *Projection for Icon*, at the international event "Cross Talk/Intermedia" in Tokyo in February 1969. Matsumoto ended up using giant helium-filled balloons as the projection surface, but his proposal speaks to the contemporaneous interest by experimental filmmakers who saw cloud-like substances as a potential technical support for expanded cinema.[12] At "Cross Talk/Intermedia," these same buoyant balloons were also used by the experimental filmmaker Iimura Takahiko and the composer David Rosenbaum.[13]

The artistic use of helium gas and inflatable, pneumatic objects had also become popular during the 1950s and 1960s. From the Gutai group artist Kanayama Akira's *Balloon* (1956) to Robert Whitman's *The American Moon* (1960) and Andy Warhol's *Silver Clouds* (1966), artists frequently made use of plastic, a synthetic material whose availability increased in the postwar years, and helium-filled objects for their installation and film projection works.[14] Similarly, the visual artist Shuzo Azuchi Gulliver used a gigantic cylindrical inflatable for his expanded cinema piece, *Flying Focus* (1969). Reminiscent of the early practice of celestial projection, images emitted from a slide projector were projected onto an upright cylinder floating against the night sky.[15]

This turn toward ephemeral screens made of vaporous particles in the air was also evident in a more commercially oriented attraction at Expo '70, the same world's fair where Nakaya Fujiko's exquisite fog sculpture covered the Pepsi Pavilion. The Pepsi Pavilion itself was also inflatable architecture (a "balloon dome"), designed to draw visitors' attention to the immersive quality of its atmospheric envelopment.[16] The Japanese Tobacco Company's Rainbow Pavilion featured an immersive smoke show that combined spectacular light and film projections with a gigantic smoke screen generated by dry ice. We can see how this smoke screen belongs to the same lineage as Robertson, Moholy-Nagy, and Matsumoto's proposals to use vaporous particles hanging in the air as projection surfaces.

VISUALIZING THE ATMOSPHERE: SCIENCE

Yet light and film projections are only one part of the lineage of visualizing the atmosphere. Fog and smoke have also served as scientific instruments inside the laboratory. Given that the industrial pollution known as *smog*—a combination of *smoke* and *fog*—is associated with a lack of aerial visibility, the use of fog and smoke for visualizing atmospheric phenomena may seem counterintuitive. However, observing and analyzing natural atmospheric phenomena, including the formations of clouds and fog, often required their mimetic replication (or simulation) inside the enclosed space of the scientific laboratory.

At the beginning of the twentieth century, the French physicist Étienne-Jules Marey made use of chronophotography and smoke as instruments for visualizing and observing the otherwise invisible atmospheric phenomena of air currents, turning the malleable and opaque substance of smoke into a means of visualization. He built glass wind tunnels attached to a smoke machine that spouted smoke streaks from a row of parallel nozzles. He then placed tiny objects in these wind tunnels to disturb the flow of air—thus altering the visible path of the smoke streaks. Marey documented the patterns created by these smoke trails in a series of stunning chronophotographs. Smoke, here, functioned as a sculptural medium for visualizing airflow and the typically invisible disturbances within it while photography worked as a graphic medium for recording this movement.[17]

Marey was by no means the first scientist to notice smoke's potential as a tool for the visualization and observation of airflow. The French aeronautical engineer Alphonse Pénaud had also observed how "dust particles lit up by the sun would give a graphic picture of the disturbance of the air around birds." In order to replicate this natural optical condition, Pénaud used jets of smoke to further study air turbulence, an experiment that anticipated the use of dust, smoke, and chemical fog by expanded cinema and light art practitioners in the mid-twentieth century.[18]

Such scientific deployment of cloud-like substances is an essential part of the history of the laboratory. Take, for instance, the invention of the cloud chamber by the Scottish physicist and meteorologist Charles Thomson Rees Wilson. The cloud chamber is a scientific instrument used by atomic, nuclear, and particle physicists to visualize otherwise invisible atmospheric phenomena such as the passages of charged particles. Wilson's original impetus for building a sealed container with supersaturated water vapor was to reproduce the cloud formations he observed as a meteorologist. The cloud chamber, in other words, was first designed to create artificial clouds in a controlled environment. To use the expression of Peter Galison, this little chamber was an instrument of "mimetic experimentation."[19]

It was these mimetic experiments—the reproduction of natural physical phenomena such as rain, clouds, fog, lightning, and snow inside the simulated and controlled environment of the laboratory—that informed the later invention of the water-based artificial fog used by Nakaya Fujiko and her collaborators for the Pepsi Pavilion. To fully understand the genealogical significance of this fog sculpture, therefore, requires that we pay attention to the technological and scientific conditions that enabled the artist to turn artificial fog into an artistic medium.

The material history of microphysics cannot be narrated without an understanding of the technical and epistemological impacts of instruments and machines that assisted scientists in their attempts to visualize, document, measure, and compute their experiments. Unpacking the invention of the fog medium in a genealogical fashion thus demands that we understand the technological apparatus that supported this artwork: the fog-making machine. Furthermore, just as the construction of scientific instruments for experiments is bound up with their institutional as well as theoretical contexts, the fog-making machine used for the Pepsi Pavilion has its own historicity (figure 1.1).

In order to understand the historicity of this apparatus, however, we must not simply look at the instrument itself but also broaden our scope to trace a literal genealogical connection: a familial connection between the artist and her father, Nakaya Ukichirō, a famed physicist

FIGURE 1.1. E.A.T.'s Pepsi Pavilion at Expo '70, Osaka, Japan. Photograph: Shunk-Kender © J. Paul Getty Trust. Getty Research Institute, Los Angeles (2014. R.20).

who invented artificial snow in the mid-1930s. While critical and historical writings on Nakaya Fujiko's fog sculpture have made customary reference to this father-daughter relationship, they hardly go beyond anecdotal interpretations of their shared interests in meteorological phenomena.[20] As we will see, however, the connection between their work goes beyond their familial connection; it is the practice of atmospheric control that binds the artist and the scientist.

ENGINEERING THE ATMOSPHERE

According to Sloterdijk, the invention of poison gas in the early twentieth century weaponized the very act of breathing air—a hitherto latent possibility.[21] The atmosphere thus became a medium for distant killing through the spread of poison gas, and along with this change came the use of smoke screens, fog machines, and fog dispersal techniques in the service of aviation.

As James Fleming notes in his incisive analysis of weather control,

"The dawn of aviation brought new deeds and challenges, with fog dispersal taking centre stage."[22] Natural fog, in other words, became an explicit object of systematic technological manipulation in aerial warfare. The rise of fog along with clouds, snow, and rain as objects of military research is intimately tied to this strategic understanding of the atmosphere as a prime battlefield in the twentieth century. Pilots especially needed a clear view of the runway, requiring fog dispersal; battleships at sea also benefited from the fog-dispersal technology.

Many scientists and engineers—one of whom was Henry G. Houghton, a physical meteorologist from the Massachusetts Institute of Technology—contributed to this emergent field of fog dispersal research that developed alongside aviation technologies. Houghton invented an experimental fog-clearing machine in the mid-1930s. Using pressure nozzles, he created "artificial fogs in his laboratory and tested means of dispersing them."[23] This early research on fog-producing pressure nozzles provided an inspiration for the technical component of Nakaya's fog sculpture a few decades later.

Not surprisingly, however, the first successful case of large-scale fog dissipation came during World War II. In 1944 the British Royal Air Force deployed what they called the Fog Investigation and Dispersal Operation (FIDO) system. The chemical engineers working on this project came up with a device to heat up the airfield so that Allied pilots could safely take off and land during foggy conditions.[24] On the other side of the globe, a team of Japanese scientists, led by Nakaya Ukichirō, embarked on a similar project to observe and disperse summer sea fog in June 1944. Having worked on several wartime research projects related to frost heaving, aircraft icing, and lightning at the Institute of Low Temperature Science in the 1930s and early 1940s, Nakaya was the scientist the Japanese military entrusted with the strategic task of developing a fog-dispersal system.

With the assistance of researchers at the central meteorological observatory, military engineers, and his students from Hokkaidō University, Nakaya directed a project studying summer sea fog. In order to collect comprehensive data on density, humidity, scale, and fog droplet size, they rode balloons provided by the Japanese Army and photographed fog droplets day after day. These photographic records provided a visual means of gauging the size and density of droplets in the atmosphere. The researchers also deployed time-lapse cinematography to document the appearance and disappearance of sea fog from the top of a nearby coastal mountain.[25] Along with the prevention of icing on aircraft propellers and frost heaving on the railroad, the clearing of the visual field for aviators became particularly urgent as Japan consolidated its territorial control over northern climate regions such as Manchuria and the Kuril Islands. The scientific study of fog was thus directly implicated in the expansion of the Japanese Empire—as well as its eventual demise.

From 1944 to 1945, Nakaya's team tirelessly gathered atmospheric data using balloons, cameras, desiccators, and daily weather maps. They finally devised a fog-dispersal truck using makeshift materials one month before Japan's surrender in August 1945.[26] The end of the war did not bring an end to Nakaya's atmospheric science research, however, as his collaboration with experts from other fields continued. After the war ended, Nakaya worked on the agricultural impact of snow, ice, and frost in hopes of improving the productivity of his war-torn nation after the loss of its overseas colonies. Later, he also worked on resource development projects and advocated for the sustainable use of water and snow.[27]

In order to continue his research on artificial snow and artificial rain, Nakaya also sought financial assistance from governmental agencies, including the Allied occupation forces and the United States Air Force. Accordingly, his involvement in both Japanese and American military-funded research drew some harsh criticism from his contemporaries.[28] Of course, it would be unfair to single out Nakaya alone for his pursuit of research opportunities. A number of Japanese atmospheric scientists and physicists had been mobilized by the wartime military regime, and many were later recruited by American universities and other research institutions during the Cold War, when Japan became a strategic ally of the United States.

Nonetheless, it is notable that between 1952 and 1954, Nakaya joined and worked for the Snow, Ice, and Permafrost Research Establishment (SIPRE), a laboratory and research facility established by the US Army Corps of Engineers in 1949. It is his institutional connection to organizations such as SIPRE that places Nakaya squarely in the transpacific nexus that bridged wartime Japan and Cold War America. To put it differently, by following Nakaya's career we can trace Japan's geopolitical reorientation from enemy nation during World War II to the closest American ally during the Cold War period.

One of the American meteorologists Nakaya knew was Vincent Schaefer at the General Electric Research Laboratory. During the occupation, Schaefer had personally helped Nakaya by procuring American film stock to reshoot his film *Snow Crystals* (1939), which documented his groundbreaking experiments with the invention of artificial snowflakes.[29] Inspired in part by microscopic photographs of natural snowflakes by Wilson Bentley, Nakaya began photographing and cataloging numerous types of snow crystals around 1932. Every winter he would climb Hokkaidō's Mount Tokachi, and take more than 3,000 microscopic photographs, in total, of natural snowflakes.[30]

Nakaya then embarked on re-creating snowflakes inside the Low Temperature Science Laboratory, which simulated outdoor climatic conditions. To produce artificial snowflakes, Nakaya and his team experimented with various materials—from a thread of silk to a strand of spider web—in order to grow snow crystals inside the laboratory environment. To his delight, rabbit hair, with its uneven surface, proved the most effective base for growing snow crystals.[31] The film *Snow Crystals* documented Nakaya's experimental techniques for making snowflakes inside the simulated laboratory environment.

At the invitation of the International Commission on Snow and Ice, Nakaya sent the print of the film to the conference in lieu of his participation during wartime in 1939. In 1947, two years after the war ended, Nakaya received an invitation to present his research along with the film at the International Commission of Snow and Ice conference in Oslo, Norway. Since the original print of the film was lost during the war, and the copy he had submitted in the 1930s had also been lost, Nakaya decided to reshoot the film at the Institute of Low Temperature Science.[32] It was Schaefer who procured the necessary funds to help Nakaya's team reshoot the film *Snow Crystals* in 1948, while working on the classified cloud-seeding project called Project Cirrus (1947–52), for which he served as a coordinator.[33]

During World War II, Schaefer—like Nakaya—worked on military research related to deicing techniques. Together with Irving Langmuir, a Nobel Prize–winning chemist who also worked for the General Electric Research Laboratory, Schaefer developed a method for cloud seeding to artificially induce precipitation. They were the literal "rainmakers" who contributed to the technology of weather modification during the Cold War.[34]

Researchers involved in Project Cirrus "conducted about 250 experiments involving modification of cold cirrus and stratus clouds, warm and cold cumulus clouds, periodic cloud seeding, forest fire suppression, and a notable attempt to modify a hurricane."[35] The promise of freely engineering meteorological phenomena seemed like a near-future reality. A 1954 *Collier's* magazine article, tantalizingly titled "Weather Made to Order," describes such futuristic scenarios as "milking rain or snow from reluctant clouds at the proper time and place."[36] The practice of weather control, in short, is described as a domestication of nature. The gendered analogy of milking rain or snow also betrays a masculine fantasy of extraction, extended to the atmosphere (figure 1.2).

The author of the article, Howard T. Orville, chairman of the Advisory Committee on Weather Control under the Eisenhower administration, speculates on the future potential of weather modification: "And before we can hope to control the weather, we must learn what causes weather. To gain this knowledge would probably require an effort as large as the Manhattan Project for the development of atomic energy. Mastery of the weather is theoretically possible if our research is expanded on that scale."[37] Orville, a retired Navy officer, also discusses the possible military uses of weather modification, such as intercepting and overseeding clouds in order to dry up crops and thus to "strike at an enemy's food supply."[38]

By the mid-1960s, such speculation became a harrowing reality. The political destabilization of Southeast Asia during the Vietnam War and the military potential of "weather warfare" seemingly convinced the Pentagon to launch weather control as part of its experimental warfare. In preparation, the US government under President Lyndon Johnson tested its secret weather modification techniques for the purportedly humanitarian project of alleviating droughts in India. Once it proved effective (or so it seemed), large-scale cloud-seeding operations were employed to steer hurricanes over Laos and Vietnam with the intention of prolonging the monsoon season and thus disrupting "North Vietnam's supply lines that snaked through the Laotian panhandle and into South Vietnam."[39] In short, the military use of weather control up in the air became a potential means of disrupting enemy logistics on the ground. This Cold War proxy war in Southeast Asia—known for the first systematic deployment of digital computers and operations research on the battlefield—was also the first to weaponize the weather as a part of military logistics.[40] This historical fact—that Asia was the test site wherein computers and weather control, already developed in tandem with one another, worked together as instruments of warfare—should not be lost on us.

Such tactical use of weather control further integrated meteorological phenomena into warfare, propelling the ongoing process of atmospheric

FIGURE 1.2. The cover of *Collier's* magazine, May 28, 1954.

explication that began with the invention of poison gas and continued with fog dispersal and its counterpart, smoke-screen technology.[41] While the commercial use of cloud seeding promised a rosy future for weather on demand—modulating rainfall to prevent flooding, feed hydroelectric power plants, or turn arid deserts into fertile croplands—the development of weather control was inseparable from its military applications.

However, this does not mean that the military use of weather control overshadowed its civilian counterpart. In 1950s and 1960s Japan, meteorologists affiliated with hydroelectric power companies supported by the state carried out numerous research projects on experimental weather control, especially on artificial precipitation. In the summer of 1954, for instance, a group of researchers at Kyūshū University collaborated with Kyūshū Electric Power Company to conduct a series of cloud seeding experiments, using air balloons. Their hope was to multiply the production of electricity needed for the nation's rapid economic recovery and further industrial growth.[42]

Regardless of its applications, however, there is one common factor that binds these diverse forms of weather control: their inseparability from the question of *security*. From its military application for warfare, to its civilian application to ensure food and water security, controlling weather became tied to the geopolitics and biopolitics of the twentieth century. The military application of weather control became inseparable from the geopolitical influences of nation-states over their given or disputed territories, as well as the biopolitical management of populations and their access to crops or water. Weather control in this sense was a dual-use technology; at the most basic level, it was an instrument for managing the environment in both peacetime and wartime, an instrument that both sustained biological life and ensured the survival of the modern nation-state.

In this regard, it is worth remembering Sloterdijk's point that explicating the atmosphere reveals the existential insecurity of living in a technologically mediated environment. With the militarization of poison gas and weather control, technological modernity intensified the sense of insecurity associated with the environment, as the air we breathe potentially contains poison, and the clouds above us are possible meteorological weapons. In a compensatory manner, this intensified sense of atmospheric insecurity further propels technological inventions to create countermeasures, such as the inventions of gas masks, air purification, and so on. The eventual establishment of the regulatory body the Weather Control Commission in the United States (directly modeled after the Atomic Energy Commission) fits this framework—the implication being that the weaponization of weather control could, like nuclear power, also be lethal.[43] The geographic range and geophysical effects of weather modification are always imprecise. Unlike other weapons—such as ballistic missiles—winds, storms, rainclouds, and plumes of air pollution do not follow preprogrammed paths. Even uncontrolled air pollution can be lethal, as indicated by deaths caused by heavy smog. Such incidents of industrial air pollution are considered to be "inadvertent weather modification" rather than an intentional practice of weather control, though both forms of atmospheric control generate a sense of insecurity, which arises from the unpredictability of atmospheric phenomena.[44]

The sense of vulnerability generated by weather modification is, however, not an exception but rather a rule of technological modernity. It is a salient example of the paradoxical process of atmospheric explication in general. According to Sloterdijk, "Modernity conceived as the explication of the background givens thereby remains trapped in a phobic circle, striving to overcome anxiety through technology, which itself generates more anxiety."[45] The explication of the atmosphere creates a vicious cycle: the more we learn about and exacerbate the vulnerability of the atmosphere, the more we turn to technology to compensate for and control this vulnerability.[46]

The military investment in the weaponization of the weather, in this regard, is part of the ongoing process of atmospheric explication that also reveals the human desire to dwell inside a climate-controlled environment.[47] The revelatory capacity of technology to explicate the atmosphere is inseparable from the artifice of human dwelling as a constant effort to engineer the environment. Needless to say, the effort to secure and expand habitable environments through engineering the land, ocean, and sky is a continuous thread, which runs through the history of industrialization and colonialism which characterizes modernity.

FOG SCULPTURE

It is against this broad context of the ongoing process of atmospheric explication that I want to situate the invention of artificial fog as an artistic medium by Nakaya Ukichirō's daughter, Nakaya Fujiko. Her innovative use of water-based artificial fog, which generated a site-specific microclimate around the Pepsi Pavilion, cannot be separated from the concurrent epistemological and technological process of atmospheric explication. It is not coincidental that the artistic use of fog became both conceptually salient and technologically feasible at the precise moment when the adverse effects of weather modification (including the inadvertent kind, in the form of air pollution) were slowly becoming clear.

To put it polemically, the atmospheric control over artificial fog that enveloped the Pepsi Pavilion is a scaled-down version of commercial, industrial, and military geoengineering that controlled and modified weather. This is not to disregard the aesthetic intention of the artist, who is known for her commitment to environmental activism and her critique of mercury pollution. Rather, my objective behind drawing this genealogical connection between the artistic control over site-specific weather phenomenon and the nonartistic control of weather elsewhere is to highlight the ambivalent duality of atmospheric explication. Here, the technologically mediated process of atmospheric explication, through artificial weather, binds together otherwise heterogeneous experiments undertaken by artists, scientists, and engineers.

Although the ultimate inventor of the pressurized, nozzle-based fog-making machine for the Pepsi Pavilion was the American cloud physicist Thomas Mee, Nakaya Fujiko sought his help and settled on this apparatus after a long process of experimentation. To better understand how the fog sculpture sits at the point of convergence between these two lines of descent (of visualizing and engineering the atmosphere), let us look closely at the technological and scientific assistance that Nakaya received to make this artwork.

The idea to envelop the exterior of the geodesic dome with artificial fog emerged at the early planning stage of the Pepsi Pavilion by E.A.T., a group to which Nakaya had belonged since her participation in the "9 Evenings: Theatre and Engineering" event in 1966.[48] Throughout the second half of the 1960s, Nakaya and other Japanese artists—including Ichiyanagi Toshi, Takahashi Yūji, Takemitsu Tōru, Isobe Yukihisa, Usami Kenji, Morioka Yūji, and Kobayashi Hakudō—participated in E.A.T. projects that included "9 Evenings" (1966), "Some More Beginnings" (1968), the Pepsi Pavilion at Expo '70 (1970), and "Utopia: Q&A 1981" (1971).[49] Among these, the commissioned project of designing the Pepsi Pavilion was by far the largest project the E.A.T. group undertook. The project involved seventy-five artists, scientists, and engineers, nurturing interdisciplinary collaborations among them.

Enveloping the dome with artificial fog was central to the group's overall objective of turning the pavilion into an interactive "living responsive environment."[50] They wanted this artificial environment to register and respond to ambient factors such as wind, temperature, humidity, and the movement of visitors in real time.[51] However, technical feasibility posed a challenge. According to Nilo Lindgren, a journalist who followed its planning stage, "No one knew whether or not it was actually possible to make a fog, but the idea persisted and survived."[52] Nakaya, who had an avid interest in the ephemeral form of clouds, became a key person in charge of executing this ambitious idea.

There are many different ways of artificially creating fog. As Nakaya notes in her essay "The Making of 'Fog,' or Low-Hanging Stratus Cloud," one can use water (as she ultimately did for the Pepsi Pavilion), chemicals, oil, or smoke. She opted for using pure water in order to accommodate the aesthetic requirements of the project. Water, rather than other substances, was more suitable for the following reasons. Nakaya writes:

> My choice was based on what I felt were the three most important requirements of the fog for our purpose:
>
> 1. Visibility: it should scatter enough light to reduce considerably the visibility of the objects behind, and, at the same time, make visible the otherwise invisible dynamics of atmosphere;
> 2. Tangibility: it should feel soft and cool to the skin;
> 3. Vulnerability: it should be subject to atmospheric conditions; it should disappear, not persist.[53]

Among these three conditions, the first (visibility) and third (vulnerability) are particularly interesting in light of the scientific investment in, and the weaponization of, fog discussed earlier. Fog—or low-hanging stratus cloud, as Nakaya calls it—is marked by its versatility. When used to conceal objects behind it, it works like a smokescreen. But it can also refract and diffuse light. Some of her later projects thus make clever use of laser beams, as in the case of her collaborative work with Bill Viola (*Fog Sculpture*, 1980), taking advantage of fog's optical effects of refraction and diffusion and serving as an ambient screen.[54]

Moreover, fog's constant metamorphosis can draw viewers' attention to ambient environmental factors such as wind, temperature, humidity, and even the movement of visitors (which makes it an ideal interactive or responsive medium for environmental art). Put another way, fog sculpture engages in the process of atmosphere explication; it renders explicit latent conditions of the atmosphere that otherwise remain imperceptible as an environmental given.[55] Generated by atomizing nozzles attached to the roof of the geodesic dome, this site-specific fog sculpture cascaded, drifted, and gathered outside the dome, responding to the ever-changing patterns and density of air currents, temperature, humidity, and light.

What is unique about the technical support of this work is its use of water-based, rather than chemically based, fog. In using water, the work *simulated* natural fog and provided the pavilion with its own microclimate. Yet this microclimate was completely artificial. Nakaya notes: "The only request I made to my partner-scientist was that I wanted dense, bubbling-out fog, as close a simulation as possible to natural fog in its physical nature, to cover the entire Pavilion, with perhaps drop-size control added to make rain once in a while."[56]

At the preparatory stage for designing the fog-making system, Nakaya spent six months gathering statistical data on the local weather patterns in the town of Senri, where the world's fair was to take place. She carefully studied the layout of the fairgrounds and the topography of the surrounding area to understand its potential physical impact on the aesthetic process of fog making. She also consulted a number of Japanese physicists and meteorologists in order to explore the technical feasibility of producing pure water fog.[57]

Two of the scientists she sought advice from were Magono Chōji and Higashi Akira at Hokkaidō University. They were both students of her father, Nakaya Ukichirō, and had participated in his wartime research project on fog dispersal in the first half of the 1940s. Nakaya Fujiko's path thus directly crossed with that of her father in her quest for the scientific and technical support she needed to create this exquisite environmental artwork.

By generating simulated fog and rain, this site-specific work, regardless of the artist's intentions, therefore can be situated in relation to the broader experimental practices of manufacturing "artificial weather" that became prevalent in the 1950s and 1960s. As I discussed in the previous sections of this chapter, attempts to visualize otherwise invisible atmospheric phenomena have generated scientific and artistic experiments since the nineteenth century. Efforts to control weather and to engineer artificial fog, rain, and snow, however, belong to a different lineage, even though both traditions share a desire to explicate the atmosphere. The technological connection between these two Nakayas points to the intersection of these two lineages.

SITE-SPECIFIC WEATHER CONTROL

Pushing the line of genealogical thinking that binds fog sculpture to weather control, I want to offer a new conception of site-specificity as a geopolitically located practice. The expanded concept of geopolitics (literally, the politics of the earth) in this regard provides a useful perspective for thinking about the specificity of a given site of weather modification. It is in this sense—of the specificity of the given environment within which the work of weather control takes place—that we may use the term *site-specificity*.

To begin, it is imperative for us to understand how the practice of engineering the atmosphere is often imagined as both site-specific and scalable. One may presumably move from modulating an atmosphere at the miniature scale of a cloud chamber, to the median scale of a pavilion, to the large scale of an entire region. However, as one moves from the enclosed space of a laboratory to the larger space of open experiments, the geopolitical configuration of the technology changes and the meteorological and climatological effects become less predictable. For weather modification can only be site-specific if the site of experiment is a strictly controlled environment (as in the case of artificial indoor weather inside the laboratory) or the scale and complexity of the experiment are relatively small. When it operates in the open, the locally modified weather interacts with broader geographical, climatological, and meteorological conditions of distant locations, inviting unpredictable and inadvertent effects. Site-specific experiments of weather control are therefore impacted by this fundamental tension between predictability and unpredictability, containment and contamination, or microclimate and macroclimate, even though the practice is, in theory, imagined to be scalable.

While the term *site-specificity* comes out of the discipline of art history and holds a privileged relationship to the field of sculpture, it is useful to think through its literal connotation, or the environmental givenness of the site.[58] When we move away from the formal or conceptual constraints of a site-specific artwork (though Nakaya Fujiko's fog sculpture surely can be analyzed from that angle) toward the geographical, climatological, and meteorological complexities of the site itself, we can also unpack its geopolitical and historical specificities.

Here, I am using the term to deliberately expand this notion to include a site's environmental constraints and affordances, wherein the broadly conceived act of engineering or controlling the atmosphere may take place. To do so is to decouple an artwork from its disciplinary context of art history and place it in a different framework of analysis; that is, the interdisciplinary context of climatic media, which technologically mediate, modify, and engineer the atmospheric phenomena such as weather in order to physically and socially "condition" and exert control over the air and people at a given site. To read the singular artwork of fog sculpture, which generates an interactive environment for the viewers, and the geopolitically determined operations of weather control side by side is to pay attention to their common ground. This ground, I argue, is the epistemological and technological conditions of mimetic experimentation, the attempt to artificially replicate meteorological phenomena.

Expanding the conceptual affordance of the term *site-specificity* beyond the history of art in this manner also allows us to attend to the multiple senses of the term *medium*. In the context of art history, the term refers to an artistic medium—the material and technical supports and formal conventions of an artwork—while the same term in the context of media studies predominantly signifies technical channels and intermediary agents of communication, transmission, and storage.

The recent recuperation of medium in the spatial and environmental sense of milieu (literally, the middle) by media scholars offers a heuristic means of rearticulating the material support of environmental artworks. Nakaya's fog sculpture thus exemplifies this etymological affinity between milieu and medium. The idea of elemental media—water, air, and sky—as communication media, proposed by John Durham Peters, for instance, pushes this line of thinking to incorporate natural physical phenomena, including the weather, back into the history of technical media.

"'Media,' understood as the means by which meaning is communicated, sit atop layers of even more fundamental media that have meaning but do not speak," writes Peters.[59] For him, "the old idea that media are environments" needs to be flipped if we are to understand media in this expanded sense, since "media are ensembles of natural element and human craft."[60] Similarly, we must radically expand the use of the term *medium* in relation to this particular artwork if we are to understand the significance of the fog sculpture through the recent scholarly turn toward elements and other environmental conditions within media studies. As I have argued throughout this chapter, this expanded sense of artificial fog as a type of climatic media allows us to consider the development of its technical apparatus through the history of science and technology as part of its genealogy. This development, moreover, is significantly inflected by the transpacific geopolitics of the twentieth century, in which site-specific and regional modifications of weather, including its weaponization, played a crucial role.

In conclusion, I want to discuss a surprising afterlife of the fog-making machine used for Nakaya's fog sculpture at the Pepsi Pavilion (figure 1.3). Originally invented by Mee and his engineers for weather control, the apparatus—the nozzles used to make artificial fog—had practical applicability beyond the realm of art. As Billy Klüver proudly notes, it "offered interesting possibilities for environmental irrigation systems, outdoor air-conditioning, and protection of crops from frost."[61] The original application of the fog machine was aesthetic, but its afterlife was not. This fog-making technology (or more precisely, the evaporative cooling process derived from it, which Mee Industries, Inc. developed after Expo '70) is used today to cool down data centers.[62] Mee's fog-making apparatus and other air-conditioning systems installed at data centers worldwide are precisely the infrastructure that sustains the electrically powered servers of today's internet and cloud computing service providers. The metaphorical clouds of networked data storage and processing systems are thus directly linked to the physical clouds of fog sculpture, by the historical path of a shared apparatus. In this regard, it is worth mentioning that the MeeFog system is installed at none other than Facebook's data center in Prineville, Oregon.[63]

To read the invention of artificial fog as climatic media through the perspective of cloud computing and infrastructure studies means to pay heed to the technological control of the atmosphere itself. Noting the ubiquitous presence of networked computational devices paired with microsensors in our environments, and both their capacity to filter data and condition our sensory experiences of the world at the imperceptible level, Mark Hansen has proposed the term *atmospheric media* to describe their taken-for-granted presence.[64] Calling on Hansen's lack of attention to the environmental cost of such atmospheric media, Peters notes: "Fantasies of what Mark Hansen calls 'atmospheric media' presupposes an electrical grid. Information is not smokeless. Google's servers burn up millions of dollars of electricity every month and produce an enormous amount of heat that requires cooling."[65]

In other words, Hansen's analysis of atmospheric media sidesteps the infrastructural issue of the energy-intensive maintenance of cloud computing that supports the operation of these ubiquitous computational devices and sensors. My use of the term *climatic media* in part is meant to accentuate the material dimensions of what Hansen calls

FIGURE 1.3. The fog machine inside E.A.T.'s Pepsi Pavilion at Expo '70, Osaka, Japan. Photograph: Shunk-Kender © J. Paul Getty Trust. Getty Research Institute, Los Angeles (2014. R.20).

atmospheric media, including the vast infrastructure of electricity and air-conditioning that enables the daily operations of cloud computing and data centers.

Critiques of the energy-intensive maintenance of cloud computing and data centers abound in media studies. More and more tech companies are also turning to cost-effective modes of air-conditioning by outdoor air, fog, and snow in cold climate regions. Yet what has not been discussed enough either in academic or industrial contexts is the geopolitical interests behind such indoor climate engineering, which relies on outdoor weather phenomena such as fog, rain, and snow. It is for this reason that I have closely analyzed the transpacific geopolitical contexts within which the inventions of artificial snowflakes, fog, and rain took place.

Writing in the immediate aftermath of the war, Nakaya Ukichirō argued that snow is a renewable resource that resource-scarce Japan needs to take seriously.[66] Currently, in the northern cities in Hokkaidō, where Nakaya conducted much of his groundbreaking research on snow and ice, the idea of recycling snow as a source of refrigeration is attracting investors and tech companies to build data centers that use the cooling effects of summer snow. Fog and snow are thus literally integrated into the material infrastructure of cloud computing.

Meanwhile, Nakaya Fujiko and a collaborator recently placed meteorological sensors at various places around an installation site in order to record ambient data such as temperature, humidity, and wind speed and direction. These data were then run through a special computer program that controlled the nozzles of a fog-making machine so that the shape of the fog directly responded to, and interacted with, the surrounding environment.[67] Here, current debates about atmospheric media come into sharp focus through the technological articulation of artificial fog and computational media.

The low-hanging cloud or fog that enveloped the Pepsi Pavilion at Expo '70 thus resurfaces, not only in Nakaya's later and similarly spectacular artworks (such as the fog sculpture for the Blur Building designed by the architects Elizabeth Diller and Ricardo Scofidio for the 2002 Swiss Expo) but also much less visibly in the walls and pipes of data centers where digital clouds are stored, accessed, modulated, and cooled. The distance between these two manifestations of artificial fog may seem great, yet, as I have argued in this chapter, they belong to the same genealogy.

Pointing out the frequent recycling of Cold War bunkers into data centers, which inherit what he calls a "bunker mentality," Tung-Hui Hu argues that data centers sit at "the border between the dematerialized space of data and the resolutely physical buildings they occupy."[68] A similar tension exists between the air-conditioning systems that support the operation of data centers and the engineering of the atmosphere by artists, scientists, and engineers that I traced in this chapter.

Arguably, this bunker mentality, oriented toward ensuring security, is itself an effect of the existential insecurity generated by the process of atmospheric explication. The repurposing of the fog-making system invented for the Pepsi Pavilion to cool down data centers also partakes in this ongoing process of atmospheric explication. Going back to Hu's discussion of the bunker mentality for a moment, we may surmise that *in*security about the loss of data stored in the digital cloud is part of what Sloterdijk has called the phobic circle of explication. As we explicate the atmosphere through technology, our anxiety about its vulnerability is amplified, which in turn prompts more technological solutions to manage and control this vulnerability.

The epistemological implications of atmospheric explication, however, are not limited to the management of anxiety and insecurity generated by technology. What I have called "the lineage of visualizing the atmosphere" is a mode of explication that also gave rise to a series of aesthetic experiments that took the ephemeral matter of cloud-like substances (e.g., smoke, mist, fog, and helium-filled balloons) as projection and installation media. The duality of fog as a screening device to conceal and to reveal, to undermine and to increase visibility of the environment, has thus served different functions in the realm of contemporary art. One may well read these artworks as symptoms of the existential insecurity generated by the technological explication of the atmosphere.

We may also situate them as integral components of the cloud-computing infrastructure, which turns computers into climatic media. To do so enables us to directly link the existential insecurity of atmospheric explication discussed by Sloterdijk to the material infrastructure of data centers. The increasing embeddedness of computational media in our physical environment and the ever-intensifying traffic of electronic signals in our everyday lives demand that we shift our perspective from the old model of technical media to intentionally include and consider atmospheric phenomena as media without collapsing metaphors and histories.

2

Data-driven predictive technologies are everywhere: from the predictive text function on our smartphones and curated YouTube and Google recommendations, to the constantly updated stock market headlines and extreme weather news, to the AI-supported astrological advice via horoscope apps, algorithmic networks of future forecasting have become part of our daily cultural experience. The exponential growth of computing power has accelerated this process of prediction. Although the prognostic art of forecasting is clearly prone to error, a search for more accurate and more precise prediction has continued apace, propelling constant upgrades to models and technologies of forecasting.

One field in which the early impact of computing on prediction has registered prominently is meteorology, or more precisely, weather forecasting. The computational practice of numerical weather prediction revolutionized weather forecasting in the 1950s. This same historical moment also saw the rise of another type of forecasting: futurology, which promised to predict and project socioeconomic trends and technological transformations. Unlike meteorologists who work on the short span of hourly and daily weather, futurologists often speculate on the future in the longer span of years and decades. Despite the temporal disparity, however, these two modes of forecasting have much in common.

At the center of these two modes of technological forecasting lies the digital computer, a quintessential instrument of numerical prediction and an object of techno-utopian fascination in the mid-twentieth century. But while technological forecasting of the future developed in parallel with digital computing, computation is not the only element that binds the two. The smooth operation of computers hinges on another important factor: air-conditioning. The infrastructural basis of technological forecasting is the air-conditioned computer rooms and data centers wherein machines are comfortably chilled and protected from excessive humidity and heat. As Nicole Starosielski argues, thermal manipulation is crucial to the material production, circulation, and operation of media, including computers.[1] It is the use of mechanized air-conditioning for computers and its genealogical relationship to the geopolitics of future forecasting that I want to explore in this chapter.

My argument is that predicting the future relies on artificial climatization. Whether it is the single computer rooms that housed mainframe computers in the early days of numerical weather prediction at the Institute of Advanced Studies in Princeton, New Jersey, and at the Japan Meteorological Agency in Tokyo, or the massive data center complexes that support today's weather, stock, and trend forecasting globally, these indoor environments must be kept not too hot, not too dry, and not too humid for the optimal performance of digital computers. Temperate indoor climates with their air-conditioned atmospheres are the hidden infrastructural supports of future forecasting.

Managing the uncertainty of the future through computation harbors a desire to acclimatize ourselves to and secure ourselves against the unknown. This thermostatic desire not only ushers in endless speculation about turbulent weather, economic turmoil, and technological breakthroughs but also continues to foster our trust in the minutely calibrated future, as if it too can be controlled like the temperature in a room, with the touch of a virtual thermostat. This view of a future that can be calibrated through computing and forecasting developed in close relation to the transpacific geopolitics of the Cold War. Examining this context will allow us to better understand how the epistemological endeavor of mathematical modeling of the future relates to techniques and technologies of atmospheric control.

Weather forecasting and air-conditioning are like habits. They have become familiar and mundane. They recede into the taken-for-granted background of our lives. Yet it is precisely this background givenness that I want to question, as their operations depend on a spatiotemporal inversion: an inverse movement of dispersive extension of the computing and air-conditioning infrastructures that support the intensification of the precision-based future forecasting. As prediction becomes faster and more precise, bigger and more complex infrastructures of air-conditioning—as well as measuring, tracking, and processing of data—are required. There is a proportional relationship between the temporal vector of forecasting and the spatial vector of infrastructures that support it.

Atmospheric control aimed at the future manifests today in myriad ways. Today we experience the proliferation of weather apps on smartphones and the marketing of hyperlocalized and often customized predictions of the weather minute by minute and neighborhood by neighborhood.[2] The same propensity toward hyperlocalization and customization characterizes the marketing of recent home air-conditioning units, which promise to offer individually curated airflows. These air-conditioning units, with built-in cameras and infrared sensors, monitor and track the minute movements of users in order to calibrate their anticipated comfort levels.[3] This anticipatory regulation of bodily temperature by smart air conditioners performs a type of future forecasting, albeit at a tiny scale. Hyperlocalized air-conditioning that individually curates airflow is the domestic and design counterpart to increasingly hyperlocalized weather forecasting, which similarly projects customized predictions of the atmospheric future at a broader scale.

In both cases, the atmosphere is broken into smaller and smaller units of microclimates to accommodate ever more precise, more individuated, and more customized forecasting of the future. The air and thereby the atmosphere are often imagined as continuous and indivisible, as if they resist a territorial logic.[4] Yet, as I aim to demonstrate in this chapter, the atmospheric future mediated by weather forecasting and air-conditioning clearly follows and embodies this territorial logic. To constantly subdivide the atmosphere into miniscule units of prediction, moreover, presupposes the mathematical logic of projection in which the model approximates the real. This mathematical approximation of the atmosphere, in turn, allows for deeper and more minute control over anticipated movements of bodies and elements such as airflow within the compartmentalized unit. This increased partitioning of the atmosphere into microclimates partakes in the mode of control that operates through the projection of a numerically calculated and projected future. In the meantime, and parallel to this, the forecasting of future socioeconomic, cultural, and technological trends continues to flourish.

How did we arrive at this proliferation of compartmentalized microclimates and customized foresights into future trends? One answer, I argue, lies in the transpacific genealogy of digital computing that binds numerical weather prediction and futurology. To trace this genealogy, I pay close attention to the geopolitical complexities that enabled the transpacific circulation of humans and machines between Japan and the United States. Like the trade winds and jet stream that aided colonial invasions and imperial expansions, these institutional currents carried elite male researchers—they were almost always men—and colossal mainframe computers across the Pacific during the height of the Cold War. Such transpacific circulations of researchers and computers were geopolitically determined. By tracking this geopolitical dimension of technological forecasting and its entanglement with air-conditioning, this chapter examines the processes of projecting, computing, and territorializing the atmospheric future.

In what follows, I first examine the development of numerical weather prediction, a subset of technological forecasting that became institutionalized due to, and thus alongside, the accessibility of digital computers. In order to tease out the epistemological framework of mathematical projection behind the technological mode of forecasting, I then turn to the rise of futurology, which was closely linked to the managerial vision of social engineering, in the same time period. What binds these two modes of forecasting together is the experimental uses of networked computing and district cooling at the simulated future city of Expo '70. This world's fair served as an exemplary testing site for urban computing and cooling. I conclude by examining contemporary examples of smart weather forecasting and smart air-conditioning technologies as part of this transpacific genealogy.

Before we turn to numerical weather prediction, let us note how air-conditioning was initially conceived as a form of producing "man-made weather." The invention of modern air-conditioning by Willis H. Carrier, an American engineer, relied on the principles of thermodynamics and involved the mechanized control of condensed vapor. Mechanical air-conditioning works through the process of removing heat and moisture from the air and subsequently circulating this filtered air in an indoor environment. Carrier's intention was not so much the production of coolness but the reduction of humidity. In 1902 he found a reliable mechanism of dehumidification—the basis of air-conditioning—and quickly turned it into a successful business of manufacturing artificial weather.[5]

Commenting on Carrier's terminological ingenuity, the architectural critic Reyner Banham notes: "The phrase 'Man-made weather' is an admirable one, not only in describing the end product of the air conditioning process, but because it also underlines the extent to which Carrier's mastery of the craft turned upon direct observation of the nature and performance of air as a component of outdoor weather."[6] The mechanical process of manipulating humidity and temperature can be conceived as the production of indoor weather. Although the term *weather* colloquially implies what is outside—up in the sky—weather understood as the elemental conditions of the atmosphere also exists inside climate-controlled environments, from office buildings to data centers. In this regard, the use of mechanical air-conditioning too functions as a site-specific practice of weather control, even if its scale and aim may seem distant from outdoor experiments of cloud seeding, fog-making, and weaponization of the weather.

This mundane technology of regulating indoor weather played a critical, though not so obvious, role in the advancement of meteorology. As meteorology turned to digital computers to increase the accuracy of weather forecasting, the new infrastructural need to create artificial microclimates to protect these computers arose. Machines, more than humans, had to be cooled and pampered for numerical weather forecasting to be operationalized.

It was during the 1950s and early 1960s that the application of the mathematical technique of numerical weather prediction changed the instrumental dynamic between humans and machines. Before the institutionalization of numerical weather prediction, the art of forecasting the weather was primarily based on skilled human forecasters' subjective interpretations of datasets gathered about atmospheric phenomena. Just as human calculators—many of whom were women—worked as skilled "computers," human weather forecasters used to be virtuoso artists whose experience and skills alone made the prediction possible.[7] As Kristine Harper notes, "Once an art that depended on an individual forecaster's lifetime or local experience, meteorology has become a sophisticated, *theoretical* atmospheric science" in the mid-twentieth century.[8] This theoretical reorientation of meteorology from art to science was brought about by the advent of digital computers.

The first experiment with computerized numerical weather prediction happened because John von Neumann, a physicist and a founding figure of digital computing, wished to demonstrate the civilian application of digital computers developed by the US military during World War II. Together with Jule Charney, an American meteorologist, Neumann founded the Meteorology Project at the Institute for Advanced Studies in Princeton, New Jersey. In 1950, Charney and Neumann used the ENIAC (Electronic Numerical Integrator and Calculator), the first electronic digital computer, to experiment with numerical weather prediction. Crucially, the US Navy provided the necessary funds to support the experiment with the hope that the precise prediction of weather would lead to its modification.[9] This is the moment when the history of computing dovetailed with that of weather forecasting and weather control. Prediction begets control, or so some hoped.

Historians of science have traced the institutional nexus between the rise of numerical weather prediction and computing back to the late 1940s and early 1950s. "Computer modeling," writes Paul Edwards, "altered meteorological institutions by establishing computer power as a critical—and scarce—resource." This resource revolutionized the field. Consequently, the profession of meteorology underwent a significant change, as its practitioners learned the grammar of computer programming, without which "the crucial, highly complex translation of mathematics into computer code could not proceed."[10]

However, as the technique of numerical weather prediction advanced and meteorologists doubled as programmers, something else happened. Adequate systems of air-conditioning had to be constructed in order to provide an infrastructural support for these computers; the machines needed atmospheric pampering for their optimal performance.[11] The ENIAC, for instance, "required a forced-air cooling system to keep from catching fire."[12] Similarly, the first computer used for the sole purpose of numerical weather prediction at the Japan Meteorological Agency required the construction of a special cooling plant. Without such an infrastructure of air-conditioning, weather forecasting could not have become a theoretical science.

NUMERICAL WEATHER PREDICTION

Like its American counterpart, weather forecasting in Japan underwent a qualitative shift after the introduction of digital computing. The use of mechanical air-conditioning was integral to this shift.

Japan had engaged in scientific observations of meteorological phenomena since 1875. These scientific observations assisted the technological modernization of Japan as a fledgling nation-state with an imperial ambition to unify and expand its territorial control in East Asia. The familiar images of weather charts, in which atmospheric conditions around the Japanese archipelago and the coastal region of the Asian continent are diagrammatically represented, are visual reminders of this geopolitical complicity between meteorology and empire building. Like cartography, meteorology had long functioned as an imperial science that aided the territorial expansion and maintenance of sovereign power. Mapping regional atmospheric conditions via weather charts is a cartographic practice inseparable from the territorial claims of the modern state.

By the 1890s, nationwide weather reports were issued daily, though the reputation of the Central Meteorological Agency suffered from its repeated failures. Because weather prediction in the predigital era relied on the subjective interpretation of human forecasters, it was also seen as an art of speculation. This is not to say that there was no theoretical advancement in Japanese meteorology before the introduction of numerical weather prediction. On the contrary, Japan's meteorologists were making substantial advances in the analysis of upper air systems—atmospheric conditions existing above the range of weather observable from land, known as surface weather systems. During World War II, for instance, military-funded research observing the upper air led to the discovery of jet streams, which enabled the launch of the infamous balloon bombs that traveled across the Pacific and landed on the West Coast of the United States.[13] There is more to say about this predigital era of weather forecasting, but one thing is clear: the introduction of numerical weather prediction was a game changer. The centrality of this technique sheds light on the transpacific Cold War geopolitics around computation and forecasting.

The Cold War conflicts accelerated meteorological research along with other adjacent fields (e.g., physics, ecology, oceanography, and cybernetics), as the superpowers competed to increase their technological capabilities to develop intercontinental missiles, rockets, and high-performance aircraft, and to weaponize the weather.[14] Numerical weather prediction, in other words, developed alongside Cold War military research in aerodynamics similarly conducted with newly available digital computers. Driven by the strategic need to understand and manage the atmosphere through which missiles and fighter jets would fly, Cold War military science brought on this qualitative and quantitative shift in the age-old practice of weather forecasting.

Numerical weather prediction in Japan began with the formation of a research collective, the Numerical Weather Prediction Group (aka the NWP Group) in 1953. The leader of the group was Shōno Shigekata, a famed meteorologist at the University of Tokyo. Shōno trained many of the elite Japanese meteorologists who would later migrate to the United States and participate in numerical weather prediction and atmospheric dynamics research projects. This group investigated theoretical possibilities for numerical weather prediction and advocated for its adoption at the Japan Meteorological Agency.

One of the meteorologists who helped with this transition was Ganbo Kanzaburō, who worked with Charney, von Neumann, and others at the Institute for Advanced Studies from 1952 to 1954, and upon his return to Japan worked for the Japan Meteorological Agency. Following the US Weather Bureau, which officially launched computerized weather prediction in 1955, Japan then became the third country in the world (after Sweden) to institutionalize numerical weather prediction in 1959.[15]

Several other Japanese meteorologists participated in this transpacific network of atmospheric scientists during the Cold War. Manabe Shukurō (aka Syukuro Manabe), a meteorologist and climatologist who worked on computer simulations of global climate change, was also a member of the NWP Group. Manabe joined the General Circulation Research Laboratory by invitation from the renowned American meteorologist Joseph Smagorinsky in 1959.[16] Another researcher, Arakawa Akio (aka Akio Arakawa), worked for the Department of Atmospheric and Oceanic Sciences at UCLA, representing yet another institutional bridge and transpacific connection. Arakawa, known for "his wizardry with numerical methods," worked on the numerical modeling of the circulation of the global atmosphere, including the formation of clouds, through the grid system.[17] There are a few other examples of the transpacific migration of Japanese researchers who participated in the so-called brain-drain class, including Kasahara Akira (aka Akira Kasahara), who was described as "the priest of numerical weather prediction" by one of his fellow Japanese meteorologists.[18]

This upsurge in the transpacific flow of elite male meteorologists moving from Japan to the United States indicates the geopolitical reorientation between the two former enemy nations as well as the strategic import of meteorology during the Cold War. These wizards and priests entered the citadel of the American military-industrial-academic complex, from which Japanese universities and scientific research institutes also benefited, at a key moment in the transformation of this complex.

Importantly, the transpacific flow of human brainpower also had its machinic counterpart, though its directionality was in reverse. As Japanese meteorologists exited, American computers arrived. In 1957 the Japan Meteorological Agency signed an agreement with IBM Japan to rent the mainframe computer 704. While a domestic computer such as FACOM-100 developed by Fujitsū was used in the initial stage of numerical weather prediction experiments, the agency opted for the IBM computer, which they deemed superior in its functionality.[19] Until the domestically produced HITAC 5020 developed by Hitachi replaced the IBM 704 in 1967, Japan's weather forecasting was run on this rented American computer, a fact that irked some domestic manufacturers. Indeed, it was partly such techno-nationalist pride that spurred the corporate-government partnership to advance Japan's computer industry.

The IBM 704 arrived in the early morning of January 13, 1959. A container carrying the package landed at the Yokohama port with much fanfare. The truck that transported the machine was adorned with a huge white banner with English signs that read: "JMA Welcome IBM 704 Electric Digital Computer" and "The First in the Orient."[20] These signs speak symptomatically to the simultaneously self-Orientalizing and patriotic gesture on the part of the Japan Meteorological Agency. Registered in the claim "The First in the Orient," for instance, is an ambivalent sentiment of quasi-colonial mimicry, in which the gaze of the United States that saw Japan as the racialized other, the military stronghold, and the ideological wingman was internalized. Such discourses were instrumental in aiding the exertion of the American economic and political influence in Asia during the Cold War. Like the exodus of the meteorologists, the transpacific journey of this electronic brain was also deeply implicated in the imperial geopolitical remapping of this region.

Once safely stored inside its brand-new computer room, this precious machine needed constant atmospheric pampering and care. The agency understood that creating the temperate microclimate for the computer was critical for the success of their numerical weather prediction. In preparation for the arrival of the IBM computer, the government had constructed a two-storied structure to hold an industrial refrigeration system and cooling towers. In order to run their prediction program, the agency also hired three "air-conditioning coordinators." The sole task of these technicians was to monitor and control the temperature and humidity inside the computer room.[21] These technicians were "human thermostats" who calibrated the optimal temperature for the machines.[22] Meteorologists from this particular era reminisce about how the gleaming computer room stood apart from the rest of the compound, especially from the run-down wooden structure where human forecasters were busy reading computer-generated weather charts.[23] The purified air and artificial coolness gave a semblance of technological progress to the otherwise unremarkable facilities.

This anecdote indicates the infrastructural importance of air-conditioning for numerical weather prediction. Without the production of indoor weather, the numerical prediction of outdoor weather was impossible. The localized microclimate control inside the computer room—a miniature version of our current data centers—is the material condition of possibility for forecasting the weather. Put another way, human-made artificial weather had to be produced and controlled *before* one could predict and control natural weather; that is, control over indoor weather precedes the computerized forecasting of outdoor weather.[24]

It is not prediction, then, that begets control, as the US Navy, who funded the first computerized weather prediction, had hoped. Rather, it is the opposite. This infrastructural reliance of prediction of outdoor weather on the control of indoor weather points to the causal reversal of the initial impetus that made numerical weather prediction possible. Moreover, this reversal of causality—that prediction is dependent on control—indicates the deeper epistemological and political stakes of the thermostatic desire that undergirds dreams and ambitions of controlling weather. It does not simply express a wish to control what is to come through prediction. Rather, it performs a more fundamental epistemic gesture of producing a knowable object (or the *object-sphere*, to use Martin Heidegger's term), and naturalizing this object as if it had always existed.

To better understand the epistemological and political stakes of both the production of future weather as an object of knowledge and this reversal of causality between prediction and control, we need to turn to the parallel development of futurology, for the idea of mathematically predicting the future exceeded the bounds of meteorology. In both Japan and the United States, there was widespread hype around the forecasting of the future within social science. As self-proclaimed futurologists debated the computability of the future, prediction became synonymous with mathematical projection, and mathematical projection gave hope to the controllability of the future.

Futurology—with its reliance on digital computers—also depends on the production and control of indoor weather by mechanical air-conditioning. Moreover, what we can glean from the development of futurology is an epistemic operation that is more fundamental to the technological forecasting of the future: the self-grounding gesture of the modern scientific subject who posits the future itself as a knowable object. The future of outdoor weather is a variant of this future *in general*. It is to this second genealogy of forecasting the future that I now turn.

FUTUROLOGY

Futurology emerged in the aftermath of World War II and gained considerable popularity in the United States, Japan, France, and the United Kingdom in the 1960s. The root of futurology as an institutionalized practice lies in Cold War strategic thinking, though it soon became a much broader trend in the civilian context. Although there were notable connections between Japanese and other international futurologists (mostly the French sociologists), the main connection I want to focus on here is that of Japan and the United States, and its relationship to the geopolitical context of numerical weather prediction—a field that similarly benefited from the Cold War strategic thinking including systems theory and digital computing.

Futurology in Japan—like elsewhere—coalesced as a loosely knit network of social scientists, economists, anthropologists, engineers, urban planners, science fiction writers, and bureaucrats. Often affiliated with newly established think tanks such as the Institute for Future Engineering in Tokyo—which wielded influence on governmental policies regarding technological innovations, restructuring of energy industries, and urbanization—this multidisciplinary network of futurologists placed a high value on information technology. As the rapid pace of postwar economic growth decreased, the government was also rolling out strategic plans for postindustrialization in the 1960s.

The major catalyst for popularizing futurology was the planning of Expo '70, the temporary "city" that served as a large-scale social laboratory and a testing site for computing and air-conditioning, among other technological experiments. Importantly, the site had all the communication and energy infrastructures of a functional city. Its administrative use of networked computing and a data communications system, moreover, was hailed as the prototype of the future system of social engineering, while its use of a district cooling system was seen as a rational step toward optimizing the use of energy in urban areas. Together, these two systems of communication and circulation—of data and coldness—projected a techno-utopian image of futurity.

In addition to architects and engineers, the main advocates of this urban experiment were futurologists and technocrats. It is their managerial vision of the future that I want to investigate here, as its logic mirrors the causal paradox of prediction and control seen earlier with numerical weather forecasting.

Like meteorology, the multidisciplinary field of futurology flourished with the arrival of digital computing. The exemplary case of future forecasting is the famous report, *The Limits to Growth* (1972), prepared by the Club of Rome, an international organization dedicated to the systematic forecasting of the future of the planet. The report made use of the system dynamics model of computer simulations developed by the systems scientist Jay Forrester at the Sloan Management School at MIT to predict future scenarios of overpopulation, economic growth, environmental resource depletion, and so forth. The organization had several notable Japanese members, including the architect Tange Kenzō.[25]

As we will see in later chapters, Tange and Metabolist architects embraced cybernetics, systems theory, and computer simulations as means of designing cities as self-regulating, living organisms with their own metabolic pathways and microclimates. Not surprisingly, it was Forrester's "world model" that also provided the theoretical basis for Tange Lab's report *Japan in the 21st Century*, published as part of the government-commissioned project of future forecasting (1970).[26] Kurokawa Kishō from the Metabolist architecture group was also a self-proclaimed futurologist who participated in a number of futurological events in Japan.

Kurokawa and other Japanese futurologists shared the concerns of their overseas colleagues—such as the British futurologist Dennis Gabor, author of *Inventing the Future* (1963), and the American futurologist Alvin Toffler, author of *Future Shock* (1970)—regarding the impact technological changes, such as computing, may have on society. Others such as Olaf Helmer at the RAND Corporation, who developed the quintessential Cold War future forecasting strategy of the Delphi Method and later cofounded the think tank Institute for the Future, were invested in finessing methodologies and models for forecasting. Meanwhile, other enterprising futurologists explored the application of future forecasting for the consulting industry.[27] Such varied approaches to futurology produced numerous techniques and methods of future forecasting regarding scientific, technological, industrial, and economic trends, each of which were brought to bear on governmental policies in the aforementioned countries.

In May 1970, two months after the opening of Expo '70, the Japanese Association for Future Studies hosted the International Conference on Future Research, under the theme of "Challenges from the Future," in Kyoto. The conference and the world's fair did not coincidentally happen at the same time but were rather intimately linked. Tracing this link allows us to examine the main advocates for these two events.

The popularity of futurology in Japan preceded the government's proposal to host Expo '70. As William Gardner argues, a civilian group of intellectuals called "Thinking the Expo Group" was an active force behind the founding of the Future Studies Research Group in 1966.[28] It was led by five men: the cultural anthropologist Umesao Tadao, often credited as the progenitor of the Japanese discourse on the information society; the science fiction writer Komatsu Sakyō; the sociologist Katō Hidetoshi; the architectural critic Kawazoe Noboru (another member of the Metabolist group); and the sociologist Hayashi Yūjirō from the Economic Planning Agency, whose book, *The Information Society* (1969), popularized the term *informatization*.[29]

This small research group quickly developed into the Japanese Association for Future Studies in 1968. The overall conceptualization of Expo '70 as a simulated future city of information and networked computing owes much to this interdisciplinary circle of intellectuals who gathered around the Thinking Expo Group. Importantly, their work emphasized the speculative and artistic dimensions of the world's fair.[30]

Like its American and French counterparts, the Japanese branch of futurology operated in close proximity to the central government's economic policy initiatives. These connections hint at the institutional basis of Japanese futurology, which encompassed a wide range of intellectuals—from Komatsu Sakyō, a prominent science fiction writer known for his dystopian visions of the future and a member of the Future Studies Research Group mentioned above, to Masuda Yoneji, an utterly optimistic technocrat who blurred the boundary between futurology and management science.

This managerial undertone of Japanese futurology is best exemplified by the writings of Kōyama Ken'ichi, a political scientist who contributed an essay, tellingly titled "The Future Society's 'Management According to Objectives,'" to the anthology, *A Proposal for Futurology* (1967). Like Hayashi, Kōyama was active in the emerging field of "social engineering" (*shakai kōgaku*) in the 1960s. Through his prolific writing, Kōyama also introduced various works of American, French, British, and Soviet social scientists and technologists under the unifying banner of futurology.

Take, for instance, *An Introduction to Futurology* (1967), in which Kōyama introduced a divergent array of thinkers he presents as "new utopian thinkers." His list of futurological works is indicative of the international scope of futurology as it was understood in Japan at the time. For instance, it includes the sociologist Daniel Bell's *The End of Ideology* (1960); the French government–commissioned report "Réflexions pour 1985" (1965), edited by the technocrat Pierre Massé; *Computers and the World of the Future* (1964), edited by the management scientist Martin Greenberger; and the works of Soviet cyberneticians and science fiction writers such as Lev Pavlovich Teplov and Ivan Yefremov. For Kōyama, these thinkers collectively represented the global promise of futurology, their national, ideological, and disciplinary differences notwithstanding.

According to Kōyama, futurology is defined first and foremost by the idea of the manipulability—or engineerability—of the future. It is this assumption of manipulability that aligns the futurological framework of future forecasting with the instrumental rationality of modern science. Kōyama writes: "Emerging out of interdisciplinary collaborations among social science and natural science, futurology is an emergent methodology that aims to analyze, conceptualize, and design the future society and humanity as totality; this is based on the viewpoint that the future is manipulatable."[31]

This idea of the future as an object of manipulation, management, and engineering appears again in the title of Kōyama's 1967 essay, "The Design for the 21st Century: The Manipulable Future" (1967). There, he argues that the future is a realm of possibilities from which one selects better choices based on calculation, prediction, and projection.[32] His argument is that only when the future is apprehended as a cluster of probable possibilities can it be manipulated. "The characteristic feature of the new utopian futurologist thinkers," he writes, "is that they posit the selectable future as a set of hypotheses."[33] However, for these possibilities or choices to be hypothesized, the future must be conceived first and foremost as a realm of projection based on past data sets.

I want to highlight the term *projection*, since it allows us to clarify an underlying epistemological assumption of Kōyama's argument, and by extension, of Japanese futurology. The future is imagined here as a project. This projected future is presumed to be a predictable, calculable, and engineerable object. Once conceived as a project, this future as an object of calculation is propelled forward like a projectile on its parabolic flight path. Such a projective understanding of future spatializes—and territorializes—it. This projected future corresponds to what Martin Heidegger calls an object-sphere.

My use of the term *object-sphere* here is intentional. For the notion of *sphere* adds spatial connotations of coverage and enclosure, which are implied in this projective prediction of the future. (As we will see in the next chapter, the notion of sphere also played a strategic role in Japan's wartime discourse on geopolitics and its imperial territorial expansionism, which is heavily influenced by its German counterpart.) An underlying operation of the projective mode of predicting the future is what Heidegger calls "mathematical projection," an axiomatic mode of thinking that characterizes the self-grounding nature of modern science. "The mathematical," according to Heidegger, "is this fundamental position we take toward things by which we take up things as already given to us, and as they must and should be given."[34] The quantitative fixity of mathematical thinking makes it uniquely amenable to calculation and projection, eliminating elements of surprise. Similarly, the future in Kōyama's theory of futurology is posited in advance as a projectile whose path is already determined, though its outcome is not yet known. It is this vectorial imagination of the future as a projectile—already hinted at in the etymological sense of *forecasting* ("throwing or hurling" something "before or in front") as a gesture of scheming or planning beforehand—that futurology presupposes.

According to Heidegger, the mathematical mode of thinking is marked by "anticipating determinations and assertions," which turns an object of inquiry—in this case, the future—into a project. To quote Heidegger again: "The project is axiomatic. Insofar as every science and cognition is expressed in propositions, the cognition which is taken and posited in the mathematical project is of such a kind as to set things upon their foundation in advance."[35] Similarly, futurology is marked by this propositional will, which sets its own epistemic object in advance. Its self-grounding gesture is discernible in the grasping of the future as an object of scientific knowledge and the futurologist as a subject who both invents and studies this object. Once conceived in this self-referential manner, the future as an object can be predicted and designed.

This self-referential making of the future as a project—and a projectile—spatializes the future as an enclosed object-sphere. By foreclosing the temporal openness of the future through the mathematical mode of thinking, which renders it calculable and knowable in advance, futurology excludes the unknowable or wholly unexpected dimension of time that is yet to come.[36] Moreover, this deterministic way of conceptualizing the future as the enclosed sphere of calculation not only spatializes but also territorializes it, as if the future can be mapped with grids and graphs.

COMPUTING

This territorialization of the future as an object of knowledge—with the futurologist as its correlate subject—lies at the basis of Cold War military science, from which futurology developed. Another indicator of the overlap between futurology and mathematical projection lies in the popularity of simulations (both computer simulations and scenario making) among futurologists at this time. Simulations are axiomatic both in the Heideggerian sense of projection and in the more narrow and technical sense of developing mathematical models. To simulate, one has to "set things upon their foundation in advance" and determine the parameters of the models on which simulations will be performed.

The concepts and methods of computer simulations based on mathematical models are deeply associated with the Cold War military-industrial-academic complex.[37] As Edwards writes, the "closed-world" discourse of the Cold War period manifested itself in the proliferation of simulations as a cultural paradigm.[38] The popularity of simulations effectively blurred the boundary between military and civilian realms of forecasting the future. Frequent discussions of simulation as a metaphor and practice among Japanese futurologists, architects, technologists, and technocrats attest to the prevalence of the mathematical mode of thinking. Moreover, computer simulations were also used for planning and design, for instance, by the Japanese architects at Tange Lab.

Within the field of Japanese architecture, Tange Lab was an early adopter of computer simulation.[39] The culminating point of their fascination with computer simulation was Expo '70, whose master plan was handled by Tange. This world's fair was conceived as "a simulation" of the future city.[40] In addition to developing a master plan for this simulated city of the future, Tange Lab made use of computer simulations to calculate and visualize the flow of visitors and vehicles based on the probability of popular attractions and waiting times at various pavilions in order to optimize the structural design of the Expo compound.[41] These simulations of pedestrian and automobile circulations served not only the purpose of designing the layout but also of devising strategies of crowd control.

Tange Lab's use of computer simulations was not only prescient, it was also suggestive of its affinity with the mathematical mode of thinking that characterized the Cold War cultural paradigm of simulation and future forecasting. Both practices conceive of the future as an object-sphere in the projective form of computer models and future scenarios. The future, in other words, is projected in advance and hypothesized about, even if such hypothesizing may fail in the end.

Tange Lab's flow simulation and data visualization of pedestrian and vehicular traffic at the Expo site indeed fell short of predicting the actual volume of traffic once the fair opened. Nonetheless, their experiments attest to the increasing importance of digital computers within future-oriented practices of forecasting, planning, and policing urban space, economy, and technology. This techno-utopian investment in the relatively new technology of digital computing also gave rise to another futurological fad: the idea of computer-aided utopia.

This imagination manifested in the frequent evocation of the portmanteau *computopia*, which grew out of the 1960s industrial and political context of techno-nationalism and social engineering, evidenced by the development of networked computing used at Expo '70.[42] Along with the members of the Japanese Association for Future Studies and Tange Lab, technocrats and industrialists who supported this idea of computopia formed the third group of futurologists. If future forecasting and simulations were the principal technical concerns of the first two groups, networked computing and its managerial potential of social control and organization captivated the third.

Expo '70's networked computer system came out of the nonprofit organization JCUDI (the Japan Computer Usage Development Institute), which began publishing a series of documents called the Computer White Papers in an effort to "encourage the business use of computers and modernize management" in Japan in the 1960s.[43] The founder of this organization was a technocrat named Inaba Hidezō, who also launched Japan's first computer magazine, *Computopia*.[44]

As was made evident in the Computer White Papers' evocation of management as the end goal of computerization, the Japanese technocrats and futurologists who eagerly imported the new discipline of management science from the United States embraced its promise of efficiency and optimization. Management science, to quote the British cybernetician Stafford Beer's book title, is the business use of operations research.[45] Emerging out of the World War II military practice of quantitative management of logistics and decision making, operations research quickly found nonmilitary applications in the business world.

While the civilian applications of operations research in the business sector were discussed among Japanese industrialists in the 1950s, the widespread interest in management science and its appropriation of information technology—the discipline of MIS (Management Information Systems) in particular—peaked in the mid-1960s in Japan. It was during this time that the corporate-government investment in Expo '70 as the prototype of a postindustrial computopia began in earnest.[46]

This managerial vision of the postindustrial society is best expressed in the 1967 book entitled *Computopia* written by the technocrat-turned-futurologist Masuda Yoneji. He argues that the information age ushers in a "new elite" class of scientific and technological experts (technocrats) who "design politics, military affairs, and economics as gigantic systems and operate them through computers."[47] He calls this future computopia, an idealized postindustrial society that harnesses "the cognitive creativity of individuals" who have universal access to "information utilities" and produce "knowledge capital." Aligning himself with historical thinkers of utopia like Thomas More, Masuda contends that "Computopia is a wholly new long-term vision for the 21st century."[48] Computopia in his view is synonymous with an affluent capitalist society where socially conditioned citizens happily perform skilled cognitive labor in efficiently networked informatic environments, engage in voluntary self-management, and express their creativity in their leisure time.

For Masuda and his fellow futurological technocrats, the key technology that would liberate workers (from the drudgery of manual labor, long hours of commuting, and the discomfort of urban density) is networked computing. It is the virtual connectivity of users-as-workers who live in green suburbs and work from home that dominates their imagination of the future.

As was the case with numerical weather prediction, this rather generic rose-colored vision of networked computing was inflected by the specific geopolitical conditions of postwar Japan. Unlike numerical weather prediction, however, the development of networked computing played more directly into the techno-nationalist sentiment and economic protectionism of the 1960s.

This geopolitical background surrounding the development of networked computing also sheds light on the transpacific nexus between Japan and the United States. This nexus manifested in the tension-filled relationship between two tech giants: IBM and the Nippon Telegraph and Telephone Public Corporation, which was privatized and rebranded as NTT in the mid-1980s (hereafter, I use the abbreviation NTT to refer to this company before its privatization).

Since networked computing provides the technical support for future forecasting—including weather prediction—understanding the transpacific geopolitical and industrial context that led to its development and showcasing at Expo '70 is critical. This means we need to approach a history of digital computing from the Japanese perspective, while attending to the relationship between Japanese and American developers.

Japan's postwar ascendancy as the powerhouse of consumer electronics and computers was due to these protectionist industrial policies developed by the Ministry of International Trade and Industry (MITI), a governmental organization widely credited for the so-called economic miracle phase of Japan's recovery and growth.[49] Indeed, it was MITI that initiated the proposal to host this world's fair in Osaka as part of its national infrastructure development and regional economic stimulus projects. In addition, NTT provided significant financial and technological support to the fledgling domestic computer industry, mainly through its foray into data communications services, and through using Expo '70 as a platform for displaying the myriad potential applications of networked computing.[50]

The postwar development of the Japanese computer industry is also shadowed by what is often referred to as IBM imperialism.[51] The threat of monopoly posed by IBM gave rise to the popular analogy of IBM as an elephant and Japanese computer firms as mosquitoes. The MITI used this analogy to plead with the elephant not to "crush the mosquito under its feet" during their negotiations over IBM's basic patents in 1960, as Japanese firms needed to use these patents to develop their technical capabilities to produce domestic computers.[52]

In the meantime, IBM started to sell its products in Japan through its subsidiary company, IBM Japan, based on a 1961 agreement. Quickly, the company became the most desired employer for recent university graduates majoring in science and engineering in Japan. Its advanced computing technology, management style, and corporate philosophy became objects of curiosity, admiration, and envy, as evidenced by numerous published articles and books, which promised to unveil the secret of its global success.[53]

IBM was, in fact, an emblem of the new era of computing *and* corporate management for many. As John Harwood argues in his analysis of the coevolution of the organizational ethos of corporate management and the industrial design of the computer, the company invented more than machines; it invented a new system of management as well. As IBM put it, its "business was how other businesses do business."[54]

As the intertwined issues of computing and corporate management were gaining wider attention, the Japanese government developed its protectionist policies to restrict the sales of foreign computers and to consolidate and subsidize research and development efforts of domestic computer firms.[55] This techno-nationalist spirit against IBM imperialism gained momentum around 1964, when IBM developed a special online data processing system for the Tokyo Olympics. This "Tokyo Olympics Tele-processing System" connected multiple terminals through a telephone line, which transmitted real-time information to the company's data center in Tokyo.

This large-scale data communications system created by IBM sent shock waves through the Japanese computer and telecommunications industries, which saw these Olympics as a national project and a project of nation building.[56] Between the 1964 Tokyo Olympics and Expo '70, the tide rapidly turned in favor of the Japanese computer industry, largely because of the corporate-government partnership to make Expo '70 into the testing ground and showcase of Japan's technological capabilities. Sparked by this, Japanese companies such as Hitachi and NTT worked to establish a networked computing system, which was deployed as the "Expo '70 Data Communication System."

This networked computing system was specifically designed to manage the daily operations of Expo '70, including processing traffic and parking information, tracking the numbers and movements of visitors, running lost-and-found booths, and managing information terminals. Linked to the multiple networks of surveillance cameras, sensors, telephones, and printers, this data communication system was envisioned as the prototype of a localized computer network, which technocrats and industrialists alike regarded as vital to the postindustrial economy.[57]

The unprecedented scale of Expo '70 as a testing site for this brand-new networked computing system left an indelible mark on Japan's information and communications technology sector in the 1970s. For instance, Kitahara Yasusada, then the vice president of NTT, advocated the post–Expo '70 vision of computopia, which he presented as part of NTT's turn toward its "post-telephone" business. Like Masuda, Kitahara sketched a rosy picture of computopia: workers complete their office work via videophones and computers while staying at their comfortable suburban homes. A father buys tickets for baseball games and pays with a credit card online, while a mother uses an interactive videotex system (called "Captain System") to select recommended cooking recipes displayed on the screen and order missing ingredients from a nearby supermarket. At midnight, when one of their children gets a fever, the parents simply contact the doctor over the phone, send the child's medical data to the hospital, and receive immediate medical advice online. The next morning, the children are seen exchanging favorite videos, texting, and playing virtual games with their friends on the Captain System.[58] The spread of the internet and smartphones, however, eventually rendered the Captain System obsolete. Yet its techno-utopian vision of connectivity deserves attention precisely for its historicity.

As Fred Turner reminds us, digital utopianism and its promise of personal liberation through computers yoked together the American countercultural movement of New Communalists to the emergent Silicon Valley technologists in the 1960s, thus forming the historical antecedent to the cyber-utopianism of the 1990s.[59] Japan's techno-utopian narrative of computopia around and after Expo '70 parallels this familiar rhetoric of computerization as emancipation that frames American digital utopianism, albeit with a more distinctively bureaucratic undertone.

However, it would be inaccurate to simply read the Japanese futurological discourse and practice of computopia as a derivative offshoot of American digital utopianism, whose anti-technocratic stance and ethos of egalitarian collaboration ironically emerged out of the interdisciplinary institutional setting of the military-industrial-academic research of the Cold War. For the presumed autonomy of the civilian sector (including the countercultural milieu of digital utopianism) from the state apparatus of bureaucracy stands in contrast to a much more blurred boundary between the two in the Japanese context. In the latter, it was precisely this bureaucratic dimension of computopia that came to the fore.

THE TECHNOCRATIC AVANT-GARDE

The American brand of digital utopianism posits technocracy and bureaucracy as the antithesis of democracy. However, bureaucracy was not always opposed to utopian thinking. For instance, bureaucracy has long served as the utopian model of the egalitarian society for the Left as in the case of the German postal service, which inspired Lenin and Kropotkin.[60] The intricate partnership not only between the state and the corporate sector but also between the administrative class of bureaucrats and the creative class of avant-garde architects, artists, and designers that characterized the planning and execution of Expo '70 as the prototype of a future computopia points to the importance of highlighting this alternate lineage of imagining utopia through bureaucracy. Many of the technocratic futurologists who straddled the line between governmental and civilian institutions operated as what I would call the "technocratic avant-garde" and worked closely with the architectural avant-garde of Tange Lab.

The concept of the *avant-garde* has long been associated with an orientation toward the future imagined as the uncharted territory lying beyond the horizon called the historical present. Its characteristic disposition toward the novelty of experimentation and utopian social transformation underscores this temporal vector of its self-fashioning through futurity. Thus we get the commonplace modernist association of the artistic avant-garde with revolutionary politics. The avant-garde understood in this revolutionary temporality of breaking out of the present in its thrust toward the future is, not surprisingly, aligned with the antibureaucratic stance. For bureaucracy as a system of organization and management relies on institutionalization, that is, the establishment and maintenance of norms, rules, and the status quo.

Yet not all avant-gardes are anti-institutional or antibureaucratic. As its conceptual root in Saint-Simonian political thought (which positions artists along with scientists and engineers as visionary leaders of the industrial society) indicates, the idea of the avant-garde is historically linked to the birth of technocracy and scientific management.[61] This administrative connotation of the technocratic avant-garde as institution builders contradicts the canonical accounts of the artistic avant-garde as insurgents who form the creative camp of the countercultural movement. In the American context, this creative camp merged with the technologists and cyber-utopianists, as Turner has cogently argued. But this camp is often seen as opposed to the administrative sector of the state apparatus: the technocrats.

The Japanese context of digital utopianism critically differs from the American context on this point. It would be remiss to ignore the symbiotic relationship that existed between the technocratic avant-garde and the artistic avant-garde in Japan. The utopian outlook of the technocratic proponents of computopia, such as Inaba, Masuda, and Kitahara—and their version of futurology—can only be understood if we step out of the anti-institutional and antibureaucratic framework of the avant-garde and turn to the Saint-Simonian lineage of technical experts as state administrators who serve as the vanguard of social engineering.[62]

Technocracy and futurology, in other words, are closely connected. What binds them is a kind of pragmatic utopianism with a faith in the power of science and technology to engineer the future. Taking on the self-appointed position of the social vanguard, these experts direct the state apparatus of bureaucracy—with its administrative orientation toward predicting, designing, and managing the future. In so doing, the technocratic avant-garde brings together bureaucracy and social vanguardism, though this may appear oxymoronic in a capitalist society. As David Graeber argues, however, bureaucracy can appear creative especially when it democratizes despotism by undertaking massive technological and infrastructural projects. Bureaucracy in its despotic feat can enchant us when it operates as a form of "poetic technology;

that is, one where mechanical forms of organization, usually military in their ultimate inspiration, can be marshaled to the realization of impossible visions: to create cities out of nothing, scale the heavens, make the desert bloom."[63] The concurrent rise of futurology and computopia thus demonstrates how the technocratic avant-garde in 1960s Japan fits within Graeber's paradigm of bureaucracy as poiesis.

At the center of this technocratic avant-garde and its futurological embrace of computopia is the digital computer: the quintessential instrument of predicting, designing, and managing the future already projected as an object-sphere and a mappable territory. The experimental city of Expo '70 was built according to this projected future wherein human brains and electronic brains—like the artistic and technocratic avant-garde—symbiotically collaborate.

Like numerical weather prediction, however, this computational experiment at Expo '70 required the infrastructural support of air-conditioning. In other words, here too the desire to manipulate the postindustrial future through networked computers relied on the infrastructural production of artificial indoor weather inside computer rooms at the fair.

This testing site, which doubled as the prototype of computopia, relied on the smooth operation of its machinic "brains" inside the Operation Control Center's computer room. To run this computopia, these machines needed atmospheric pampering, just like the computers at the Japan Meteorological Agency. Atmospheric control of the microclimate inside the Operation Control Center's computer room, in short, was needed in order for this temporary computopia to be functional. Running below telecommunication cables and radio waves were underground water pipes, which delivered chilled water to cool down the fair's Operation Control Center's computer room and other facilities. These underground pipes formed a parallel network where coolness—instead of data—circulated. It is to this infrastructure of cooling, which supported the technocratic avant-garde's computopia, that I will turn to next.

REGIONAL AIR-CONDITIONING

The principal architect who took charge of designing the fair's regional air-conditioning system was Ojima Toshio, an environmental engineer with personal connections to Tange Lab.[64] He considered Expo '70 to be the ideal testing site for Japan's push for district cooling, which he saw as crucial for reducing the cost and infrastructural redundancy of air-conditioning in densely populated urban spaces. Instead of letting each pavilion install its own air-conditioning system, the architect opted to unify the thermostatic regulation of this temporary city by providing a centralized district cooling system composed of three refrigeration plants.[65] Taking place during the massive reorientation of the nation's energy industry (from coal to oil and nuclear power) and amid the increasingly palpable effects of urban air pollution, the Expo '70's experiment with regional air-conditioning naturally generated heightened anticipation.

Ojima was one of the leading voices who frequently discussed the idea of climate engineering and various possibilities for indoor and outdoor air-conditioning, including designing climate-controlled domed cities with carefully manufactured indoor weather. The idea that Ojima emphasized in many of his writings was the relationship between humans and "artificial climates."[66]

Like the transparent gigantic bubble that covers over the city of New York in Buckminster Fuller and Shōji Sadao's unbuilt project "Dome over Manhattan" (1960), Ojima and other Japanese architects' sketches for future cities from this era often highlight technologically produced microclimates as their defining feature. The domed-over city, according to Fuller, will "keep out rain, snow, and storms as well as exterior industrial fumes, while collecting all the rainwater in reservoirs," and the "temperature inside the dome will be so stabilized that a semitropical atmosphere will exist."[67] Similarly, the designers of Expo '70 initially harbored an analogous vision of hermetically sealing this temporary city inside a synthetic membrane.[68] Such a vision aimed to turn the entire urban space into an indoor microclimate whose temperature and humidity could be regulated like a glass-walled greenhouse (figure 2.1).

Although this ambitious plan never came to fruition, Expo '70 still succeeded in demonstrating the possibility of designing a large-scale air-conditioning system. Crucial to the construction of this system was another type of urban membrane: the informatic system of networked computing. Ojima recalls how essential the continuous supply of coolness to the Operation Control Center's computer room was, even in the chilly days of mid-March when the fair opened.[69] If not the city and its urban dwellers, at least the machines inside the computer room received constant atmospheric pampering. Inside these architectural bubbles sat domestically produced mainframe computers, which ran the prized data

FIGURE 2.1. Dome over Manhattan (1960) by Buckminster Fuller and Shōji Sadao. Courtesy of the Estate of R. Buckminster Fuller.

communication system that technocratic futurologists hailed as a sign of the coming computopia.

In the end, the Expo '70 experiment with regional air-conditioning failed in practice because the coolness was unevenly distributed. Computer rooms were not shut down, but some pavilions received complaints that they were too hot, while others were too cold. This uneven implementation of atmospheric pampering aimed at visitors also points to the subjective perception of temperate microclimates. What is comfortably cool or warm to one person might not be the case for someone else nearby. Unlike the computing machines, the perception of temperature for their human counterparts fluctuated according to their embodied perception of the surrounding atmosphere. Their comfort level was harder to predict compared to the functional level of their machinic counterparts. The eventual course of air-conditioning technology, in other words, seemed to lie in the more customized mode of predicting this embodied perception of ambient comfort.

To follow this transpacific thread of the genealogy of mechanical air-conditioning a step further, the final section of this chapter turns to contemporary examples of weather forecasting and air-conditioning. In these examples, we find an intensification of the thermostatic desire that posits the atmospheric future as an object of technological control. This desire continues to drive technological and financial investments in precision, optimization, and localization of atmospheric prediction and control, which often manifest as microtemporalization of prediction (faster intervals) and hyperlocalization of prediction (smaller microclimates).

While tending toward localization and optimization (often associated with the rhetoric of smartness), these contemporary examples of weather forecasting and air-conditioning also exhibit a spatiotemporal paradox. The intensification of the localized prediction requires an inverse movement of dispersive extension—or environmentalization—of the computing and air-conditioning infrastructures that support this precision-based forecasting. The territorial and technocratic understandings of the future—as an object-sphere and a pragmatic utopia—have turned into the mundane practice of atmospheric control as in the case of smart air conditioners. I argue that the political valence of this transformation is no longer directly shaped by the transpacific geopolitics of the Cold War but nonetheless inherits its epistemic and infrastructural conditions.

HYPERLOCALIZED WEATHER FORECASTING AND SMART AIR-CONDITIONING

To further examine the shift toward customized air-conditioning and weather prediction that inherits and builds on the Cold War paradigm of future forecasting, I return here to the contemporary examples of atmospheric control present in our daily environments through smart weather forecasting and air-conditioning technologies. Instead of the centralized model of thermostatic regulation, which characterized the regional air-conditioning system at Expo '70, today's smart air-conditioning technology aims to partition the atmosphere into discrete microclimates that respond to the fluctuating temperatures of individual bodies.

Similarly, the centralized system of network computing that Expo '70 featured has developed into a much more dispersed assemblage of multiple networks of smart devices that double as data-capturing sensors. Ambient computing and the customized prediction of weather—both artificial and natural—are simultaneously pushing atmospheric control into the background and hyperlocalizing it. This double move of ambient dispersion and hyperlocalization is accompanied by the acceleration in speed and increased mathematical precision with which constant forecasting of the nearest future happens.

The mid-twentieth-century dream of technological future forecasting finds its latest incarnations in smart weather forecasting and smart air-conditioning businesses today. Take, for instance, IBM's vertically integrated systems of monitoring and managing weather, business, and urban infrastructure. In 2016 IBM stepped up its involvement in the field of weather forecasting by purchasing The Weather Company, the largest private weather service provider. Combined with the AI-powered Deep Thunder program, which IBM has developed since the mid-1990s, the company is pitching a customized hyperlocal microweather forecasting service.[70] With the acquisition of The Weather Company, which owns the popular commercial weather reporting service Weather Underground, IBM made a full foray into the weather business.[71]

Making use of machine learning technology, IBM aims to provide precision weather forecasting to "help a business make smarter logistical, planning and operational decisions, faster and with more confidence." From managing urban traffic to the operation of wind farms, IBM's weather service aspires to "dovetail with other analytics-driven projects such as Smarter Cities."[72] IBM Japan also acquired a license to provide commercial weather reports from the Japan Meteorological Agency and established the Asia Pacific Forecast Center inside its headquarters in Tokyo in 2017. With its access to data sets gathered by the Japan Meteorological Agency's AMeDAS (Automated Meteorological Data Acquisition System), it promises to provide hyperlocal weather prediction to the region.[73]

To run numerical weather prediction, the Japan Meteorological Agency currently relies on a Hitachi supercomputer. Hitachi is also one of the leading manufacturers of AI-operated smart home air-conditioning units. While IBM markets hyperlocalized and customized smart weather forecasting for businesses, Hitachi markets hyperlocalized and customized airflows for consumers to provide, in theory, individually curated indoor weather.

Hitachi's residential air conditioners, such as the wall-mounted Shirokuma model, are equipped with near-infrared LED and thermal sensors and pattern recognition software to monitor and identify the positions, body temperatures, and durations of users in the room. The multiple cameras and sensors not only track down individual movements of multiple users but also map the layout of the room in order to find the most efficient pathways and intensities for multiple airflows that aim to create personalized microclimates for each individual user. The system keeps track of how long the user stays immobile or active inside the room in order to achieve the optimal comfort level of the user—not too cold, not too hot. If one of the users leaves the room for more than ten minutes, or comes back wearing a different outfit, the clock gets reset. Users can also control the system remotely with their smartphones.[74]

Hitachi developed this "life camera AI" system by repurposing some of its proprietary image-processing technologies used for security and surveillance systems. The company, for instance, markets high-speed detection and tracking technology using artificial intelligence, which can ostensibly "distinguish an individual in real time using features from over 100 categories of external characteristics such as sex, color of clothing, or carried items."[75] Hitachi brings together the biometric mode of governance (including facial recognition) and the marketing of individually curated indoor weather, which respond to the neoliberal ideas of personalization and customization. The technocratic model of social engineering and district cooling, which characterized the experiments at Expo '70 (for which Hitachi provided digital computers) has today morphed into the neoliberal model of individuated atmospheric control. However, the managerial undertone of the mathematical projection and engineering of the future, which characterized the fair fifty years ago, is still present in Hitachi's AI-supported air-conditioning and surveillance systems.

IBM's hyperlocalized weather forecasting and Hitachi's personalized air-conditioning are just two examples of contemporary forms of atmospheric control. There are many others that can be cited and analyzed, though I have focused on these two companies, which had a considerable impact on the planning and operation of Expo '70, in order to emphasize the genealogical continuity. The constant monitoring, tracking, and processing of data pertaining to weather and bodies are central to this continuity, which follows the same epistemological framework of projecting and territorializing the atmospheric future.

Accompanying this territorializing model of projecting the future is the extractive operation of capitalism. Like the earlier practices of settler colonialism and imperialism through which Japan and the United States extracted natural and human resources in order to accumulate capital, the current drive toward atmospheric compartmentalization follows the similarly extractive logic of positing the atmosphere as an untapped resource frontier. Ever-smaller divisions of the atmosphere into the grids of calculability engage in the mathematical projection that not only delivers on the corporate promise of customization but also retraces the colonial practice of territorialization.[76] In other words, in spite of this tendency toward customization, neoliberalism as a historical framework of analysis is insufficient. For the managerial vision of engineering, the atmospheric future is inseparable from the geopolitics of territorialization.

A hint of atmospheric territorialization in meteorology is found in the prevalence of grid-based methods of computer modeling used in numerical weather prediction (e.g., the Arakawa grid system). The mathematical approximation of the real by computer modeling using grids has an epistemological as well as geopolitical affinity with the territorial imposition of order. For the grid is a regulatory method of partitioning and organizing space, be it the geometric grid used to produce perspectival drawings or the topographic and township grids used in colonial settlements.

The visual use of grids to organize space is an old technique, yet it found a new application in the management of things and people through modern settler colonialism and capitalism. The cultural technique of the grid first gained governmental applications in the European New World colonies. The township grid used by the colonial government of the United States, for instance, not only rendered dispossessed lands from the Indigenous populations into commodities—available for settler purchase and registration—but also served as the standard unit for "taxation, census, electoral districts, and road construction."[77] In other words, the grid became the indispensable technique of government by managing both the territory and the populations within it.

While automatically computing the next hour's weather and adjusting the intensity of coolness might seem far removed from this long tradition of partitioning and territorializing the land, today's smart weather forecasting and air-conditioning technologies, which rely on hyperlocalization and microtemporalization, inherit the territorializing proclivity to partition the atmosphere. Such atmospheric territorialization replicates the imperial and colonial process of exerting control over territories and populations through the orderly projection of minutely divisible units of measurement. The mathematical projection of the future with the aim of taming its unpredictability similarly haunts these mundane contemporary technologies.

Just as the trade winds that sailed European colonialists to the Americas, and like the jet stream that sent balloon bombs from Japan to the United States, the breeze of technological forecasting of the future that smart weather and air-conditioning businesses advertise is navigational; it too steers and directs us toward a future that is already posited as extractable. What they promise of this extractable future, moreover, is the potential for gaining control over unpredictability.

The extractive gridding of the atmosphere, in other words, primes the unpredictability of the future itself as a commodity. The contemporary forms of technological forecasting generate new markets in which projected futurity circulates as commodities, not unlike the minimization of risk through the futures market within financial capitalism.[78] In this sense, the technological forecasting of the future turns what is uncertain into calculable risks. In fact, the curtailing of anticipated risk through prediction—from the potential economic damage of turbulent weather on businesses to the potential bodily discomfort of too much cold air—is what the hyperlocalized and microtemporalized weather forecasting and air-conditioning businesses sell. In so doing, they transform uncertainty and the temporal openness of the future into calculable risks and exchangeable commodities.

As Orit Halpern, Robert Mitchell, and Bernard Dionysius Geoghegan write: "We live in a world of fundamental uncertainty, which can only ever be partially and provisionally captured through discrete risks."[79] Increasingly, they argue, smart technologies are called for to anticipate and preemptively account for what is uncertain instead of what is predictable. Yet in the case of weather forecasting and air-conditioning, "smartness" is not about uncertainty but rather prediction and control. In this context, the technological forecasting of the future operates as if uncertainty can still be managed like a room's temperature.

Moreover, this technological forecasting of the future is bolstered by the causal reversal of control and prediction. Behind the mundane, taken-for-granted presence of weather apps and home air conditioners that have receded into the ambient background of our daily lives are the hidden infrastructures of computing and cooling, which have become vast, dense, and diffuse. As the speed and precision of localized prediction increases, so too must its infrastructure also grow larger—from the increasing ubiquity of environmental sensors to more robust cable networks, satellites, and data centers, which require, as we now know, ever more air-conditioning. Intensified future forecasting increases the spatial expansion and environmental impacts of its infrastructural base. This inverse relationship between the temporal acceleration of forecasting and the spatial expansion of infrastructure outlines the current state of future-directed thermostatic desire.

The genealogical roots of this thermostatic desire for technological forecasting and controlling the future, as I have argued, trace back to the geopolitics of territorialization and mathematical thinking, through which the future is projected as a knowable object. The projective act of designing the future based on prediction and control, furthermore, informed the pragmatic utopianism of the technocratic avant-garde who collaborated with the architectural and artistic avant-garde for the state-initiated experiments with urban planning, networked computing, and regional air-conditioning at Expo '70. Behind this unprecedented scale of futurological experimentation were the transpacific Cold War geopolitical conditions of the mid-twentieth century. It was within this specific spatiotemporal context that meteorology, futurology, and bureaucratic vanguardism coalesced around the utopian promises of digital computers and the symbiotic collaboration between human brains and their machinic counterparts in predicting the future.

While the mundane practices of checking the weather or turning on air conditioners on hot days may not appear to tell us much about the geopolitical and epistemological conditions of atmospheric control, we gain a critical perspective when unfolding the genealogies of such practices, techniques, and technologies. In so doing, we can begin to think beyond the projective, extractive, and territorializing framework of imagining the future, expanding it once again to its radical temporal openness.

3

TO THE GREENHOUSE:
WEATHERPROOF ARCHITECTURE
AS CLIMATIC MEDIA

In downtown Seattle sits a massive greenhouse: three glass-covered spheres that are part of Amazon's headquarters. Amazon Spheres, as they are called, reflect the entrepreneurial ambition of its founder Jeff Bezos who, aside from his massive e-commerce and logistics businesses, is also financing his own private aerospace company Blue Origin to develop orbital space colonies. This retro-futuristic structure, Spheres, is visually reminiscent of the iconic lattice-shell architecture—such as geodesic radar domes in the Arctic and the Biosphere 2 project in the Arizona desert—associated with American military and scientific research facilities. The interior environment of this corporate greenhouse attempts to replicate the distant tropical climatic zone of Hawai'i, while physically located in the foggy and cool northwest coastal city of Seattle.

More than three thousand species of plants, many from tropical and subtropical cloud forests, grow inside this spherical conservatory. Echoing the equally retro-futuristic vision of Blue Origin's space colonies (also designed to simulate the climatic conditions of Hawai'i while orbit-

FIGURE 3.1. Amazon Spheres. Joe Mabel, CC BY-SA 4.0, https://creativecommons
.org/licenses/by-sa/4.0 via Wikimedia Commons.

ing between Earth and the moon), Amazon Spheres presents a terrestrial
version of an entirely engineered indoor climate.[1] The company hires
full-time horticulturalists to curate and tend to these indoor plants. The
temperature inside is kept around 75 degrees Fahrenheit (23–24 degrees
Celsius) with 60 percent humidity in order to comfortably house both
plants and the Amazon employees who work inside these structures.
Some of the tropical plants are misted by the Spheres' proprietary fog
system (figure 3.1).[2]

The architectural practice of incorporating tropical greenhouses inside corporate buildings began and spread in North America during the
1960s, when mechanized air-conditioning of office space became the
norm. As David Gissen writes, architects and scientists hired by corporations reimagined "the modern office building's plentiful light and atmospheric features as a representation of divergent geographic zones,
and landscape architects and horticulturalists sought to identify those
species of plants that would thrive in the unusually consistent indoor
climate."[3] This deliberate incorporation of gardens inside urban offices
resulted in the reconceptualization of the indoor atmosphere as a replication of geographically distant climatic zones. It also facilitated the
horticulture business of cultivating tropical plants in South America

and other geographically distant places to be exported to North America for use in their climate-controlled office buildings. Mechanized heating, ventilation, and air-conditioning systems were key not only to the production of artificial weather, but also to the global logistics of the indoor plants trade. Amazon Spheres is a fitting example of this logistical connectivity and the latest iteration of these corporate greenhouses, albeit on a more grandiose scale.

I begin this chapter with Amazon's corporate greenhouse in order to highlight the relevance of air-conditioning and engineering of indoor climates to the logistics and geopolitics of territorial expansion. Lush with palm trees, ferns, and flowers even on the wintery days, the greenhouse (or "hothouse") is an architectural embodiment of the thermostatic desire to control the indoor atmosphere in order to cultivate living organisms inside an enclosed environment with its own microclimate, sheltering them from the elements of outdoor weather. During the nineteenth and twentieth centuries, these architectural techniques and technologies of sheltering also served colonial settlers and aided imperial scientists. Equally reminiscent in the Amazon's spherical greenhouse, therefore, is the expansionist desire of earlier imperial botanists—such as the British, Germans, and Japanese—who brought exotic flora from warmer climate regions back to the colder metropoles and cultivated them inside glass-roofed enclosures.[4] The greenhouse, with its historical associations with imperial botany, operates as a form of climatic media by combining the architectural and horticultural techniques and technologies of shielding what is inside from what is outside, while cultivating the plants therein. Both symbolically and materially, the greenhouse functions as a medium of separation, and this separation produces an enclosed indoor microclimate within which the transplanted flora are made to thrive.

Within the context of the points above I also draw attention to the similarities between the architectural practice of sheltering and cultivating human life and the horticultural practice of cultivating plant life inside air-conditioned microclimates in this chapter. Horticulture relies on a set of techniques and technologies such as irrigating, heating, tending the soil, and managing light. As exemplified by the greenhouse, it also works closely with architectural techniques and technologies of building walls and shelters, designing and managing light, ventilation, humidity, and temperature.

"There is no such thing as *the* house, or the house as such; there are only historically and culturally contingent cultural techniques of shielding oneself and processing the distinction between inside and outside," writes Bernhard Siegert in his analysis of cultural techniques as media.[5] The greenhouse as an ensemble of cultural techniques and technologies also operate as media, which generate material and symbolic distinctions between the life deemed worthy of protection or in need of careful management from the life that falls outside such protection and management. Accordingly, the greenhouse and other forms of architecture as media are implicated in the production and maintenance of biological, racial, gendered, economic, national, and geopolitical hierarchies and orders. The weatherproof walls of the greenhouse, whether be it imperial or corporate, not only exert atmospheric control over the plants and people inside them, but also uphold symbolic orders that socially condition and govern the lives on both sides of the walls.

Since the mid-twentieth century, the architectural metaphor of the greenhouse—with its connotations of separation and management— has taken on an added climatological dimension: the greenhouse effect. Earth itself is now analogized to a gigantic greenhouse with its atmosphere substituting for glass roofs and walls. Amid concerns about the climate crisis on this planetary greenhouse, aerospace speculators like Bezos have opted to invest in space settlements that promise to expand the living sphere of humanity beyond its earthly limits. This escape from the terrestrial greenhouse to extraterrestrial greenhouses in the form of space colonies is a path that is familiarly modern and imperialist. We have heard this narrative of territorial expansion before. Greenhouses and space colonies are genealogically connected; they are weatherproof architectures of settlement that rely heavily on the material and symbolic productions of indoor atmospheres, which simulate and replicate the climatic conditions of geographically distant places.

The metaphors of the sphere and the greenhouse are also prevalent in Peter Sloterdijk's analysis of the existential stakes of capitalist modernity, with which he reinterprets Martin Heidegger's philosophy of being and dwelling. The spherical greenhouse that encloses its interior exemplifies an air-conditioned mode of dwelling that Sloterdijk attributes to modernity. His analysis, which highlights both existential and physical sheltering of humans inside air-conditioned spheres, foregrounds the symbolic functions of architectural enclosures. Furthermore, for Sloterdijk, the historical development of greenhouse architecture is inseparable from a theological shift away from the heavenly realm of gods to the terrestrial realm of humans that Europeans experienced as they sailed away from their homelands to "discover" and colonize distant lands. These voyages, from which these European explorers brought back exotic flora, mark the dawn of capitalist modernity as the age of globalization.[6]

However, Sloterdijk's unabashedly Eurocentric narrative of modernity, with its settler colonial framing (emphasizing, for instance, the colonial voyages of "discovery" by Christopher Columbus and others that initiated this theological shift), ignores the complex transpacific contexts of capitalist and imperial modernity.[7] The aim of this chapter is to put a critical and transpacific spin on Sloterdijk's proposition that modernity is an age of globalized air-conditioning, while attending to the influence that a German theory of geopolitics had on Japanese imperialism. The wartime alliance between Japan and Germany was followed by Japan's subsequent postwar security alliance with the United States, which led to the reorientation of its geopolitical positions on the one hand, and to its ambitious explorations of the polar regions during the Cold War on the other. By tracing this connection between the wartime and Cold War geopolitics of territorial expansion via architecture, I take my exploration of indoor climate engineering into the realm of designing built environments.

Specifically, this chapter reads Tange Lab and its affiliate Metabolist architects' involvement in Cold War scientific expeditions in the polar regions through earlier wartime geopolitical discourses surrounding the expansion of the living sphere of the Japanese Empire. The cold climate regions played an important geopolitical role as Japanese architects and researchers reoriented their investment in designing houses and cities in Manchuria, Sakhalin, and other northern territories of the Japanese Empire to the international territories of the Antarctic and Arctic after the end of World War II. International attention to the polar regions increased during the early Cold War period not only due to their strategic potential for military security but also for their scientific potential as test sites for space settlements. Since then, geodesic domes and other modular architectures built to withstand the extreme environment of the polar regions have served as terrestrial analogues of outer space colonies.[8]

My intention here is to genealogically situate the retro-futuristic architecture of the Amazon Spheres and the Blue Origin space settlement project within this geopolitical context of the Cold War space race, where some of Tange Lab's important architectural experiments also took place.

By taking the analogy of the greenhouse and its idea of climatic shelter-ing as a point of departure, this chapter thus shifts its focus from plants to humans to chart out a transpacific context of territorial expansions aided by climatic media. Instead of bringing exotic flora from the tropics back to the metropole, the Japanese architects and scientists designed portable "greenhouses" (in the form of capsule housing and domed cit-ies) for explorers and settlers in the cold climate regions. To trace this transpacific genealogy of greenhouse-like architectures to which space colonies belong, however, we need to first understand the geopolitical conditions of Japanese imperialism and how it informed Tange Lab's and Metabolists' architectural experiments.

TANGE LAB AND METABOLISM

When the Japanese Empire collapsed in 1945, it lost most of its overseas colonies and semicolonial territories. This sudden reduction in land left Japan to turn inward to maximize its resource extraction, logistical co-ordination, and economic productivity through various means in order to compensate for its territorial contraction.[9]

Tange Lab and its affiliated Metabolist architects responded to this ter-ritorial contraction with novel proposals. Turning their attention inward, these architects, working with the state, proposed developmental proj-ects that optimized the use of the available territory in order to expand Japan's habitable space through horizontal and vertical extensions.[10] They saw the sea and the sky as "future sites for human habitats."[11] Com-bining the idea of reclaimed land with skyscrapers, for instance, they suggested constructing floating megastructures over the sea. Another Metabolist strategy to literally increase the territory was to build up ver-tically and stack platforms of "artificial ground." Proposed by Kawazoe Noboru, artificial ground (or artificial land) became one of the unifying concepts behind the diverse works that the Metabolist group presented at the 1960 World Design Conference.[12] These architects also regarded transportation, logistcs, and information management as key compo-nents of urban planning, and embraced cybernetics and systems theory.

Coalescing around Tange Lab at the University of Tokyo, led by the renowned architect Tange Kenzo and his protégés, Metabolism is likely the most celebrated and well-known Japanese architectural movement to date. These architects envisioned cities as living organisms and ap-proached urbanism through biological and cybernetic metaphors and analogies of organic growth, metabolic cycle, homeostasis, ecosystem, information, and communicative feedback in the 1950s and 1960s. Tange's and the Metabolist group's affirmation of the organic growth and constant metamorphosis of the city echoed an international trend in urbanism led by European and American architects, which similarly put forward an organicist approach to urban planning in the 1950s.[13] Yet, to fully understand their investment in expanding the territorial limits of Japan, we have to look beyond the immediate postwar context of urbanism, and into the wartime context of colonial architecture and urban planning.

The idea of expanding human habitats into unfamiliar territories is a crucial component of empire building. Noteworthy in this regard is Tange's wartime collaboration with the military regime. For instance, in 1942 he participated in the design competition for the Commemorative Building Project for the Construction of Greater East Asia (or the Greater East Asia Co-Prosperity Sphere Monument).[14] During the war, Asada Takashi—one of the early members of Tange Lab and the unofficial mentor to the Metabolist group—also discussed the security need for expanding the Japanese Empire's "living sphere" by fortifying national defense systems, multiplying production facilities, and extracting natural resources in the north.[15] I will come back to the geopolitical concept of the living sphere shortly, but for now it suffices to note that Tange and Asada were fully aware of Japan's imperial ambition to expand its territory and its need to ideologically and logistically unify the region under the banner of the Greater East Asia Co-Prosperity Sphere.

The connection between Tange Lab and the legacy of Japanese imperialism is also found in the biopolitical undertone of its Cold War architectural projects. From Tange's analysis of housing as the minimal unit of the reproduction of labor force to Asada's development of prefabricated housing for explorers and researchers in the Antarctic, Tange Lab's architectural projects after the war explicitly and implicitly aimed to cultivate the biological life of populations deemed worthy of protection. Tange was also involved in the unrealized project of designing a massive domed city in the Arctic, another polar region that played a strategic role during the Cold War. For these projects, the architects drew on earlier wartime studies of national land planning, environmental engineering, demography, and economic productivity conducted for the expansion of the empire.[16]

Tange Lab's connection to the scientific legacy of the Japanese Empire is particularly evident in Asada's design of the cold climate housing at Japan's Shōwa Station in Antarctica. Japan dispatched an expedition team to build a permanent research facility near the South Pole as part of its participation in the International Geophysical Year (1957–58). The station was established primarily for the purpose of peaceful observation and data collection of meteorological, geographical, and climatological conditions. For this expedition project, Asada and his team designed prefabricated proto-capsule housing, while drawing extensively on the knowledge of environmental engineering and climatological experiments undertaken by cryospheric scientists at Hokkaidō University's Institute of Low Temperature Science.[17] As we saw in the previous chapters, this institute played a foundational role in advancing Japan's cryospheric and atmospheric research, first in competition with the United States during World War II and later in collaboration under their Cold War security alliance.

Some of the research conducted at the Institute of Low Temperature Science as well as the Institute of Scientific Research in Manchuria was designed to facilitate Japanese agricultural settlements in Manchuria and other semicolonial and colonial territories located in the cold climate regions.[18] These earlier studies of ice, frost, and snow offered valuable knowledge to Asada and his team who were tasked to design efficiently insulated and lightweight shelters which were easy to transport and assemble in the extremely harsh and cold Antarctic environment. The knowledge and technologies of constructing climate-controlled shelters to expand the Japanese Empire's territorial reach were repurposed for designing climate-controlled shelters for ostensibly peaceful scientific expedition.

Present within these climate-controlled shelters, which aimed to expand human habitats into the polar regions, is the same proclivity toward territorial expansion that characterized empire-building during the war and the postwar experiments with artificial lands and megastructures. The extreme environment of the polar regions, moreover, served as a terrestrial analog to the harsh environment of outer space. Collectively, these architectural projects exhibit the thermostatic desire to control the indoor atmosphere. What connects them all is the idea of expanding the habitable environment through architectural design and engineering, which aim to reproduce geographically distant climatic zones, whether they be of the metropoles or Earth itself.

As the architect Yatsuka Hajime argues, Tange and the Metabolists' interest in artificial lands and megastructures extending into the sea and the sky inherited Japan's imperial ambition to expand its "living sphere" (*Lebensraum*), a uniquely geopolitical concept whose historicity deserves close examination.[19] In the early twentieth century, Japanese imperialists borrowed the German word *Lebensraum* to express their expansionist orientation. Curiously, the Japanese translation of the concept of *Lebensraum* as "living sphere" slightly differs from the common English translation of this German word as "living space." The German discourse on geopolitics and its doctrine of *Lebensraum* provided an important conceptual ground for wartime Japanese architecture. Variously translated into Japanese as *seizon ken*, *seikatsu ken*, and *seikatsu kūkan*, this geopolitical concept helps contextualize the imperial roots of Tange Lab and Metabolism and their climatological and biopolitical concerns with extending the human habitat.

Coined by the German geographer Friedrich Ratzel at the end of the nineteenth century, the geopolitical concept of *Lebensraum* was first introduced to Japan through a review of the Swedish political scientist Rudolf Kjellén's book *The State as Form of Life* (1916) in the mid-1920s. As I discussed in the introduction to this book, the Kyoto School philosopher Watsuji Tetsurō was one of the Japanese intellectuals who engaged with Ratzel's and Kjellén's theories of climatology and their analogy of the state as a living organism in his own climate-determinist analysis of Japanese national culture.[20]

Ratzel and Kjellén, like many others of their generation, incorporated the perspective of evolutionary biology into their fields of study. They also held an organicist view of the state whose healthy growth was bound to its environment or living sphere.[21] In his earlier work in geography, Kjellén had already argued that modern states endowed with limited territory must compete to extend their borders through colonial conquests and annexations of foreign lands. Kjellén's book *The State as Form of Life* cemented this organicist idea of the state and its geographical expansion as the basis of geopolitics and the protection of its population within its territory.

Importantly, the historical emergence of geopolitics as an academic discourse that foregrounds the territorial power dynamics of interstate relationships was intimately tied to the modern usage of another term:

biopolitics. The classical concept of geopolitics thus developed in close association with the idea of biopolitics, an understanding of politics as operating through the governance of the biological life of the state's subjects. It was Kjellén who first used the term *biopolitics* in this sense of governance with which we are familiar.[22]

By the 1930s, this organicist view of the state, combined with the biopolitical rhetoric of expanding the living sphere of the nation by effectively cultivating the biological life of its population, was avidly taken up by German and Japanese intellectuals. In Nazi Germany, the doctrine of *Lebensraum* advocated by the German school of *Geopolitik* provided an ideological alibi for the fascist regime in conjunction with the eugenic discourse on the racial purity of the German people. The Japanese school of geopolitics in turn was developed in close dialogue with the work of Karl Haushofer, a central figure in the German school of geopolitics. His theorization of autarchy and the living sphere drew on the previous work of Ratzel and Kjellén. Haushofer lived in Japan as a military officer from 1908 to 1910 and published several studies of Japan's economic and military ascendency. In Haushofer's geopolitical view of the world order, based on panregional hegemony, the Japanese military regime found a convenient theoretical justification for its ambition to construct the Greater East Asia Co-Prosperity Sphere.[23]

In the 1940s, Japanese geopoliticians and political scientists began to translate the term *Lebensraum* as "living sphere" (*seikatsu ken* and *seizon ken*) instead of "living space" (*seikatsu kūkan*) as it had customarily been done in the past. This semantic shift from *space* to *sphere* in translation was likely deliberate as it helped justify the regional conception of Greater East Asia, not as a clearly demarcated geographical space but as a contingent and imagined sphere of influence and survival.[24] The Japanese branch of geopolitics was developed, in this manner, as a quasi-scientific discipline in order to promote "the organic unity" of the imagined sphere of Greater East Asia, which covered not only East Asian nations, but also those in Southeast Asia and the South Pacific.[25]

As a result, the living sphere of the Japanese nation, on which the survival of the "Japanese race" hinged, was redefined from the bounded sovereign territory to the unbounded potential sphere of political influence, economic activity, and logistical coordination, supported by the imperial networks of railroads, telegraphs, and ports. To put it differently, the spherical thinking embedded in wartime geopolitics allowed a critical shift in redefining the national territory from the realm of *actuality* to that of *potentiality*. The geopolitical potentiality of expanding the empire overrode the geographical actuality of the empire. It is notable that, toward the end of the war, the German term *Lebensraum* was also translated as "life sphere" (*seimei ken*) and "survival sphere" (*shikatsu ken*), further escalating the sense of urgency. Such a discourse created the impression that the very existence of the Japanese nation was dependent on the continuous expansion of its living sphere.[26]

The rhetorical use of the geopolitical concept of the living sphere also affected Japan's wartime national land planning activities, in which a number of notable architects and colonial bureaucrats were involved. Some of the studies conducted for the wartime national land planning also informed and impacted the postwar developmental projects in which Tange Lab and Metabolist architects participated. In the minds of those architects and bureaucrats who were concerned with the national land planning and other developmental projects, moreover, Manchuria occupied a special place, for this semicolonial territory was regarded as a conceptual tabula rasa and a prime testing site for experiments in governance and urban planning.[27]

To borrow Louise Young's turn of phrase, Manchuria was "a kind of social laboratory, a controlled environment in which to test out theories of social transformation."[28] As a social laboratory, it attracted not just the right-wing military and business investors but left-wing architects and Marxist engineers as well. Designed by this politically hybrid group of modernizers, newly built cities in Manchuria were fully equipped with "running water and sewer systems, gas and electricity, telephone and telegraph lines, and a road network connecting to the railway station."[29] The colonial cities also boasted modern amenities such as public squares and parks that were still rare or nonexistent on the Japanese mainland; they served as prototypes for the Japanese cities of the future.

BIOPOLITICAL MANAGEMENT OF COLONIES

Colonial cities within the Japanese Empire such as those in Manchuria were not simply the models or prototypes of future cities. They also functioned as social laboratories and test sites for the biopolitical management of urban populations. One of the colonial bureaucrats who played a pivotal role in this culture of experimentation in the colonies and semicolonial territories was Gotō Shinpei, the so-called founding father of Japanese urban planning. His audacious experiments with colonial administration and city planning in Manchuria and Taiwan, according to Yatsuka, were the direct precursors to Tange and the Metabolists' postwar urban projects.[30]

Gotō studied medicine in Germany and served as the head of the Civil Administration Bureau in colonial Taiwan in the 1890s. He then became the first director-general of the South Manchurian Railway Company in the early 1900s. In the immediate aftermath of the Kantō earthquake in 1923, Gotō took charge of the reconstruction plan for the heavily damaged city of Tokyo. His infamous career as a colonial administrator in Taiwan, director-general of the South Manchurian Railway Company, twice-appointed communications minister, first chairman of the Urban Studies Association, mayor of Tokyo, and first director-general of the Tokyo Broadcasting Station suggests how closely his interests in empire building, urban planning, and telecommunication and transportation infrastructures were intertwined.

During his tenure as the director-general of the South Manchurian Railway Company, Gotō established a proto–think tank in the form of the research department of the company, which undertook a wide range of research activities related to the management of the informally occupied territory, from studying the Soviet model of planned economy to collecting geological data for agricultural purposes to developing housing projects for Japanese settlers.[31] In the early 1940s the researchers at the South Manchurian Railway Company's think tank collaborated with scientists from the Institute of Low Temperature Science in order to study logistical challenges posed by the cold climate, such as the prevention of frost heaving that inflicted seasonal damage on the railroad infrastructure.[32]

In Gotō's writing we also find the nascent biopolitical understanding of governing populations, including both settlers and colonized populations. His biopolitical view of governance is registered not only in the systems of medical policing he proposed but also in his mobilization of biological tropes to discuss geopolitical strategies and governmental techniques. For instance, Gotō developed Japan's colonial policies on public hygiene, which strongly reflected the then-prevalent view of social Darwinism couched in quasi-scientific tropes borrowed from biology.[33]

Gotō famously advocated a model of colonial management based on the biological principles of evolution and adaptation. His biopolitical vision of scientific colonial management is articulated in his book *Principles of National Hygiene* (1889). Largely based on the organicist model of the state and the study of the German medical police, the book argues for the systematic establishment of hygienics and a centralized police system to regulate the health of the population in order to protect the life of the "superior organism" of the state. For Gotō, all the activities of the state fall under the category of hygiene insofar as they promote the physiological happiness of the population. Following the work of the German jurist Robert von Mohl, Gotō calls the hygienic function of the state "police," which, using the German terminology, he also calls *Polizei*.[34]

As Michel Foucault reminds us, the biopolitical undertone of the concept of *Polizei*, as it developed through the seventeenth and eighteenth centuries, was directed toward a wide range of human activities before it became a modern institutional apparatus. Regulating these activities for the sake of strengthening the state was the principal objective of the police, since the state's strength—and wealth—was dependent on the productivity of its population: "If the governmentality of the state is interested, for the first time, in the fine materiality of human existence and coexistence, of exchange and circulation, if this being and well-being is taken into account for the first time by the governmentality of the state, through the town and through problems like health, roads, markets, grains, and highways, it is because at that time commerce is thought of as the main instrument of the state's power and thus as the privileged object of police whose objective is the growth of the state's forces."[35] While the rationality for policing was later modified with the rise of economic liberalism and the discourse of civil society, the management of the population as the main target of policing did not disappear. As Foucault writes, "The development in the second half of the eighteenth century of what was called *medizinische Polizei*, public hygiene, and social medicine should be re-inserted in the general framework of a 'biopolitics'; the latter aims to treat the 'population' as a set of coexisting living beings with particular biological and pathological features, and which as such falls under specific forms of knowledge and technique."[36] This new domain of knowledge and techniques of government presupposed the biological conception of humans as a species.

The biopolitical production of knowledge and techniques related to colonial governmentality generated by imperial bureaucrats like Gotō, however, was not limited to the realm of medical police. His effort to modernize telecommunication infrastructures was as crucial to his vision of colonial administration and the "welfare" of the Japanese Empire. Not surprisingly, then, his twin obsessions with communication and biology informed the very language he used to frame the importance of imperial infrastructures. Telecommunication and transportation networks were logistically vital, as both were instrumental in the rapid development of Japan as a modern nation-state and an imperial power. The wealth and strength of the nation, vying to become an imperial force, were dependent on the possession and control of communication infrastructures. Gotō reframed this infrastructure development as a biological—and hence natural—demand of the state as a living organism.

In Gotō's view, the state is the most superior form of organism "through which the satisfaction of the biological needs of the individual are realized."[37] This hierarchical view of the state as the superior organism appears again in his text, *On Japanese Expansion* (1916). Foreshadowing the later discourse of geopolitics, Gotō argues in the vitalist philosophical framework that the constituents of the nation belong to the same ethnic group or "race," and every race has its own "vital desire" or "expansionist desire." Competitions among modern nation-states are thus displaced onto race struggles based on the biological desire for the vital expansion of their environment.[38] This is how he understood and justified the vital expansion of the Japanese Empire as a living organism, a view that later developed into a more explicitly geopolitical discourse of expanding its living sphere.

In his discussion on the colonial governance of Manchuria, for instance, Gotō resorts to the biological analogies of the vertebrate animal and the nervous system. Complaining about the lack of a unified administrative system for the Office of the Kwantung Governor-General, Gotō advocates for the centralization of all administrative units through biological analogies: "The current state of colonial Manchuria in the empire is characterized by its disunity, which is comparable to the de-centralized nerve ganglia of a lower form of animal life." In his view, this office needs to function as the "brain" of Japan's imperialist expansion in Asia, and must be restructured by unifying its judiciary, police, civil engineering, and telecommunications apparatuses. Only then can these administrative apparatuses properly function as the "central nervous system" of the empire, which he analogizes to the intelligent "vertebrate animal."[39]

Gotō's comparison of the Japanese Empire and its governmental apparatuses to the nervous system of the vertebrate animal is just one example, but it points to the historicity of biological tropes that postwar Japanese architects like Tange and the Metabolists used to describe their visions of urban planning. Tange, for instance, often compared the growth of the nation to that of the vertebrate animal and the communications infrastructure to the central nervous system.

As a young architect, Tange contributed to the modernist architectural experiments undertaken in the colonial cities of Manchuria.[40] While he rarely spoke about his wartime experience with empire building, it nonetheless informed Tange's postwar projects and, by extension, those of the Metabolist architects Tange trained. While it is tempting to attribute Tange and the Metabolists' view of the city as a living organism solely to the postwar language of cybernetics and systems theory (and therefore label it "postmodern" as some critics do),[41] its genealogical root is already found in the much earlier imperial and settler colonial discourses on geopolitics, colonial administration, and urban planning.[42] The biological metaphors and analogies they frequently deployed were already part of the geopolitical theory of the state as a living organism, whose drive to expand the living sphere became the ideological basis of imperial expansionism. It is in this context that Tange and the Metabolists' postwar architectural experiments with artificial lands and megastructures that attempted to extend human habitats into the hitherto uninhabited spaces of the sky and the sea should be understood. Keeping this genealogical context in mind, let us turn now to Tange's postwar writing on architecture and urban planning.

TANGE'S BIOLOGICAL METAPHORS FOR COMMUNICATION SYSTEMS

Tange's writing from the early and mid-1960s cites the operations of the nervous system and blood circulation as analogical models for the smooth flow of an urban communication system, especially that of traffic.[43] For instance, his proposal to restructure the city of Tokyo in the unrealized yet celebrated *A Plan for Tokyo, 1960*, introduces the idea of a "civic axis," which he compares to the spine of the vertebrate animal (figure 3.2).

Tange argues that Tokyo's existing centripetal pattern radiating from the city center to its periphery cannot accommodate the postwar explosion of this metropolitan population. What is needed, in his view, is to increase the mobility of people, goods, and information along the linear axis of highways stretching from the inner city of Tokyo into the artificial land extension built across Tokyo Bay. Tange suggests relocating the

FIGURE 3.2. Tange Kenzō with a model of *A Plan for Tokyo, 1960*. Photo: Akio Kawasumi. Courtesy of Tange Associates.

central administrative and financial district onto this offshore spine of the city, together with some recreational and welfare facilities as well as major technology research laboratories, which would support the future economic and social activities of the nation.[44]

A set of metaphors Tange prefers to use in describing this organic growth of the city comes from cell biology. For instance, he writes, "The evolution of radial cellular bodies into vertebrates and the metamorphosis of eggs into bodies are instances of the sort of development we have in mind, and they illustrate its necessity."[45] In order to underscore his point about the merits of his linear model of urban development, he, like Gotō before him, contrasts the radial communication system of the "primitive forms of life such as amoeboid protozoa and starfish" to the linear communication system of the vertebrate animal. From arteries to nerves, argues Tange, the communication system of intelligent vertebrate animals that evolved from primitive forms of life run along the spinal axis. The future design of Tokyo—and the Japanese archipelago by extension—thus needs to follow this evolutionary pattern.[46]

Tange also notes that "Japan can only maintain its 'organic life' by eventually turning into a single colossal city through the linkup of physical, social, and information networks into a single 'central nervous system.'"[47] Hailing the arrival of the second industrial revolution (or the "communication revolution"), Tange envisions the future of the entire Japanese archipelago as a single megalopolis, which maintains its homeostatic balance through a built-in social and economic feedback system. The two elements he highlights as central to this feedback system along these lines are transportation and telecommunication networks.[48] The influence of Norbert Wiener's cybernetics, which he cites, is clear in this text. Tange's language thus borrows some of the vocabularies from cybernetics, while inheriting and repeating the biopolitical vision of urban planning from Gotō and other colonial administrators.

The historicity of the biological metaphors and analogies deployed by Tange in his discussion of telecommunication networks should also be noted. For instance, he frequently used the neural analogy of telecommunication networks as a nervous system that had been circulating in Japan for a long time. This analogy first developed in Europe as scientists found operational similarities between the workings of the electric telegraph and the human nervous system based on the transmission of electric signals. By the 1850s, this association was well established and became a common trope in Europe and North America.[49] Within Japan, it began to appear soon after 1854, the year when the experimental demonstration of telegraph technology took place. Fukuzawa Yukichi, a Meiji intellectual and fervent advocate of modernization, called it "the nervous system of the nation" as he celebrated the completion of the central telegraph office in Tokyo in 1878.[50] Invoking the organicist view of the state, he contended, "As Japan sharpens its new nerve system, its body gains new vitality."[51] For intellectuals like Fukuzawa, implementing the infrastructure of telecommunication was critical not only for Japan's successful transition to capitalist modernity but also for its geopolitical competition with Western nations.

Not long after Fukuzawa's celebratory comment on the construction of the telegraph office, Japan as a fledgling modern nation-state embarked on its imperialist ambition to colonize resource-rich nations in Asia. Building and controlling telecommunication networks inside and outside the Japanese archipelago was regarded as critical to the success of its empire building. Many viewed the infrastructural development of telecommunication networks as essential to fortifying the "imperial vision of an integrated East Asian sphere under Japan's leadership."[52] While the discourse of geopolitics served to justify the regional unity of the Greater East Asia Co-Prosperity Sphere, the strategic effort to control telecommunication networks in the areas under Japan's military and political influence offered a practical means to realize this regional unity. The gradual takeover and wholesale management of submarine cables linking Japan, Korea, China, and Sakhalin indeed gave Japan concrete logistical tools for expanding its geopolitical sphere of influence.[53] Control over telecommunication networks in Asia in turn allowed Japan to establish, at least partially, "informational hegemony" in the region, which until then was largely dominated by European telecommunication companies.[54] Telegraph and telephone cables along with railroads, in other words, were indispensable for Japan's imperialist expansion of its living sphere.

To sum up, the imperial vision of the Greater East Asia Co-Prosperity Sphere was made possible through a combination of the spherical thinking of wartime geopolitics and network thinking based on the logistical infrastructures of railroads and telecommunication cables. Both of these infrastructures were compared to the biological structures and functions of a living organism, especially those of the nervous system, on which the healthy growth and operation of the empire depended. The empire was analogized to the living organism itself, whose propensity toward expanding its living sphere was further justified as its innate biological need. In short, the geopolitical need to expand its territory was naturalized through the language of biology.

Taking this genealogical understanding of the colonial expansion of the living sphere a step further, I want to return to the Cold War architectural projects of designing climate-controlled shelters and domed cities in the polar regions. These projects, I suggest, are genealogical successors of colonial architecture and cities, designed to acclimatize and protect the life of Japanese settlers, and thereby biopolitically and geopolitically strengthen the empire. These Cold War projects were not overtly colonial

"spherical thinking"

or imperialist; nonetheless, they still operated on the biopolitical view of sheltering the life deemed worthy of cultivation inside greenhouse-like architectures and settlements. These settlements helped expand the living sphere of their inhabitants and, by extension, helped advance the geopolitical and economic interests of the states and corporations that financed these projects.

ARCHITECTURE FOR THE POLAR REGIONS

The telecommunication and transportation networks that helped expand the Japanese Empire's living sphere were not the only "media" that facilitated the movements of goods, people, and ideas. Architecture as media, especially greenhouse-like insulated housing as climatic media, also helped Japanese colonial settlers acclimatize in the cold climate regions. (I keep my focus on the cold climate region of the northern territories, in particular Manchuria, because of the direct institutional connection between researchers at the Institute of Low Temperature Science at Hokkaidō University and architects affiliated with Tange Lab, even though there were Japanese colonial settlements in the southern tropical regions as well.)

The research division of the South Manchurian Railway Company collaborated with the Institute of Low Temperature Science in studying causes and mechanisms of frost heaving that damaged the railroad every winter in Manchuria. The physicist Nakaya Ukichirō, who visited Manchuria to collect data on frost heaving during the war, for instance, recalls how Japanese agrarian settlers struggled to acclimatize to the extreme cold climate, including adjusting to the continental style of housing made of bricks and giving up on their attachment to straw-mat floors.[55]

Recall, this institute provided expert knowledge on the cold climate to help Asada Takashi, the Tange Lab architect, design his proto-capsule housing for the Japanese explorers and researchers at the Shōwa Station in the Antarctic in the 1950s. "Capsules" are lightweight, modular, and often recyclable units that Metabolist architects analogized to biological cells of a living organism. A prototype of capsule housing designed by Metabolist architects is often traced back to Asada's design of this prefabricated rectangular house at the Shōwa Station.

In preparation for designing the housing for the researchers at the station, Asada's team gathered scientific data on extreme cold climate living by relying on the research conducted by scientists at the Continental Science Institute in Manchuria as well as the Institute of Low Temperature Science.[56] For example, the insulated observatory that Nakaya built to study the phenomenon of the icing of propeller airplanes as they flew through clouds during winter provided a practical inspiration for Asada's design. Asada also studied construction techniques used by Japanese agrarian settlers in Manchuria, many of whom were young men without carpentry experience. The design for their dwellings, which they had to build with their own hands, was thus simplified, minimizing the amount of materials they needed to carry.[57]

Focusing on minimizing energy costs and morphological flexibility, Asada's team initially proposed a donut-shaped building composed of a raised floor and aluminum membranes in 1956.[58] Its spaceship-like appearance and aluminum membranes gave it a futuristic look and anticipated the nonlinear shapes of inflatable pneumatic structures that became fashionable in the late 1960s. This innovative plan was abandoned, however, due to protests by the Antarctic expedition team members who wished to live in a more ordinary panel building. The architects thus adjusted their plan and proposed a rectangular house made of wood panels, which were insulated with polystyrene foam made in Germany. These lightweight prefabricated panels were easily transportable by helicopters and designed in a way that the expedition team members, who were amateur builders, could easily assemble in the extreme cold weather.[59]

If Asada's Shōwa Station housing forms the southern pole of Tange Lab's experiment to expand human habitats into the extremely inhospitable cold environment through climate-controlled dwellings, Tange's involvement in the design of *The Arctic City* (1971) forms its northern pole. Although unrealized, this project indicates Tange's own interest in climate-controlled greenhouse-like dwellings. Formally, its proposed use of a pneumatic roof resonates with Tange Lab's design of the similarly air-supported polyester roof that covered the Festival Plaza at Expo '70.

The principal architect for *The Arctic City* was Frei Otto, a German architect known for pioneering tensile and pneumatic structures using synthetic fabrics as their membranes. After his spectacular design of the German pavilion at Expo '67 in Montreal, Otto was approached by Farbwerke Hoechst, a German chemical company that manufactured synthetic fabrics. Their proposal was to design a fully insulated weatherproof domed city to shelter a mining community of 45,000 residents in the Arctic, a site that was attracting international attention for its untapped resources of oil, gas, and minerals. Like the Japanese settlers' houses in Manchuria, the expansion of human habitats into the Arctic through the domed city with its own artificial microclimate was motivated by the potential economic and geopolitical gains. To develop this project, Otto formed an international team of architects, including Tange. Their plan was to cover the entire city with a transparent plastic membrane made of synthetic fabrics in order to control its indoor atmosphere.

Powered by atomic energy, this Arctic domed city was also to be filled with lush green vegetation. As David Crowley puts it in his analysis of the project, "The effects of the long Arctic winter on the inhabitants and the plant-life would be offset by a massive artificial sun moving on tracks suspended below the surface of the dome."[60] *The Arctic City*, in other words, was envisioned to be the ultimate greenhouse. A combination of the imperial architecture of greenhouse and settler housing, this weatherproof domed city is also an Arctic counterpart to Buckminster Fuller and Shōji Sadao's proposal to cover Manhattan with a plastic dome to shelter it from elemental conditions such as rain, wind, and snow. Moreover, this weatherproof Arctic domed city, covered entirely with translucent membranes and thus hermetically sealed, can also be read as a terrestrial analog of space colonies. Like the retro-futuristic image of orbital space colonies with lush green trees and agricultural lands that Blue Origin promotes—a vision that Bezos borrowed from the American physicist Gerard O'Neill's popular book, *The High Frontier: Human Colonies in Space* (1976)—*The Arctic City* promised to replicate a geographically distant climate of the warmer metropole at the polar edge.[61]

What these projects all have in common is the idea of an air-conditioned and insulated dwelling inside a weatherproofed architectural bubble. The underlying assumption is that a select group of human settlers would live and thrive like the tropical flora transplanted from the colonies and cultivated by imperial botanists in the metropole—only the direction of travel is reversed. Settlers bring with them the climate of their home—or one they regard as ideal—and engineer the interior atmosphere of these shelters and domed cities to suit their biological and social needs. These projects are marked by the same thermostatic desire to control the indoor atmosphere and its climatic conditions. In this regard, they follow a long genealogical line of greenhouse architecture as climatic media.

In every case, the production of an artificial microclimate designed for the survival of biological organisms housed inside is central. Architectural techniques for building walls and roofs, along with other engineering technologies for climate control and insulation, were developed to ensure this survival and help cultivate the life housed inside the greenhouse-like capsules, domes, and spheres. The same biopolitical vision of fostering and managing the life of the population within the air-conditioned enclosures is reflected in *The Arctic City* as well as contemporary projects of space settlements. The plan for this semispherical domed city is both a material and symbolic embodiment of the geopolitical imaginary of territorial expansion and colonial settlement, which rely on nested spheres of control.

To put it differently, the underlying rhetoric of expansion that the geopolitical concept of the living sphere helped establish is present not only in Tange Lab's projects but also in the numerous projects of the polar and outer space explorations and settlements, including the one currently proposed by Blue Origin. Polar regions and outer space—along with the deep sea—are what Crowley calls "edge situations," which are known for their biologically inhospitable and extreme environments. The Tange Lab and Metabolist projects of designing capsules, megastructures, and domed cities that extended human habitats into the sky, sea, polar regions are survivalist architecture at their core.[62]

While the Tange Lab and Metabolist projects that I examine in this chapter are not directly linked to outer space explorations and settlements, the geopolitical and conceptual overlapping between the polar regions and outer space as edge situations makes it possible to analyze architectural proposals for both situations as comparable and genealogically related. The terrestrial edge situation of the polar regions and the extraterrestrial edge situation of outer space also share conceptual similarities as the resource-rich "frontiers" located in extreme environments. As Crowley writes, under the threat of nuclear catastrophe, many of the Cold War architectural experiments that took place in the polar regions also reflected "the fear that mankind's conventional habitat faced destruction: humanity would have no choice but to colonize hitherto uninhabited environments like the seabed or, of course, distant planets."[63]

Space colonies, greenhouse-like capsules, and domed cities—which aim to shelter and cultivate the lives of colonial settlers, explorers, researchers, and workers—all exhibit the same thermostatic desire to separate and secure the welfare of a certain population deemed worthy of

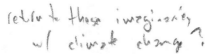
refer to those imaginary w/ climate change?

protection and survival, while inflicting violence, dispossessing, and excluding other populations. The symbolic and material operations of architectural enclosures are intertwined with the biopolitical and geopolitical projects of managing and governing the settler life. With its promise of lush green scenery and the optimal climatic comfort for its inhabitants, Tange and Otto's Arctic City too is deeply marked by these geopolitical and biopolitical projects. Their proposal to reproduce the climatic conditions of a geographically distant metropole is akin to contemporary proposals to colonize distant planets and terraform them (for instance, terraforming Mars by melting the ice that covers its surface to release carbon dioxide in order to make its atmosphere more Earth-like).

Architecture as climatic media sheds light on these intertwined lineages of greenhouse building, air-conditioned dwelling, and terraforming, which today continue apace with privatized and state-funded space exploration projects, including those financed by Silicon Valley tech tycoons. Understood in this genealogical context of settler colonialism and terraforming supposedly "inhospitable" edge environments, the connection between Blue Origin's space settlement and Amazon's corporate greenhouse—the Spheres—which pamper human workers and plants alike inside the air-conditioned artificial climate, becomes clearer; the air-conditioned and climate-controlled greenhouse is a terrestrial counterpart to an extraterrestrial space colony. Both present carefully engineered interior atmospheres in order to cultivate and manage the biological life housed inside them.

In this chapter, I situate contemporary North American aerospace investors' imperial ambition to expand human habitats into outer space within the transpacific context of Japanese empire building and Cold War explorations of the polar regions. Tange and Otto's unbuilt Arctic City and Blue Origin's space colony projects are genealogically tied to the dream of weatherproof architectures for colonial settlements. These architectural enclosures are iterations of the greenhouse, which attempts to reproduce subtropical and tropical climates elsewhere, often in the metropole's harsh and cold environments. The corporate greenhouse, like the Amazon Spheres, also follows this lineage. With Blue Origin—financed by Bezos, who owns Amazon—the targeted life of climatic pampering shifts from plants to humans, as the colonial vision of settlement comes forward.

In his discussion of space colonies, Bezos analogizes the temperate artificial climate inside these sealed buildings to "Maui on its best day, all year along. No rain, no storms, and no earthquakes."[64] This reference to Maui—one of the Hawaiian Islands in the Central Pacific—as the model of future space settlements should not be overlooked. Hawai'i occupies an important place within the transpacific geopolitics and its attendant histories of settler colonialism and imperialism. It is home to Kanaka Maoli, the Indigenous Hawaiian people, and a site of Euro-American colonial explorations, missionaries, sugarcane plantations, and tourism, which brought waves of migrant laborers and settlers from Japan and other Asian countries. Its history is deeply marked by the transpacific movements of colonial settlement, militarization, and the ongoing decolonial struggles of its Indigenous people.[65]

All the more reason, then, to read this reference to Maui in light of the transpacific genealogy of climatic media in which techniques and technologies of building shelters, greenhouses, and domed cities played a key supporting role in imperial territorial expansions. This genealogy also points to an enduring fantasy of scalability. Atmospheric control through the climatic media of weatherproof architecture, as examined in this chapter, is imagined as a scalable technique, even though in reality such scalability is unattainable. From shelters to domed cities to orbital space colonies to terraformed planets, the scales of atmospheric control shift but they exhibit the same thermostatic desire, and a belief that these built enclosures can generate perfectly controlled artificial climates that expand the living spheres of their inhabitants.[66]

Scalability

4

SPACESHIP EARTH:
PLASTICS AND THE
ECOLOGICAL DILEMMA OF
METABOLIST ARCHITECTURE

Plastics are filling up the planet, and have been doing so for decades. In the mid-twentieth century, the petrochemical industry started to mass-produce cheap plastics. While some of these became the iconic plastic commodities of the 1950s and onward, such as Tupperware, plastics also became the new construction materials for architects and industrial designers experimenting with lightweight, flexible, and pre-fabricated forms.[1] From air-supported pneumatic roofs to tensile canopies to capsule houses, brightly colored and smoothly textured synthetic materials overtook the allure of other construction materials, such as concrete, glass, and steel.

The Metabolist architects associated with Tange Lab turned to plastics in their design of capsule architecture in the 1960s. Some of the Metabolist capsules and their predecessors, such as Asada Takashi's prefabricated housing for the Antarctic, were constructed as shelters. Reflecting the Cold War bunker mentality as well as its expansionist geopolitics in polar regions and outer space, these capsules aimed to protect inhabi-

tants from harsh external environments.[2] While sheltering the inhabitants inside climate-controlled bubbles, the capsules were also bound
up with planetary-scale climate change caused in no small part by the
very proliferation of petrochemical products that supplied the plastic
membranes and other synthetic components used to build the Metabolist capsules.

Building on the previous chapter's examination of weatherproof
domes and capsules designed during the Cold War, this chapter digs
deeper into the elemental lineage of Metabolist architecture with an
emphasis on its use of plastics. It further explores how their operation
as climatic media intersects with the planetary issues of environmental pollution, greenhouse gas emissions, and climate change. My aim is
to rethink Metabolist capsule architecture through contemporary critiques of petrochemicals and geoengineering. More specifically, I turn
to Metabolism's entanglement with the petrochemical industry and the
oil economy that continues to accelerate the damaging effects of climate
change. The primary genealogical thread that I trace here is that of the
biochemical concept of metabolism, which the Tange Lab architects adopted as their group's namesake in 1960.

Famously, the Metabolists borrowed the term *metabolism* from Karl
Marx and Friedrich Engels's discussion of the material exchanges between humans and nature as mediated by labor.[3] This biochemical concept of metabolism also centrally features in contemporary Marxist
theories of the anthropogenic climate crisis (variously called "metabolic
rift," "ecological rift," or "biospheric rift").[4] Reading Metabolists' experiments through the mediation of this ecological Marxist discourse thus
allows us to better understand the materiality of Metabolist capsules,
and its connections to Japan's petrochemical industry, environmental
pollution, and waste management.

In what follows, I hence bring the biochemical and architectural concepts of metabolism together to contextualize Metabolism, interrogating
the climatological consequences of their purportedly environmentally
conscious design projects. This requires situating Metabolist capsule
projects within their material historical conditions—namely, the plastics with which they are built, which rely on the petrochemical industry,
which in turn is supported by the oil economy. Kurokawa Kishō is the key
figure I use to weave together the two genealogical threads of biochemical and architectural metabolism. Furthermore, where the architectural
experiments of Metabolism and the political economy of petrochemicals

meet in the present is in the revived interest in geoengineering as the ultimate technological fix for anthropogenic climate change. In theory, geoengineering aims to mitigate greenhouse gas emissions by targeting climate engineering at the planetary scale. And yet, geoengineering by and large ignores the root cause of the climate crisis, which is capitalism itself. The Metabolists's capsules, as we will see, present a strikingly similar ecological dilemma.

PLASTIC CAPSULES

One of the salient examples of Metabolist capsules is Ekuan Kenji's *Plastic Ski Lodge* (1963), designed specifically to withstand cold winter weather. He built this tangerine-colored synthetic capsule with the assistance of Komatsu Kasei, a manufacturer of polyvinyl chloride (PVC) pipes. This project was followed by the *Yadokari Hermit Crab Capsule Lodge* (1969), a compact orange capsule that Ekuan built in collaboration with Nikko Kasei, a manufacturer of thermoplastic resins.[5] Both capsules were designed with the following architectural challenge in mind: maintaining a habitable indoor environment against the extreme climate conditions of outdoor environments such as the Antarctic, deep sea, and outer space.[6]

This is not to say that all capsule housing was designed for exceptional environments. Kurokawa Kishō's *Capsule House* (1970) exhibited at Expo '70, for instance, was designed to promote the flexible lifestyle of urban dwellers. Made from fiberglass-reinforced polyester, the three petal-shaped orange-and-red capsules were joined at the center, which was a large circular room. These capsules served as independent rooms for different family members, each of which containing a separate bathroom unit and a sleeping pod. Similarly, his most iconic capsule project, the *Nakagin Capsule Tower* (1972), composed of concrete boxes with plastic interior parts, aimed to enhance the metabolic cycle of the city. Instead of demolishing the entire building when it gets old, the residential capsules were to be periodically replaced. Once every few decades, new capsules, in theory, could be manufactured and plugged back into the core of the tower. Capsule architecture in this regard was supposed to contribute to the sustainable development of urban space such as the densely populated city of Tokyo. In spite of such differences in their climate preparedness, however, what these capsule houses all had in common was their reliance on plastics for exterior and interior construction materials (figure 4.1).

FIGURE 4.1. Nakagin Capsule Tower (1972) by Kurokawa Kishō.
Photo: © Vincent D. Feldman.

Capsule architecture designed by the Metabolist architects is emblematic of the contradictory forces behind the thermostatic desire to control both interior and exterior atmospheres. While these architectural bubbles made of plastics keep their inhabitants inside air-conditioned and insulated microclimates and protect them from being exposed to extreme weather and other exterior climatic conditions, plastics are also materially responsible for escalating greenhouse gas emissions that offset the macroclimate of the planet, including the increasingly severe weather.

Plastics, to quote Heather Davis, are "the substrata of advanced capitalism." Their pervasive presence in our daily environment—from utensils to clothes, from smartphone cases to shopping bags—has become habitual.[7] Yet these commonplace plastics hold a close ecological relationship to the material processes of fossil fuel extraction, greenhouse gas emission, and the pollution of air, water, soil, and the internal organs of living organisms. Seen in this light, capsule architecture based on plastics is intimately connected to the changing geological and climatic conditions of the planet.

In addition to polyester capsules, there was an international boom of pneumatic domes, polyester roofs, and tensile canopies made with synthetic fabrics in the 1960s. Designed by a team of Tange Lab architects, the pneumatic roof of the Festival Plaza at Expo '70, for instance, used layers of translucent polyester films filled with air.[8] Polyester, plexiglass, synthetic rubber, vinyl, polyethylene terephthalate, and other kinds of plastic materials were rapidly entering urban and domestic environments in the form of walls, roofs, bathtubs, furniture, clothes, toys, insulation, and food packages, just as the Metabolist and Tange Lab architects began experimenting with these new construction materials.

After the sharp rise in oil prices following the 1973 oil crisis, the popularity of inflatable roofs and plastic bubbles as eye-catching architectural forms in Japan and elsewhere dropped. Partly, it was the rising cost of petrochemicals, but it also had to do with their environmental toxicity. As the production of plastics increased, so did the public's concerns about industrial pollution and the perceived limits of nonrenewable natural resources including fossil fuels, from which plastics are made. Among the Metabolist architects, Kurokawa responded to these environmental concerns by turning to the ecosystemic view of managing planetary resources and waste recycling, though his holistic vision was sharply undercut by the environmental footprint of plastics and investment from the petro-economy that financed some of his capsule projects.

THE METABOLIST GROUP

Individual Metabolist architects interpreted the central concept of their movement differently. In general, however, they all agree that metabolism is a biological concept, often synonymous with the Japanese translation of the English word *metabolism* as *taisha* or *shinchin taisha*. Metabolism, understood biologically, signifies the biochemical renewal of the cells and tissues of living organisms, including their growth and death. The group's use of capsules to accommodate the "organic growth" of buildings, megastructures, and cities expressed the idea of metabolic renewal. In so doing, they analogized the architectural process of designing built structures to the biochemical process of growing organic cells. Moreover, they often compared the smooth circulation of energy, transportation, and information through urban infrastructures to the metabolic pathways that circulate oxygen, blood, nutrients, and hormones within living organisms.[9]

In 1960 the members of the Metabolist group published a manifesto that would make the group known internationally. The members of the group at the time of the publication of the manifesto were Kawazoe Noboru (architecture critic), Ōtaka Masato (architect), Kikutake Kiyonori (architect), Maki Fumihiko (architect), Ekuan Kenji (industrial designer), Awazu Kiyoshi (graphic designer), and Kurokawa Kishō (architect). Most of the members were affiliated with Tange Lab, having either studied under Tange Kenzō or collaborated with other lab members. Although not officially a member, Asada served as a mentor to the Metabolist group, and the architect Isozaki Arata also kept close connections with them.

Presented in the context of the World Design Conference overseen by Tange (who was away in the United States visiting MIT and Harvard University at the time), this manifesto would come to define the group and their collective vision. In one of its most crucial passages, the manifesto presents the group in the following terms:

"Metabolism" is the name of the group, in which each member proposes future designs of our coming world through his concrete designs and illustrations. We regard human society as a vital process—a continuous development from atom to nebula. The reason why we use such a biological word, *metabolism*, is that, we believe, design and technology should be a denotation of human vitality.

We are not going to accept metabolism as a natural historical process, but we are trying to encourage active metabolic development of our society through our proposals.[10]

If the last phrase recalls the Marxist understanding of the movement of history, this is likely not a coincidence. One of the main critics and a driving force behind the manifesto, Kawazoe Noboru was a self-described Marxist. Moreover, he often noted that the very turn to the term *metabolism* by the group was motivated by Engels's use of it in *Dialectics of Nature* (1883).

In order to better understand the ecological dilemma of Metabolist architecture, we need to look closely at the historicity of this metabolism concept, tracing both its relation to the recent ecological Marxist interest in the "metabolic rift" as well as the scientific background of Marx's own interest in the biochemical concept of metabolism. The Metabolist movement's relation to Marxism—while not necessarily espoused by members of the group who do not explicitly draw this connection—is crucial to understanding the theoretical relevance of Metabolist architecture to current debates on climate change.

My aim in introducing the Marxist take on the metabolism concept, however, is not to dwell on philosophical debates about the dialectical understanding of nature and labor. Rather, I argue that this Marxist perspective allows us to reevaluate the Metabolist architectural movement's ecological vision—and Kurokawa's vision in particular—in light of its own reliance on plastics and thus the oil economy. In other words, the Marxist perspective allows us to shift the term *metabolism* away from its associations with a holistic view of nature-human relationships, and put the emphasis instead on the political economy of production, the rift between humans and nature, the ecological consequences of the petrochemical and chemical industries, and the real environmental footprint of Metabolist architects. It also allows us to see some of the crucial differences between the historical contexts of the metabolic rift in Japan versus Europe, where Marx and Engels based their observations.

Coined by the sociologist John Bellamy Foster, the phrase *metabolic rift* and its associated idea of the material historical separation between humans and the earth has been widely adopted by contemporary Marxist thinkers interested in addressing anthropogenic climate change and expanding the ecological critique of industrial capitalism from Marx and Engels's work. The idea of the metabolic rift has both material and ontological connotations. That is, this rift manifests as the material "separation" between humans and the earth mediated by labor on the one hand, and as the ontological state of alienation or estrangement from nature experienced by these human subjects on the other.[11]

Unlike the concept of *ecology*, which more broadly addresses interactions among organisms and their relations to surrounding environments, the concept of *metabolism* is about biochemical processes of converting matter into energy. Since the mid-nineteenth century, metabolism has commonly come to signify chemical reactions through which cells, tissues, and organs synthesize and break down molecules through catalytic mediations of oxygen and enzymes. These chemical reactions in the body are at work not only to process food, water, and air but also to regulate the body's homeostasis—for instance, temperature, blood circulation, and hormone balance. In the mid-twentieth century, system ecologists also deployed the term to refer to various biological interactions within the ecosystem.[12]

Importantly, the term *metabolism* was first used by physiologists to describe the respiratory process. In 1842 the German scientist Justus von Liebig applied it to biology in order to discuss cellular-level biochemical processes within living organisms. Marx, who carefully followed scientific discourses and theories, borrowed this concept of metabolism from Liebig. As Foster argues, Marx responded to Liebig's metabolic analysis of the impoverishment of soil nutrients by formulating his historical materialist critique of industrial capitalism. The displacement of nutrients from the soil is a symptom of the larger historical condition of capitalism, which causes the metabolic rift between humans and the earth.[13] Marx's use of the concept of metabolism thus gave him "a more solid—and scientific—way in which to depict the complex, dynamic interchange between human beings and nature, resulting from human labor. The material exchanges and regulatory action associated with the concept of metabolism encompassed both 'nature-imposed conditions' and the capacity of human beings to affect this process."[14]

The concept of metabolism borrowed from biochemistry thus offered an important conceptual affordance to Marx's theory of capitalism. Accordingly, Marx theorized the correlations between industrial capitalism and urbanization that caused the systematic impoverishment of soil nutrients. He did so by calling this situation the "irreparable rift" in metabolism, which later thinkers such as Foster dubbed the metabolic rift.[15]

The development of industrial capitalism not only relied on the colonial practice of dispossessing the land, natural resources, and bodies through settler colonialism, transatlantic slavery, and indentured labor, but it also ushered in the systematic displacement of the agrarian population through enclosures of the commons, private ownership, and other means of expropriation in the metropole.[16] To summarize Foster's interpretation of Marx, as industrial capitalism developed, workers migrated to urban centers where they consumed crops and clothes made of organic fibers (e.g., cotton) that were grown in the countryside. To yield these agricultural products requires fertile soil. Without regularly replenishing essential nutrients, such as nitrogen, phosphorus, and potassium, the soil loses its fertility over time. The assumption here is that, in the preindustrial era, there was a more or less metabolic balance between the fertility of the soil and agricultural production, as human waste and used cloth would often return to the land where the crops were produced. However, with the increased concentration of the human population in urban centers, more crops were brought to the cities and turned into waste there. As a result, the soil nutrients were never returned to the countryside. Moreover, this metabolic rift in nature, according to Marx, is structurally related to the metabolic rift in society; the rift manifests as both biochemical imbalance in the soil and political economic problems of social inequity.[17]

To be sure, the density of urban populations, who consumed large quantities of agricultural produce, did not always lead to the immediate impoverishment of the soil. As Brett Walker has shown, in the case of early nineteenth-century Japan, the capital city of Edo (renamed Tokyo in 1868) had a sophisticated system of collecting human excrement and transporting it to the countryside as natural fertilizer. This system kept the city much more sanitary than its European counterparts such as

London where human waste polluted the nearby rivers.[18] In contrast to Tokyo, where farmers and "night-soil" collectors had developed an organized system of collecting and grading this precious commodity based on class provenance (e.g., waste from wealthy neighborhoods where residents supposedly had a better diet were sold at a higher price than those from poor neighborhoods), London did not have systematic waste management.[19] While Japanese farmers relied on various types of natural fertilizer, including dried fish and animal manures, the systemic collection of "night-soil" helped to sanitize densely populated cities, and to avert severe water pollution.

Commenting precisely on this metabolic problem of industrial cities, Liebig argued for the need to recycle nutrients from human waste: "In the large towns of England the produce of English and foreign agriculture is largely consumed; elements of the soil indispensable to plants do not return to the fields—contrivances resulting from the manners and customs of the English people, and peculiar to them, render it difficult, perhaps impossible, to collect the enormous quantity of phosphates [and nitrogen as well as other nutrients] which are daily, as solid and liquid excrements, carried into the river."[20] These chemical elements, rather than being collected, went on to pollute both the river and the ocean.

This metabolic problem of industrial dislocations of soil nutrients played out a little differently in Japan. Arguably, Japan's metabolic imbalance of soil nutrients in the nineteenth century was less drastic in comparison to Europe as it cyclically returned human waste produced by the urban population to the farmland in the countryside in the form of natural fertilizer. However, this metabolic cycle, which hinged on the robust business of commodifying the waste that provided the soil nutrients along with other natural fertilizers such as fish bones, was disrupted by the rapid spread of chemical fertilizer. In the early twentieth century, chemical fertilizers in the form of factory-produced nitrogen and phosphate became popular and brought down the price of human excrement as natural fertilizer.[21] That is, the development of petrochemical and chemical industries in Japan was central to the metabolic rift in the biochemical balance of the soil. And these industries were also behind the production of plastics, which became the construction materials of the Metabolist capsules.

The historical connection between the development of chemical fertilizer, petrochemicals, and plastics is directly bound to the material and economic conditions that led to Metabolist architects' experiments with plastics and their reliance on oil. To understand the latter, then, we need to explore the systematic dislocation of chemical elements beyond the narrow context of the impoverished soil and urbanization that informed Marx's theory of the metabolic rift in nineteenth-century Europe.

The production of chemical fertilizer and petrochemicals is intimately related and can be glimpsed through the metabolic chain reactions of chemical elements, which caused notorious cases of environmental and industrial pollution in the mid-twentieth century. At stake in this metabolic cycle is the systematic dislocation of elements such as nitrogen, mercury, sulfur dioxide, and carbon dioxide that move through soil, water, air, and the bodies of living organisms. This process of displacement is also inseparable from the capitalist economy of fossil fuel extraction, petrochemical production, and subsequent industrial pollution. The local effects of this capitalist cycle of industrial metabolism became glaringly visible as pollution-related diseases in Japan in the 1960s and 1970s.

By the early twentieth century, the metabolic pathways of Japan's capitalist industrialization, urban waste management, and agricultural development intersected and manifested in the increased rate of environmental pollution. In 1911 the government began constructing modern water and sewage systems in Tokyo in order to prevent contagious disease epidemics. Even then, the management of human excrement was largely left to the private collectors and farmers who recycled it as a form of natural fertilizer.

Around the same time, however, chemical fertilizer was introduced into the field of agriculture. Along with the infrastructural development of water and sewage plants, this shift from natural to chemical fertilizer changed the metabolic cycle of the city. By the early 1920s, the demand for natural fertilizer had decreased significantly, and the city had begun dumping human waste into the ocean, which led to seawater and seafood pollution. Eventually, the government constructed wastewater treatment plants to process the excess waste.[22]

In contrast to the declining business of natural fertilizer, the emergent business of chemical fertilizer grew rapidly. One of the major players in this field was Chisso Corporation (aka Japan Nitrogen Fertilizer

Corporation). Founded in 1908, the company led the development of Japan's chemical industry by producing nitrogen-based fertilizers as well as other chemicals such as calcium carbide and acetylene, which fueled bicycle lamps and the helmet lamps that miners used to extract fossil fuels and other minerals from the ground. During the early twentieth century, the Chisso Corporation expanded its chemical business into Japan's colonial and semicolonial territories by building fertilizer and munitions factories, hydroelectric dams, and ore mines in Korea, Manchuria, Taiwan, and Hainan Island.[23] The chemical company was directly involved in the Japanese Empire's resource extraction and territorial expansion of its living sphere.

By the 1930s, the Chisso Corporation had also entered the burgeoning business of manufacturing industrial chemicals used for the production of plastics. In the 1950s, it made a foray into the production of plasticizers, such as dioctyl phthalate, which was then used to make the most widely available plastic material: polyvinyl chloride (PVC, more commonly known as vinyl).[24] Chisso's postwar venture into the plastics business follows the trajectory of the government's initiative to grow petrochemical and chemical industries as the cornerstone of its postwar economic recovery and growth.

The 1951 report from the Ministry of International Trade and Industry (MITI)—"Concerning the Oil-Based Organic Synthetic Chemical Industry"—set the stage for subsequent policies to protect and promote Japan's petrochemical and chemical industries.[25] With the government's strategic support and the transpacific exchange of technology from American petrochemical giants such as Dow Chemical and DuPont, the Japanese petrochemical and chemical industries flourished. By the mid-1950s, major conglomerates, including Mitsubishi and Sumimoto, were building gigantic petrochemical complexes in Japan's coastal cities.[26]

By the late 1960s, Japan was a leading global producer of plastics. From toys to fabrics, petrochemical products were replacing their nonsynthetic counterparts. This is when the Metabolist architects turned to plastics to build their iconic capsules. It was also at this time that the severity of industrial pollution caused by petrochemicals began to garner public attention. The petrochemical complexes—customarily referred to as *kombinat* due to their association with Soviet industrial complexes—built along the coastal cities were the principal culprits of infamous cases of devastating industrial and environmental pollution in the 1960s and 1970s.[27]

The rise of "Yokkaichi asthma" among local residents near the Yokkaichi petrochemical industrial complex—containing an oil refinery and a petrochemical factory on reclaimed land—is a well-known case of such pollution. Local residents suffered from a range of respiratory diseases due to the toxic smog generated by the emission of sulfur dioxide from the oil refinery.[28] The polluted air killed and injured those who inhaled it.

But the air was not the only environment to bear the brunt of industrial pollution; the seawater did too. Another notorious case of industrial pollution from this era was a form of methylmercury poisoning known as Minamata disease.[29] Chisso Corporation was directly responsible for this case. At one of its chemical factories, Chisso Corporation used inorganic mercury as a catalyst to produce acetaldehyde, a toxic chemical compound used to manufacture plastics; methylmercury was a by-product of the chemical reaction. As a result, Minamata disease caused severe neurological damage among its victims, many of whom were directly or indirectly engaged in the fishing industry in Kyūshū where Chisso Corporation's factory was located.[30]

The toxic food chain started with the release of methylmercury into the seawater and continued with the metabolic process of fish and shellfish absorbing and filtering oxygen and other chemical elements from the seawater. Human consumers who ingested mercury-spiked seafood were in turn poisoned. This massive displacement of mercury from the factory into the marine environment caused a series of metabolic biochemical chain reactions. As Walker writes, the mercury poisoning caused by Chisso Corporation demonstrated how "the hybrid causation takes the form of intertwined biological and industrial metabolisms, a system comprising cascading layers of ecological relationships in the marine food web."[31]

I highlight the exemplary case of Chisso Corporation here in order to overturn harmonious connotations of renewal and sustainable growth associated with the concept of metabolism that Metabolist architects such as Kurokawa proposed. For Metabolist architecture, especially their compact design of brightly colored plastic capsules, is deeply implicated in this chain of chemical displacements because of its reliance on the manufacturing of plastic-based construction materials and the oil economy. When we take a hard look at the materiality of plastics and industrial metabolism, including the effects of environmental pollution, it is difficult to accept Metabolists' utopian vision of sustainable growth and renewal of buildings and cities. Considering these material and economic conditions of biological and industrial metabolisms, the metaphor of *metabolism* loses all harmonious connotations.

While the devastating effects of methylmercury poisoning by Chisso Corporation might be experienced locally, the ecological impact of petrochemical and chemical industries is not. Oil refineries that pollute the air with sulfur dioxide, chemical factories that contaminate the sea with mercury, and the consumption of oil and plastics that emit carbon dioxide into the atmosphere are all part of the global chain of the metabolic rift. Metabolist capsules may look like or be imagined to function like the biological cells of living organisms, which grow harmoniously. Yet they too are implicated in the biochemical circulations of chemical toxins and waste. The displaced sulfur dioxide in the air and methylmercury in the sea damaged the respiratory systems, nerve cells, and soft tissues of organs in humans and animals alike. Meanwhile, greenhouse gases emitted into the atmosphere by the production and consumption of plastics and fossil fuels continue to raise the temperature of the planet. The metabolic pathways of chemical elements cut across the molecular level of cell biology to the planetary level of climate change. Our elemental analysis of Metabolist architecture as a type of climatic media, then, needs to account for this shift in scale.

To attend more closely to this planetary scale of industrial metabolism, let me turn to Kurokawa's holistic vision of renewable capsule housing before moving on to his engagement with the work of the American economist Kenneth Boulding, who is known for his analogy of "Spaceship Earth." After highlighting the continuity of the holistic view of metabolism—from the cellular to the planetary—in Kurokawa's ecological understanding of this concept, I then turn to the historical context of the oil economy that financed some of Kurokawa's and other Metabolist architects' projects in the 1970s.

MOVABLE CAPSULES

Like shipping containers, which revolutionized the logistics of supply chains worldwide in the 1960s, Metabolist capsules such as Kurokawa's work were logistically optimized; they were designed as prefabricated and standardized boxes ready to be shipped, assembled, and quickly installed at the construction site. Kurokawa's signatory design of *Nakagin Capsule Tower*, for instance, "consists of 144 capsule units, manufactured and assembled at a factory that makes shipping containers."[32] These

黒川紀章　Oh！サイボーグの掟

1. カプセルとはサイボーグ・アーキテクチュアーである。　人間と機械と空間が対立関係を超えて、新しい有機体をつくる。　人工内臓をとりつけた人間が、機械でもなく人間でもない新しい秩序をつくるように、カプセルは、人間と装置を超える。建築は、これからますます装置化の道をたどるであろう。　この精巧な装置は、道具としての装置ではなく、生命系に組み込まれる部分であり、それ自身が目的的存在となる。

2. カプセルとはホモ・モーベンス——動民　のためのすまいである。　アメリカでは都市部の住民の転居率・移動率　は年間20％を越えた。　我国でも20％ラインをこえるのは、そう遠いことではない。　都市の勢力はもはや夜間人口で把えることはできず夜間人口と昼間人口の差、あるいは、24時間の生活時間の軌跡こそ生活の実態を示す指標となる。　土地や大邸宅という不動産を、人々はしだいに欲求しないようになり、より自由に動ける機会と手段を見出すだろう。　カプセルは、建築の土地からの解放であり、動く建築の時代の到来を告げるものである。

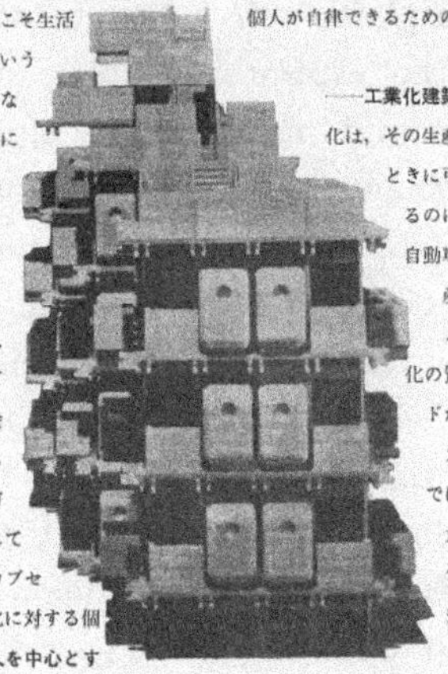

3. カプセルとは多縁性社会を指向する。　われわれは、個人の自由が最大限に認められる社会、選択の可能性の大きい社会を目指す。　組織が、社会や都市の空間を決定していた時代、システムとしてのインフラストラクチュアーが、都市の物理的な環境を形成した。　生活単位としてのカプセルは、個人の個性を表現する。　カプセルは組織に対する個人の挑戦であり、画一化に対する個性の反逆である。

4. カプセルは個人を中心とする新しい家族像の確立を目指す。　夫婦を中心とする住宅単位は崩壊し、夫婦、親子といった家庭関係は、個人単位間のドッキングの状態として表現されるようになるだろう。

5. カプセルはふるさととしてのメタポリスをもつ。　カプセル相互間のドッキングが家庭であるとすれば、カプセルと社会的共用空間とのドッキングの状態が社会的空間を形成する。　宗教空間として、権威の象徴として、或いは商業の場としての広場は崩壊し、個人の精神的原点としての公共空間が新しいふるさととメタポリスを形成する。　24時間の生活行動が、地域的に完結しているという自己完結型のコミュニティは消滅しなくてはならない。　ふるさとは、具体的な日常空間を超えた精神的領域となるだろう。

6. カプセルは、情報社会におけるフィードバック装置であり、場合によっては、情報を拒否するための装置である。　われわれの社会は工業社会から情報社会へ移行する。　工業中心型の産業パターンが、知識産業、教育産業、研究産業、出版、広告、軌道産業、レジャー産業を中心とする情報産業型の産業パターンに変化し、われわれは、あらゆる多様で大量な情報の洪水の中で生活することになろう。　このような情報過多現象と情報の一方通行から、個人の生活を守るためには、フィードバックのメカニズムと、情報を拒否するメカニズムを持つことが必要となる。　カプセルは情報社会の中で、個人が自律できるための空間なのだ。

7. カプセルは、プレハブ建築——工業化建築の究極的な存在である。　工業の工業化は、その生産プロセスが従来の建築産業と絶縁したときに可能となる。　そしてその先導部門となるのは、車両産業であり、航空機産業であり、自動車産業であろう。　T型フォードが、量産の意味をメタモルフィックに転換したように、カプセルがはじめて建築の工業化の質的転換を可能とするだろう。　フォードが、ムスタングの量産で示したように、カプセルの量産は、規格、大量生産方式による、パーツの組合せにより選択的大量生産方式となるだろう。　量産は規格化を強要するものではなく、量産による多様性の時代が到来する。

8. カプセルは全体性を拒否し、大系的思想を拒否する。　体系的思想の時代は終った。　思想は崩壊し、言葉に分解され、カプセル化される。　ひとつの言葉、ひとつの名前が、拡がり、変身し、浸透し、刺激し、大きく時代を動かす。　建築は部分に分解され、機能単位としてカプセル化される。　建築とは、複数のカプセルの時空間的なドッキングの状態として定義されるだろう。

●くろかわ・のりあき／建築家

カプセル宣言1969

50

FIGURE 4.2. Kurokawa Kishō's manifesto, "Capsule Declaration 1969." Published in *SD* (March 1969), 50.

residential capsules are habitable containers—an architectural variant of shipping containers whose standardized size and shape are aimed at ease of transportation as well as assembly. This similarity between shipping containers and residential capsules suggests how the Metabolist conception of renewal partakes in the economic shift toward optimizing urban logistics (figure 4.2).

The logistical ease of the standardized production and assembly was one of the defining features of Asada's design of the modular proto-capsule housing in the Antarctic.[33] It was also an important selling point of Kurokawa's prefabricated residential capsules. Unlike the utilitarian shelter for explorers and scientists in the Antarctic, however, Kuroka-wa's capsule houses for urban dwellers included additional features that ensured domestic comfort and convenience. Each of the concrete capsules with plastic interior parts at *Nakagin Capsule Tower*, for instance, came with an option to preinstall an air conditioner, telephone, audio equipment, bathtub, sink, and other appliances. Each capsule, in other words, was impeccably furnished with the basic comforts of urban living. Similar to trailer homes and motor homes, which were popular in North America around the same time, Kurokawa imagined these architectural capsules as a timely accommodation for the increasingly mobile urban population whom he playfully labeled *Homo movens*.[34] This emphasis on mobility as well as comfort was crucial for the compact yet optimized lifestyle projected by capsule architecture.

These capsule units were also designed to be replaceable, just as cells in the body of living organisms are replaced over time. This cycle of replacement or renewal is a crucial component of Kurokawa's holistic view of architectural metabolism. Instead of demolishing the entire apartment complex, in other words, each living "cell" or capsule can be replaced when necessary. He advocated this replaceability as an ecologically sustainable and economically sound way of maintaining the metabolic cycle of the city: "Just as the human body, such as the skin, nails, hair, blood, and organs daily undergo metabolic processes of renewing their freshness, houses, buildings, roads, and cities are constantly metabolizing in reality."[35] Yet, unlike the human body in which metabolic pathways—from the cellular rejuvenation of skin and blood circulation to the homeostatic maintenance of body temperature—operate autonomically and without our conscious effort, the metabolic pathways of built structures and cities must be consciously maintained. The use of prefabricated capsules was thus seen as one way to optimize the metabolic process of renewing the urban infrastructure (figure 4.3).

If the domestic comfort and convenience of capsule architecture re-

FIGURE 4.3. Kurokawa Kishō's design featured on the cover of *Kenchiku bunka bessatsu* (June 1995), where biological forms are arrayed alongside architectural diagrams.

sembled that of motor homes and recreational vehicles, equipped with appliances such as a stovetop, refrigerator, sink, foldout sofa, and so forth, the sheltering function of these capsule units resembled space capsules for astronauts. The term *capsule*, as Hyunjung Cho suggests in her analysis of Metabolism, "conjures up either a capsule containing medicine or the living quarters of an astronaut." The capsule as the envelope of a sealed environment differs from other kinds of containers: "A rupture in the capsule, however small, would instantly upset the internal equilibrium and destroy the strictly controlled environment in it."[36] Built at the height of the Cold War space race, the Metabolist capsules also reflect this dual logic of security and survival through containment in the inhospitable environment of outer space, binding the analogy of the space capsule to that of Earth as spaceship.

There is a parallel here between the synthetic membrane of space capsules—and spacesuits—which protect the lives of astronauts in a vacuum, and the atmospheric membrane of Earth, which protects living organisms on the planet. This similarity between the enclosed spaceship and the enclosed planet was concisely captured by the notion of Spaceship Earth, which gained popularity in the mid-1960s, intersecting with the holistic view of metabolism that the Metabolist architects espoused. Capsule architecture, in other words, emerged at the historical moment when plastics were gaining wide attention as a novel construction material and a source of environmental toxicity; when logistics was being revolutionized by standardized and intermodal shipping containers, which made transportation of goods easy and fast; and when the atmospheric enclosure of Earth was analogized to that of a spaceship. While these events may appear unrelated at first, they nonetheless significantly determined the material, conceptual, and economic conditions of the Metabolists' architectural experiments.

THE SPACEMAN ECONOMY

The ecosystemic understanding of managing Earth's finite resources caught the attention of the Metabolist architects. Kurokawa, in particular, was fond of the comparison between the planet and a spaceship. As we saw in the previous chapter, these architects were engaged in the task of expanding Japan's living sphere through the construction of artificial lands and megastructures in the sea and above ground after the loss of its overseas colonies and territories. Given their shared interest in expanding human habitats beyond the terrestrial surface of the Japanese archipelago, it is not surprising that they gravitated toward the aeronautical imaginary of the astronaut and spaceship. The similarity between Metabolist capsules and space capsules also points to an important transpacific nexus between their understanding of metabolism and the systems approach to ecology and economics.

Exemplified by Kenneth Boulding's call to shift from the extractivist "cowboy economy" to the sustainable "spaceman economy" in his widely read essay, "The Economics of the Coming Spaceship Earth" (1966), international awareness of the finitude of Earth and its ecosystemic management gained traction around this time. Together with the work of Buckminster Fuller (whose experiments with prefabricated shelters, domes, and tensegrity structures also paralleled the works of these Japanese architects), Boulding's idea of Spaceship Earth as a closed ecological system in need of economic management was warmly received by Japanese intellectuals. Similar to *The Limits to Growth* (1972)—an influential report that projected future scenarios of economic and population growth, shortages of natural resources, and environmental pollution, published by the Club of Rome (of which Tange was a member)— Boulding's work resonated with the Metabolist architects concerned with the issue of sustainable economic growth and the optimized use of available land and resources (figure 4.4).[37]

While Fuller popularized this spaceship metaphor in his book *Operating Manual for Spaceship Earth* (1969), it was Boulding who first analogized the closed ecosystem of the planet to that of the spaceship in the aforementioned essay, "The Economics of the Coming Spaceship Earth." Along with Ludwig von Bertalanffy, Boulding is known as one of the early proponents of general systems theory and served as the inaugural president of the Society for General Systems Research (1957–58).[38] The essay contrasted two models of capitalist economy:

> For the sake of picturesqueness, I am tempted to call the open economy the "cowboy economy," the cowboy being symbolic of the illimitable plains and also associated with reckless, exploitative, romantic, and violent behavior, which is characteristic of open societies. The closed economy of the future might similarly be called the "spaceman" economy, in which the earth has become a single spaceship, without unlimited reservoirs of anything, either for extraction or for pollution, and in which, therefore, man must find

成長の限界

ダイヤモンド社

ローマ・クラブ「人類の危機」レポート

The Limits to Growth

D・H・メドウズ／D・L・メドウズ
J・ラーンダズ／W・W・ベアランズ三世——著

大来佐武郎——監訳

FIGURE 4.4. The cover of the Japanese translation of *The Limits to Growth* (1972).

his place in a cyclical ecological system which is capable of continuous reproduction of material form even though it cannot escape having inputs of energy.[39]

Boulding's call to shift our understanding of economic productivity from the old settler colonial image of the open frontier (wherein settler-cowboys pillage and kill) to the equally colonial but futuristic image of the enclosed capsule (within which astronauts are trapped) advocates for the sustainable development of capitalism.

While there are other theorists whose work contributed to the popularization of ecosystem thinking in Japan, Boulding's work had a notable impact, in part because of his personal affiliations with Japanese academic institutions. From 1963 to 1964, Boulding was a visiting professor at the International Christian University in Tokyo, and in 1970 he returned to Japan in order to give a series of talks at the invitation of the public broadcast company NHK.[40]

One Japanese architect on whom Boulding's vision had a strong impact was Kurokawa Kishō. Upon meeting Boulding, Kurokawa enthusiastically endorsed his view of the sustainable management of Earth as a closed ecosystem with finite resources. Commenting on Boulding's work, Kurokawa writes: "Boulding's ecosystem approach is based on the theory of the earth as a closed system composed of ecological, economic, and social circulations. When combined with a theory of environmental metabolism, his approach offers an important hint on how to address and resolve the fundamental problems of pollution." Architects, Kurokawa contends, must learn from Boulding and his critique of the nonsustainable logic of the cowboy economy that presumes that land and resources are limitless. Under this expansionist model of the cowboy economy, we endlessly build more cities, extract more natural resources, and dispose of more waste into the environment without care or concern for the future.[41] In contrast, astronauts (or "spacemen") manage to survive with limited resources and recycle air, water, and other vital elements inside the enclosed environment of a spaceship or space capsule.

The Metabolist architects like Kurokawa who were acutely aware of Japan's loss of its overseas colonies after World War II took notice of Boulding's theory, which emphasized the limited territory and finite resources available on Earth as a whole. Boulding's call to imagine the economy as a closed ecosystem in order to better manage and optimize its finite resources to sustain capitalist growth and human life on the planet appears to have struck a chord with these architects, who were already thinking hard about the problem of finite resources inside Japan's territorial limits. Their turn to this ecosystem theory of economics—which called for a conceptual as well as pragmatic reorientation from the open cowboy economy to the closed spaceman economy—should be understood in this historical context.

To better understand this context, it is useful to note the rise of general interests in systems theory and cybernetics among Japanese architects, urban planners, industrialists, and policymakers in the 1960s, when Boulding's theory of Spaceship Earth appeared. The decade is heavily marked by the twin revolutions in logistics and information technology, as Japan shifted its economic orientation from the imperial model of territorial expansion (to acquire more land and resources through colonial theft) to the postindustrial model of informational intensification (to optimize the speed and efficiency of economic productivity by upgrading transportation, telecommunication, and energy infrastructures). The developments of digital computers, satellites, bullet trains, fax machines, shipping containers, and other iconic technological innovations of the decade were central to Japan's postindustrial information economy. This reorientation from space to time is, of course, not unique to Japan; it is also part of the historical transformation of capitalism. Postindustrial capitalism is marked by the integration and intensification of information, communication, and transportation infrastructures.

Cybernetics and systems theory, for instance, found immediate applications in the field of management theory and helped develop the field of business logistics in Japan in the 1950s and 1960s. The indirect impact of cybernetics and systems thinking on management theory, for instance, is evident in the transformations in production undertaken by Toyota, Japan's largest automobile manufacturer, which developed its "just-in-time" production system during these decades.[42] This system involved a transformation in inventory management and worker-led feedback mechanisms such as the "kanban" card meant to improve the efficiency of production. Instead of being held in warehouses on site, materials were to be delivered to workers on the assembly line as they were needed—just in time, as it were.

As Deborah Cowen argues, "Until the introduction of a systems approach, physical distribution was concerned exclusively with the movement of finished products."[43] However, as the revolution in logistics took place and business logistics developed as a field, a new understanding of the relationship between production and distribution was born. Distribution moved from being a mere process that starts where production stops, to being an essential part of the production process itself, as half-made items are shipped to a second or third location to complete construction. "The revolution in logistics," as Cowen puts it, "saw transportation conceptualized as a vital element of production systems rather than a separate domain or the residual act of distributing commodities after production; it thereby put the entire spatial organization of the firm, including the location of factories and warehouses, directly in question."[44] Factories and companies such as Toyota began to see business logistics as "a total approach to the management of all activities" from procuring, transporting, and storing raw materials to producing, stocking, delivering, and selling of products. Systems theory was key to this total approach to the logistical management of manufacturing and other businesses.

This logistical management and approach to cutting costs and time was later inherited by retail and e-commerce companies such as Amazon, Walmart, and Seven Eleven, which invest heavily in business logistics in order to squeeze more profit out of speed of distribution.[45] But this corporate investment in reducing wasted time was not the only outcome of the systems approach to logistics. Ecosystem thinking applied to the growth of capitalism also came out of systems theory and management techniques that drew on the cybernetic logic of feedback. As such, the very same patterns of thinking that led to optimization of time for delivery led to the rhetoric and practices of sustainable development, which presumes the continued existence of capitalism—sometimes under the moniker "green capitalism"—rather than its end.

It is within this historical context that I situate the intellectual appeal of Boulding's theory of Spaceship Earth in Japan and to Metabolist architects in particular. Architectural metabolism as imagined by Kurokawa shares the ecosystemic view of optimally managing finite resources inside an enclosed environment.[46] His theory of Metabolist architecture also adopts Boulding's ecological-economic perspective regarding the optimal management of industrial and household waste. Kurokawa lists waste management as the number one ecological challenge of his generation, and argues that his architectural theory of Metabolism is meant to address the issue of recycling waste. The recycling of waste binds his earlier conceptualization of capsules as organic cells to his later conceptualization of capsules as miniature ecosystems. Kurokawa contends that the challenge he took up in the 1960s as he participated in the Metabolist group was to think critically about recycling as an integral aspect of architecture and urban planning.[47]

Interestingly, Kurokawa states that he has pursued the question how to integrate the process of recycling waste into the design practice of Metabolic architecture since the group's inception. He writes: "The biggest challenge of the 21st century is how to recycle waste products and integrate them into the system of circulation. The topic I grappled with in the 1960 theory of Metabolism was precisely this system of recycling. What I called the 'metabolic cycle' at the time was to break down various parts that compose architecture (such as core and capsule) into segments based on durability and spatial needs. And in so doing, introduce systems of circulation and reproduction into architecture."[48] Kurokawa speculates that the industry specializing in waste management will boom in the future as the global consumption of plastics continues to grow. The reach of such waste management as an industry, he contends, will also be global since when a recession hits, domestic production of waste may go down, but companies can always import trash from other countries. Waste, in short, will become a lucrative commodity. Although he does not reference the preindustrial practice of collecting and selling human excrement as natural fertilizer, the logic of monetizing waste remains the same.

To support this vision of the global metabolic (re)cycle of waste as a commodity, Kurokawa cites Boulding's notion of Spaceship Earth. Just like the efficient management of waste inside the enclosed environment of the spaceship is crucial to the successful survival of the astronauts in outer space, the industrial waste on Earth needs to be carefully managed.[49] To be sure, the ecological conditions inside the space capsule, architectural capsule, and the planet operate differently, and this managerial vision of an enclosed ecosystem cannot be scaled up so easily. However, attending to this mediating role of Boulding's work in Kurokawa's own analysis of Metabolism allows us to make sense of the otherwise counterintuitive leap in his writings from metabolic metaphors of connectivity operating at the scale of bodies or buildings to that of the planet. It also draws our attention to the political implications of enclosure and containment that the image of the capsule evokes. This image of the capsule as an atmospherically enclosed environment that needs systemic management connects Boulding's analogy of Spaceship Earth to Kurokawa's holistic vision of capsule architecture.

THE OIL ECONOMY

In reality, however, the material reliance of capsules on plastics and oil money that financed his projects is in stark tension with Kurokawa's vision of ecologically harmonious architecture and sustainable development. Following the 1973 Arab-Israeli war, the Organization of Arab Petroleum Exporting Countries (OAPEC) declared an oil embargo against the United States and other countries, including Japan, that they regarded as supporters of Israel. This embargo caused a sudden rise in oil prices, leading to the 1973 oil crisis that triggered a global recession.

Japan's geopolitical relationship with the Middle East and its oil economy is complicated.[50] Since the late 1950s, both the Japanese government and corporate conglomerates have developed close trade relations with oil-producing countries in the Middle East. For instance, the Japan Petroleum Trading Company, with the diplomatic backup of the Japanese government, received permission to establish the Japanese-owned Arabian Oil Company in Saudi Arabia to extract oil and build shipping facilities by promising to pay 56 percent of the revenue to the country. Throughout the 1960s, other companies followed suit, helping build oil wells and refineries in Middle Eastern and North African countries and making deals to exchange engineering and architectural supports with crude oil.[51] The steady flow of crude oil arriving from the region pumped petrochemical and plastic production into Japan.

The 1973 oil crisis temporarily halted this flow. In order to tread the fine diplomatic line between its geopolitical alliance with the United States (which supports Israel) and its friendly relations with the majority Arab states of OAPEC, Japan accelerated its financial investment in the Middle East in order to prove its political neutrality vis-à-vis the Israel-Palestine conflict. In 1974, for instance, the Japanese government made a deal to loan $1 billion to Iran in exchange for 160 million tons of oil over ten years. They made a similar pledge, offering $1.5 billion, to Iraq. These countries in return sought technical assistance in industrial and oil-refinery developments from Japanese corporations and engineers. By the end of the year, Japan's infrastructural investment in the region helped lift OAPEC's oil embargo.[52]

The 1970s was also the time when domestic financing of large-scale architectural projects by Tange Lab and the Metabolist architects inside Japan dwindled. Having already established an international reputation as "starchitects," however, they received invitations to work on various architectural and urban-planning projects in the Middle East, North Africa, and Southeast Asia, many of which were financed by the petroleum sector. For instance, Tange cultivated a friendship with the Saudi royal family, in particular Faisal bin Abdulaziz Al Saud (king of Saudi Arabia from 1964 to 1975). Faisal commissioned Tange to work on several unfinished projects, including the monumental stadium in Riyadh and temporary accommodation facilities for pilgrims visiting Mecca.[53] For the latter project, Tange enlisted the help of Ekuan.[54] After Tange designed the Kuwait embassy in Tokyo, he developed a close relationship with the Kuwait government. In the 1970s Tange and his team also worked on projects in Syria, Iran, and Qatar.[55]

Kikutake Kiyonori, another member of the Metabolist group, was involved in the tourist industries of oil-exporting countries, working on megastructure projects such as floating luxury hotels in Abu Dhabi (1975) and Saudi Arabia (1977). The Floating Infra-Cassette (1977), a platform that contains factories, oil tanks, power stations, houses, and other residential facilities in Libya, is another example. Meanwhile, Kurokawa opened a local office in Abu Dhabi to expand his architectural business networks in the Middle East and North Africa. The continuation of Kurokawa's capsule-design principle is evident in many of these projects, including the proposed development of luxury capsules in Iraq (1975).[56] In 1979 he also won the competition to develop a master plan for Sarir New Town in the desert of Libya, located near an oil field.[57]

While many of these projects were never completed due to political and geopolitical instabilities, they nonetheless attest to Tange and the Metabolist architects' deep entanglement with the global oil economy. Although similar economic dynamics existed between Tange Lab and Metabolist architects and Asian countries such as Singapore, Malaysia, and China, their relationship to the Middle East is unique insofar as oil was the main source of financing for their projects there. Tange and Metabolist projects were directly implicated in the unsustainable practices of fossil fuel extraction and the petroleum industry.

Plastics used to build capsules, then, were not the only material connections these architects had with petroleum and petrochemical industries, which manifest as environmental pollution, greenhouse gas emissions, melting of polar ice, sea level rise, and other symptoms of climate change. Architecture as climatic media in the case of the Metabolist group is also inextricable from the planetary metabolic cycles of matter and energy through which biochemical and economic flows of oil and petrochemicals circulate.

GEOENGINEERING AS ATMOSPHERIC CONTROL

Once deemed incredible and unrealizable, the idea of geoengineering Earth's climate has recently seen a notable comeback in both the scientific and journalistic communities focusing on climate change. Geoengineering is increasingly viewed as a viable option to offset the metabolic rift by cooling down the planetary atmosphere and alleviating a plethora of ecological problems, ranging from the melting of polar ice and rising sea levels to severe storms and the extinction of certain species in the biosphere.

Geoengineering in the nascent form of weather control, as we saw in earlier chapters, was weaponized during the Vietnam War. While the weaponization of the weather was quickly banned and geoengineering lost its sheen in the ensuing decades, climate geoengineering as a remedial solution for greenhouse gas emissions has regained support among scientists, researchers, and industrialists. Paul Crutzen, the Dutch atmospheric chemist who popularized the geological concept of the Anthropocene epoch, for instance, is one of the most vocal proponents of geoengineering as a way to reset the planetary thermostat.[58] His proposal is to inject sulfur dioxide—the very same material that causes air pollution—into the stratosphere to reflect solar radiation away from the surface of Earth. From fertilizing the ocean with iron to grow more carbon-absorbing algae to refreezing the Arctic ice by seeding the clouds with salt particles in order to block the incoming sunlight, various proposals to mitigate the future impact of climate change have been debated and tabled over the past decade.[59]

At the base of such proposals is the same assumption that regards Earth as a closed ecosystem analogous to that of a spaceship, which needs constant management and intervention through design. Although the atmospheric membrane of the planet and the plastic membrane of capsule architecture differ in material composition and scale, it is useful to underscore the conceptual resonance between the ecosystem approach to geoengineering and the Metabolist approach to capsule architecture. For the enclosed atmosphere of the planet and the enclosed atmosphere of the architectural capsule are conceptually parallel and ecologically bound.

A paradox of geoengineering, however, is that it often relies on the same mechanism that has caused anthropogenic climate change. Toxic particles of sulfur dioxide, for instance, are emitted by burning fossil fuels and thus create smog. Many cities in the world are combating the problem of air pollution, yet some have argued that this pollution "is helping to cool the planet," and that "cleaning up the air would, over a brief decade, lead to an unprecedented increase in global temperature."[60] Scientists who support planetary geoengineering have counterintuitively proposed to use the same logic to cool down the atmosphere by injecting sulfate aerosols into the stratosphere as if to mimic the albedo effect of volcanic explosions and industrial air pollution in order to absorb less sunlight. It is often compared to painting the roof white to keep the temperature of the interior environment lower.

With this architectural metaphor of a roof we have come full circle, so to speak. If the greenhouse effect is largely due to the burning of fossil fuels that emit chemical compounds such as sulfur dioxide and carbon dioxide into the atmosphere, and if the production and consumption of plastics are dependent on petrochemicals, Metabolic architectural experiments are caught in the same ecological and biochemical cycles of chemical displacements. These cycles—in ecological Marxist parlance—contribute to the ongoing metabolic rift of the planet. Plastic capsules and pneumatic roofs designed by Tange Lab and the Metabolist architects are part of this planetary metabolic rift. To push this speculative conclusion a step further, we may regard technologies of geoengineering as a logical extension of architecture, an extension of architectural techniques and technologies for designing and building walls, roofs, and capsules to engineer the interior climate.

Air-conditioning and insulation of capsules are, like building a greenhouse, exemplary technologies of atmospheric control. Albeit operating at vastly different scales, cloud seeding and spraying of sulfur particles into the stratosphere to block the sunlight are also part of this technical assemblage aimed to regulate and engineer the planetary atmosphere. The same thermostatic desire for controlling the climatic future undergirds both architecture and geoengineering. Architectural experiments by Metabolists therefore present the same material contradiction that also accompanies geoengineering as a technophilic solution to the current climate crisis. Here, the contradiction emerges between the architects' ecological interests and hope for the sustainable development of cities, and their material and economic dependency on fossil fuels and petrochemical industries, whose effects are ecologically degrading and undermine the very idea of sustainability. To attend to this contradiction surrounding their architectural experiments is to read the defining metaphor of metabolism through the lens of the material histories of plastics, chemical fertilizers, and oil. A similar contradiction marks the debates over geoengineering.

What geoengineering proposes is to continue the same metabolic cycle of displacing chemicals from one sphere to another without radically challenging the underlying problems of extraction and pollution—and capitalism. It is here that I see a parallel ecological dilemma between the current discourse on geoengineering and the earlier discourse on Metabolist architecture. Both are based on the same metaphors of an enclosed capsule and the planet as an enclosed ecosystem. Both see the metabolic rift as *fixable through design*, and design becomes an ultimate solution. Understood in this manner, the historical lesson of Metabolist architecture goes beyond the field of architecture and draws our attention to the ethical and political stakes of imagining our planet as a gigantic capsule. Metabolist architecture made of plastics reminds us of the danger of imagining and designing capsules without paying attention to their oil-based materiality and toxicity, both of which result from the capitalist mode of resource extraction. In the absence of such attention, danger arises less in a breach of the capsule's seal and more in the very matter of the seal itself.

5

CLOUD CONTROL:
TEAR GAS, CYBERNETICS, AND
NETWORKED SURVEILLANCE

Tear gas, like its direct military counterpart poison gas, is a type of climatic media. The chemical fog of tear gas acts as an insidious form of air-conditioning that changes the physicochemical composition of the local atmosphere, and acts as an instrument of social conditioning. The use of tear gas often operates as a violent technique of controlling protesters and managing crowds that the police deem disruptive to the authorities. Often framed by police, lawmakers, and manufacturers as a less lethal agent of crowd control than firearms, tear gas "explicates the atmosphere," to borrow Sloterdijk's formula again. Like smog and other pollutants in the air, inhaling tear gas brings to the fore the lethal potential of breathing air contaminated with toxins. By adding harmful compounds to the air, tear gas creates a perilous feedback loop of respiratory injuries and other physiological damage: the more chemically conditioned air you breathe, the more suffocated and incapacitated you become.

Networked systems of urban surveillance similarly rely on the cybernetic logic of feedback and operate as atmospheric means of policing and regulating social conduct. Like tear gas, which governs the conduct of crowds by directly conditioning the air with chemicals, urban surveillance too relies on the medium of air, but only indirectly. Tear gas and networked surveillance work together using chemical elements, data, and the air as conduits of atmospheric control. From the ubiquitous presence of security cameras to thermal scanners to geosurveillance of cellphones to facial recognition software, urban crowds encounter numerous and ever-upgraded tracking and monitoring systems in public and commercial spaces today.

Many of these networked systems of urban surveillance operate through wireless signals; they are atmospheric in the literal sense of being carried by radio waves in the air. For instance, wireless signals and data passing through cellphones, cell towers, and satellites, which law enforcement uses to identify geolocations of protesters and monitor their movements, are literally mediated by the air and often routed through virtual clouds stored in data centers. While invisible to our eyes, these signals electronically saturate the urban atmosphere.[1]

Surveillance is also increasingly integrated into urban design. As architects, developers, local municipalities, and states promote projects related to the current wave of smart urbanism, they also design urban infrastructures that are better equipped for digital surveillance. From security cameras at parks to sensors that monitor traffic flow, various modes and systems of networked surveillance are increasingly integrated into the built infrastructures of urban environments. Even if this integration is partial, and prone to failure, smart city initiatives all over the world are accelerating the infrastructural integration of surveillance, at least in theory. Along with other increasingly automated components of urban infrastructures, such as smart energy grids and smart water meters, these networked systems of surveillance contribute to political climates of cities as the developers and planners address and respond to climate change. As infrastructural forms of social conditioning, they too function as climatic media, albeit in a more indirect manner than the types of climatic media analyzed in the previous chapters.

The architectural icon of urban design with such built-in networks and infrastructures of urban surveillance is the *control room*. And the defining logic of the control room is *feedback*. This chapter traces the transpacific geopolitical context behind the development of these networks of atmospheric control by focusing on tear gas, cybernetics, and control rooms. Specifically, I foreground the institutional nexus between the American cybernetician Norbert Wiener and Japanese cyberneticians and architects.

Some of the early demonstrations of these networked surveillance technologies, such as closed-circuit television and computerized facial recognition, took place at world's fairs in the 1960s and early 1970s.[2] Examining the experimental use of computers and surveillance cameras inside the control rooms at Expo '67 in Montreal and Expo '70 in Osaka alongside the Tange Lab architect Isozaki Arata's experimental design of the "cybernetic environment," this chapter maps out how cybernetics and computing changed the way urban security was envisioned, managed, and enforced in Japan and North America at the height of the Cold War.

Today, many of these technologies have become mundane and prevalent, but when they first entered the streets of metropoles in the 1960s, they were still seen as experimental tools of urban governance. The 1960s was also the time when Cold War geopolitical conflicts led to the first computerized warfare in Vietnam, a war that made ample use of chemical weapons including tear gas and the herbicide Agent Orange. It was then urban police started to apply these chemical weapons in the form of tear gas to quell political protests—by New Left student activists and citizens opposing both the renewal of the Japan-US Security Treaty as well as the Vietnam War in Japan, and by civil rights activists and New Left protestors opposing the Vietnam War in the United States. It is against this geopolitical backdrop of the Cold War that I want to situate the increased use of tear gas and networked surveillance in Japan and analyze how they relate to the cybernetic turn of architecture and urban design.

TEAR GAS

Tear gas—the direct civilian application of the poison gas used on battlefields—is extremely harmful. As Anna Feigenbaum sharply puts it, tear gas is an object specifically "designed to torment people, to break their spirits, to cause physical and psychological damage."[3] While the use of CS gas (composed of chemical compounds called 2-chlorobenzylidene malonitrile), the most common ingredient in tear gas, is currently prohibited on the battlefield by the Chemical Weapons Convention, tear gas canisters and grenades, which have the same chemical components as some of these weapons, continue to be accepted as "humanitarian" alternatives to firearms.[4]

Tear gas as a means of atmospheric control is not only immersive but also communicative. Attacking the respiratory tracts of those affected by its toxic vapor, the police use of tear gas operates as a one-way communicative medium; it sends a message, meant to break the will to protest. Within the context of warfare, bombing has similarly functioned as a communicative act of sending a message to the enemy other. Commenting on the American military's use of strategic bombing as an instrumental mode of communicating with the enemy other during the Vietnam War (which widely deployed digital computers and cybernetic models of control and communication), Paul Edwards writes: "Strategic bombers attacked military targets in an attempt to 'communicate' with the North Vietnamese, holding in reserve the possibility of attacks on cities in case they did not respond with the correct reply. Of course, though American bombers broadcast the message repeatedly and in increasingly horrific terms, the enemy never did receive it—or more accurately, received it but simply did not agree with its terms."[5] Like bombing, the use of poison gas on the battlefield and tear gas on urban streets sends a message. It functions as the semiotic process of communication as well as the physical process of suffocation. Tear gas as a climatic medium in this regard is doubly mediatic.

It is important to underscore the geopolitical context of Asia during the Cold War, which informs this parallel operation of bombing on battlefields and tear gassing on urban streets. Japan's participation in the Cold War arms race was uniquely inflected by its postwar constitutional renunciation of the use of armed forces for settling international disputes. This renunciation did not, however, mean demilitarization and was soon followed by the signing of the Treaty of Mutual Cooperation and Security Between Japan and the United States of America (colloquially known the Japan-US Security Treaty). This treaty stipulated the establishment of the Self-Defense Forces and the expansion of US military bases on Japanese soil, which enabled material support for US forces during the Korean War and the Vietnam War. Signed toward the end of the Allied Occupation (1945–52), the pact effectively brought Japan into the orbit of the Cold War conflict as a satellite state of the US-led coalition. The twin questions of security and militarization became the focus of recurrent mass protests against the Japan-US Security Treaty, first renewed in 1960 and then again in 1970. In an effort to curtail these street protests, the conservative Liberal Democratic Party (LDP)–led government expanded police powers and personnel and passed various legislative measures to suppress street-based direct actions.

Throughout the 1950s and 1960s, police use of tear gas gradually increased on both sides of the Pacific. The first well-known case in which Japanese police used tear gas against protesters was during the Bloody May Day Incident in 1952. Taking place only three days after the US-led Allied occupation officially ended, the police liberally used tear gas to disperse protesting workers.[6] By conditioning the air with harmful chemicals, tear gas was used to attack, subdue, and forcibly modify the conduct of the protesting crowds, while sending the political message that the authorities would not hesitate to use violence against civilians.

The gradual frequency of the police usage of tear gas in Japan was accompanied by increased news reports on the United States, both on the military's use of tear gas and smoke bombs in Vietnam and the police use of tear gas against African American civil rights protesters. This transpacific nexus between domestic use of toxic gas against civilians is emblematized by the Japanese police's deployment of tear gas against student demonstrators in the city of Sasebo, who gathered at its port to protest against the docking of the nuclear ship USS *Enterprise* on January 17, 1968.[7] This direct action was aimed at both criticizing and undermining the fact that the Japanese port of Sasebo had become a strategic base for American military actions in Vietnam.

Another spectacular use of tear gas by the Japanese police took place in January 1969 to end the campus barricade and occupation of the University of Tokyo's Yasuda Memorial Clock Tower that began in 1968. A series of other street protests also brought on the police use of tear gas in the city of Tokyo, where pedestrians were often seen covering their faces with handkerchiefs, still feeling the aftereffects of tear gas even after protesters had been dispersed.[8] Tear gas was frequently found in the urban atmosphere of metropolitan cities where political protests against the government were unfolding daily. Similarly, political demonstrations continue to unfold on urban streets today, as protesters around the world continue to be exposed to chemical fog discharged from tear gas canisters.

Tear gas, however, is not the only instrument of atmospheric control, nor is it the only type of climatic media used for the purpose of urban governance, which enact the circular logic of the feedback loop. In the mid-twentieth century, cybernetics and systems theory also changed the way urban planners and architects envisioned and designed the city and helped develop today's densely networked surveillance as an instrument of atmospheric social conditioning. The cybernetic understanding of feedback was folded into the emergent technologies of surveillance, such as closed-circuit television and networked computing, which offered the means to constantly track and monitor urban crowds.

If tear gas was an extraordinary technique of policing that corresponded to perceived moments of crisis in civic order, a system of networked surveillance—connecting remote sensors, cameras, and computers under the watchful eye of security guards and the police—was its ordinary counterpart. Security cameras and networked computing became atmospheric and climatic in the sense of being pervasive, invisible, and environmentally diffuse. These discrete networks of climatic media quietly spread through urban space in the mid-twentieth century and have become part of the mundane infrastructures of contemporary cities.

The transpacific geopolitical context of this second type of climatic media, tailored for the day-to-day governance of urban populations, suggests a critical role that Wiener's cybernetic theory of communication played in the field of architecture and urban planning.

CYBERNETICS

Architects and media theorists took cybernetics—the study of systems of communication and control between living things and machines—seriously, as cybernetics emerged as a transdisciplinary model of automatic control based on feedback mechanisms. Among those were Tange Kenzō and Marshall McLuhan.[9] By the mid-1960s, architects and urban planners across continents were collectively developing a new paradigm of urban design based on insights gleaned from cybernetics and communication theory. The architects Constantinos Doxiadis and Jaqueline Tyrwhitt, for instance, gathered an interdisciplinary international group of scholars in order to analyze urban planning in relation to information flow and communication networks.[10] It was then that the very idea of the network became integral to architecture, and Tange was among those who participated in this international effort to rethink urban design through the lens of cybernetics.

According to Mark Wigley, "Tange drew on cybernetics to discuss the influence of all the contemporary systems of communications—arguing, in McLuhanesque fashion, that there has been a second industrial revolution, an information revolution that prosthetically extends the nervous system in the same way that the first one physically extended the body."[11] Popularized by the work of Wiener, cybernetics draws parallels between the information-processing machine and the biological nervous system. Wiener did not simply draw a comparison between social organization and biological organization; he collapsed the two by redefining both through their internal communicative capacities to fight entropy or disorder through feedback loops.[12] This structural parallel between the communicative capacities of the city and those of the living organism appeared frequently in Tange's own writings in the 1960s.

We find references to Wiener in Tange's work from the mid-1960s onward. For instance, the book *The Future of the Japanese Archipelago* (1966) opens with a lengthy discussion of Wiener's idea of the second industrial revolution. Tange elaborates on the need to efficiently organize and restructure Japan's society and economy through the use of feedback and control mechanisms. The task of the architect or urban planner lies in predicting the future growth of the nation, thus optimizing the design of cities to efficiently organize the metabolic processes of energy, capital, goods, and human circulation.[13]

The influence of the North American cybernetics discourse on Tange and other Japanese architects, however, cannot be solely attributed to the mediating role of McLuhan, whose writings gained popularity in the 1960s.[14] Tange's embrace of cybernetics predates his encounter with McLuhan, and is more in line with the earlier introduction of Wiener's work to Japanese readers. Wiener's theory of cybernetics was already well known in Japan through translations. By 1957 five books by Wiener— including *Cybernetics or Control and Communication in the Animal and the Machine* (1948) and *The Human Use of Human Beings* (1950)—had been translated into Japanese. The principal translator of these books was the Japanese mathematician Ikehara Shikao, who studied and worked with Wiener at MIT in the late 1920s and early 1930s. To understand the transpacific context behind this cybernetic turn of architecture in Japan more fully, we need to zoom in on the earlier reception of Wiener's work in Japan.

Besides Ikehara, another ardent supporter of Wiener was a statistician and information theorist named Kitagawa Toshio. In 1953 Kitagawa organized a discussion-based workshop on cybernetics for the members of the Science Council of Japan. Emphasizing the interdisciplinary scope of cybernetics, Kitagawa argued for the need to "make cybernetics popular in this nation" and to position it as a general "science of control" akin to the adjacent fields of operations research and quality control.[15] The published account of this workshop suggests that the interests of its participants ranged from operations research and statistical mechanics to computing and electroencephalography in neuroscience.

In his memoir, Kitagawa devotes a full chapter to Wiener, whom he calls the "alpha" or the origin of his scholarly life. He fondly traces his personal encounter with Wiener's work on general harmonic analysis to 1932, while he was a student of mathematics at the Imperial University of Tokyo. In addition, Kitagawa recounts his relationship with Ikehara, who was teaching at the Imperial University of Osaka and through whom he was able to access Wiener's earlier research papers.

In the summer of 1935, Wiener made a brief stopover in Japan on his way to China, where he was planning to spend a year as a visiting professor at Tsinghua University. Ikehara, Kitagawa, and other Japanese academics gathered at the faculty club in Tokyo to welcome Wiener. Kitagawa describes Wiener as surprisingly chubby, friendly, and a little dorky for a mathematician. He admits that he imagined this genius mathematician to be slender and more neurotic.[16]

From 1941 to 1945, as Japan entered the war with the United States, the communication among academic researchers within the two countries was halted. After the war was over, Kitagawa discovered that Wiener had published several new works, including *Cybernetics or Control and Communication in the Animal and the Machine*, which he borrowed from the Civil Information and Education (CIE) library run by the Allied occupation forces in Tokyo in 1949. Kitagawa went on to organize the aforementioned workshop on cybernetics for the Science Council of Japan and several other events in the 1950s.[17] Then, in 1954, the year Ikehara's translation of Wiener's *The Human Use of Human Beings* appeared in Japanese, the major newspaper company Asahi organized a roundtable on cybernetics from the perspective of its relevance to theories of mass communication.[18] The Japanese reception of cybernetics thus dovetailed with the concurrent reception of mass communication theories from the United States.

It was in this political climate that Wiener made his second visit to Japan on his way back home from India in May 1956. Unlike the first time in 1935, Wiener's second visit received significant media coverage. Ikehara, the Japan Mathematics Society, and other academic organizations collectively invited Wiener to deliver lectures on his theory of cybernetics. Ikehara secured the official sponsorship for his trip by the Nippon Broadcast System (NHK) in exchange for the exclusive right to broadcast Wiener's lectures on radio and television.[19] Ikehara was pivotal in arranging Wiener's visits to Japan in 1935 and 1956, and his efforts to introduce the work of his mentor paved the way for the attention that cybernetics received from the academic community and the public in Japan.

Ikehara's correspondence with Wiener from the 1930s through the 1960s offers a useful vantage point from which to analyze the geopolitical complexity behind this transpacific reception of cybernetics. Although Peter Galison has detailed the military origins of cybernetics in his analysis of Wiener's involvement in the antiaircraft system, how the cybernetic logic of feedback resonates with wartime geopolitics between Japan and the United States has not been studied.[20] To supplement Galison and other historians' analyses of cybernetics with this transpacific perspective, I read the epistolary correspondence between Ikehara and Wiener from the 1930s through the 1960s in detail below.

Amid the rising military tension around the city of Beijing, which would soon be invaded and occupied by the Japanese Imperial Army in 1937, Wiener embarked on his trip to the Republic of China in the summer of 1935. On his way to China, he made a one-week stopover in Japan at the enthusiastic request of Ikehara.

The mounting conflict between Japan and China can be gleaned from the letter sent to Wiener from a colleague at the Office of the Dean of Engineering at MIT (signed only as V. Bush, though most likely it is Vannevar Bush, the inventor of the computational device called the differential analyzer) right before his trip. Bush begins his letter by noting: "After talking with you on the telephone the other night, I discussed the subject of your Chinese visit with Dr. Compton, particularly in regard to the situation in North China and the possibility that this might affect your plans."[21] Karl Compton, a physicist and then president of MIT, was to lead the National Defense Research Committee's Division on Detection, Controls, and Instrumentation in a few years when World War II began.[22] Bush, for his part, was soon to become the head of the Office of Scientific Research and Development, with which MIT and other universities conducted military research.

Given Bush's prominent involvement in government and military research, it is not surprising that he is careful to consult the State Department about Wiener's trip to East Asia. Indicating that there is no imminent diplomatic or physical problem for this trip, Bush nonetheless underscores the strained relationship between Japan and China: "The present activities on the part of Japan involve primarily insistence that Chinese officials in the vicinity of Peiping and Tientsin be changed in personnel to include individuals who would be favorably disposed toward the Japanese."[23] After speculating that Wiener would be safe even if Chinese students demonstrated against the Japanese, as long as Wiener stayed politically neutral, Bush suggests that Wiener make "a firm resolution before starting, not to express any political opinions while in the East." He further advises Wiener to exhibit "a complete lack of interest on all political matters whenever you make contacts. This may be a little difficult to combine with your complete frankness, but I think it is a good policy and those in the East will appreciate and respect complete reticence of this sort when you are on a scientific mission."[24]

In his letters following Wiener's visit to Japan in 1935, Ikehara does not mention the political tension between Japan and China. In contrast, his letter from July 1939—written two years after the Sino-Japanese War had started and as censorship was tightening—hints at the escalating military conflict: "Often I wish to drop in to see you and listen to your lectures. Under the existing conditions, I don't know when I can ever visit Cambridge again. . . . In spite of the unfortunate warfare in the Orient the country is rather peaceful. For we don't know anything about the 'war' except the news in the papers, which amount to little or nothing."[25] We know from history, this semblance of peace that Ikehara felt (or feigned) did not last long. The onset of the Pacific War in 1941 set Japan and the United States on opposing sides of the conflict.

During the war, Wiener worked on an antiaircraft control mechanism, which calculated and anticipated the future position of an enemy plane. His wartime research on this servomechanism, funded by the National Defense Research Committee, became the basis of Wiener's theory of cybernetics. Galison succinctly summarizes how he arrived at this feedback-based logic of cybernetic prediction and control:

> In the course of characterizing the enemy pilot's actions and designing a machine to forecast his future moves, Wiener's ambitions rose beyond the pilot, even beyond the World War. Step by step, Wiener came to see the predictor as a prototype not only of the mind of an inaccessible Axis opponent but of the Allied antiaircraft gunner as well, and then even more widely to include the vast array of human proprioceptive and electro-physiological feed-

back systems. The model then expanded to become a new science known after the war as "cybernetics," a science that would embrace intentionality, learning, and much else within the human mind.[26]

Cybernetics, in short, was developed to predict the behavior of enemy pilots, including those who served in the Japanese Imperial Navy Air Service. The key to this cybernetic servomechanism was its future orientation. It relied on past data sets to predict future events.

The mathematical theory of prediction, based on the antiaircraft predictor that Wiener and his collaborator Julian Bigelow developed, was distributed as a classified document for the National Defense Research Committee; the document with its yellow cover was nicknamed the "Yellow Peril," a racist and xenophobic epithet that positions East Asians as a threat to Western civilization and gained renewed traction during the wartime.[27]

When the war ended, Wiener was deeply troubled by the use of atomic bombs and the ongoing militarization of science.[28] Even though Wiener does not discuss politics in his letters to Ikehara, the shadow of the war loomed large in their correspondence. Ikehara's letter dated November 1945, for instance, gingerly mentions his fearful experience of aerial bombing by the Allied forces. While Wiener was busy collecting data on the flight patterns and statistical behaviors of bomber pilots in order to predict and accurately gun down enemy planes, Ikehara occupied the position of the target that Wiener's antiaircraft machine was supposed to destroy.[29]

In 1944 Ikehara took up a new position at the Tokyo Institute of Technology as head of the Department of Mathematics. Throughout the occupation period and after, Ikehara frequently corresponded with Wiener to arrange and secure the rights for Japanese translations of his books, first *Cybernetics or Control and Communication in the Animal and the Machine* and then *The Human Use of Human Beings*.

As part of the Cold War security and economic alliances fostered between Japan and the United States, sealed by the Japan-US Security Treaty, Ikehara joined the Japanese government's sponsored convoy of scientists and bureaucrats to the United States.[30] Taking place during the occupation period, such visits were often arranged between the two countries in order to facilitate the swift economic recovery of Japan under the banner of science and technology. In one of his letters, Ikehara expresses his ambition to nurture and increase collaborations among

Japanese and American scientists: "My personal wish is how to plant the spirit and organization of M.I.T. in Japan whose salvation must come from science and its consequences."[31] Wiener shared Ikehara's sentiment. In his letter from April 1955, for instance, Wiener writes: "I very much want to see Japan again and I have been struck by signs of Japanese recovery and of Japan's readiness to take a great moral status in the world."[32] Cybernetics, in due course, became the model science of organization and management, enthusiastically embraced by Japanese mathematicians, industrialists, policymakers, and architects.

I have lingered on Ikehara and Wiener's correspondence in order to underscore the point that the development and reception of cybernetics is inseparable from transpacific geopolitics and Japan's reorientation from the former empire, which colonized Asian nations and waged imperial wars, to the defacto satellite state of the United States, which waged proxy wars in Asia in order to ascertain its imperial power in the region. Introduced during Japan's postwar overhaul and reorganization of governmental, economic, academic, and social institutions, cybernetics also became something more than a fringe theory.

The cybernetic model of communication and control in part spurred debates on optimizing the defeated nation's economic productivity through its intensification, namely, the intensification of information exchange and logistics. Its affinity with the management discourse of organization fit perfectly into the postwar Japanese regime, run by the technocratic avant-garde and futurologists. While the technocrats and futurologists embraced cybernetics as a governmental model of management and organization, its logic of feedback inspired avant-garde artists and architects as a utopian model of communication and interactivity.

As Wiener himself warned, however, cybernetics as a political technique of control operates differently than a purely mathematical theory of communication and control. Used as a technique of government, cybernetics—like other theories such as game theory, with which it shares an epistemological framework—can turn into an apparatus of war.[33]

The problematic of government is, in fact, at the heart of Wiener's own theorization of cybernetics. As its etymological root in the Greek word *kubernesis* (meaning "steersman") indicates, the question of how to govern is folded into its epistemological framework. Like the steering engine of a ship that operates on the mechanisms of feedback, cybernetics, as Wiener himself saw it and as many critics have argued, provided a model of government with political implications that went far beyond the domain of science and engineering.[34]

This governmental undertone of cybernetics and its affinity with organization and logistics was not lost on Japanese readers of Wiener's work. Tange was one of them. It is to this organizational spin on the Japanese reception of cybernetics by Tange Lab architects that I now turn, as it offers an additional historical context in which to understand the emergence of networked surveillance as an atmospheric means of governing and conditioning urban populations.

ORGANIZATION AND LOGISTICS

As we saw in the previous chapters, Tange had already held an organicist view of the city as a living organism endowed with its own nervous system before his encounter with Wiener's cybernetics. But cybernetics offered an updated model that allowed him to connect communications infrastructure to other mechanisms of social organization. Following Wiener, Tange argued that every organism strives toward organization through the communicative processes of information management and feedback. Applying this argument to urban design, he placed the architectural planning of traffic, energy, and information networks as the key element of Japan's future development.[35] Urban planning for him was all about organizing space in order to maintain an effective communication or circulation of elements within the living organism of the city.[36]

Tange writes: "Organization is neither a perfect container for freedom nor a despotic mold. Rather, it is a living organism that voluntarily controls the process of feedback between freedom and order. I believe that a modern society is a highly developed form of a living organism. Its growth resembles an evolutionary process of development from plant to animal to human, as it has developed its own nervous system within social organizations, and started to engage in brain activities."[37] The modernist discourse on urbanism had long relied on organic, cellular, and evolutionary metaphors of the city, but Tange along with other architects supplemented these metaphors with the theory of cybernetics.[38]

What cybernetics offered Tange was an updated perspective to reimagine the city not only as a living *organism* but as a self-regulating *organization* in which networks of communication and control played the central role of abating entropy or disorder. Quoting Wiener, Tange notes that the task of an urban planner is "to resist the strong current of nature that leads to disorder, to construct orders and systems based on free will, and to build organizations."[39]

Organization, as Reinhold Martin among others has argued, gained the attention of architects and corporate designers in the United States following World War II along with the epistemological shift brought on by cybernetics, information theory, operations research, and system engineering.[40] The situation was not much different in Japan. It is not surprising that Tange foregrounds organization as a problem of design.

Moreover, the cybernetic metaphor of the city as a self-regulating organization resonated with, and was in significant part influenced by, the futurological discourse on information society, postindustrialization, and the logistics revolution. Promoted by a group of sociologists, economists, architects, and policy makers—some of whom were Tange Lab associates—the futurological discourse on the information society applied the concepts of prediction, feedback, and control to the realm of urban planning, the economy, business, government, and civic society. In addition to automation and computation, operations research and logistics gained the attention of these futurologists since it appeared indispensable to streamlining and optimizing the economic productivity of Japan. This collective investment in automation, operations research, and logistics critically inflected the way in which Tange Lab architects interpreted cybernetics.[41]

These futurologists' interest in information and the logistics revolution can be glimpsed in the opening chapter of *Japan's Information Society: Its Vision and Challenges* (1969).[42] The book covers a wide range of topics, including the rise of the information industry, the computerization of banking systems, strategies for business management, the impact of automation on the labor market, and the introduction of computers into educational institutions as well as transformations in logistics and the subsequent distribution of commodities. This last topic—logistics—deserves special attention since it holds a direct relevance to the research activities of Tange Lab.

Broadly defined, logistics concerns the management of movement and the coordinated flow of both things and military operations. The term derives from military usage, but it has come to be associated with the post-Fordist capitalist mode of production and distribution through the expansion of business logistics in the 1960s and 1970s. Business logistics also focuses on supply chain management, a field that grew rapidly upon the introduction of computers and operations research, the innovation of the container ship, the corresponding reconfiguration of transport infrastructures, and the application of cybernetics to the manufacture and distribution of goods.

In Japan, the nascent logistical approach to manufacturing and distribution began to circulate in the early 1960s through popular books such as the economist Hayashi Shūji's *A Revolution in Distribution*.[43] Indeed, the 1960s was the period when operations research, systems theory, and the technocratic discourse of the information society all converged around a set of related issues: logistics, computerization, and urban transportation and communication infrastructures.[44] All of this left an indelible mark on Japanese architectural criticism and informed its embrace of cybernetics.

Moreover, if cybernetics can be broadly defined as "the field concerned with information flows *in all media*," architecture was cybernetic even before architectural criticism embraced its vocabulary.[45] In this regard, Tange Lab's systematic studies of information and energy flows in the 1950s and early 1960s warrant attention. For instance, in 1963 Tange Lab conducted a comprehensive analysis of "the connections between the more than 100 departments and bureaus of the government and the movement of 10,000 workers inside the [Tokyo Metropolitan Government] building."[46] They tracked the flow of documents and people in order to optimize its bureaucratic organization. Optimization and organization are two concerns that characterize Tange Lab's work from this period. Throughout the 1960s, Tange showed his interest in the coordinated management of the flow of things as an essential component of urban design. This coincided with the economic rationality of information society discourse and, furthermore, dovetailed with governmental investment in the studies of information traffic.

The history of government, as Foucault reminds us, is marked by the quest of economic forms and techniques of administering the population, territories, and the market.[47] As is evident in the number of state-led development projects, market regulations, and social security systems, the liberal government of postwar Japan retained its wartime regime of the welfare state. Arguably, the cybernetic model of control accommodated postwar Japan's political regime, which embraced a hybrid form of economic management, combining state interventions and free market competition.[48]

Two architects trained at Tange Lab—Shimokōbe Atsushi and Ōba-

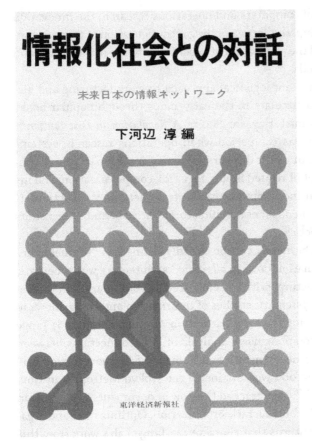

情報化社会との対話

未来日本の情報ネットワーク

下河辺 淳 編

東洋経済新報社

FIGURE 5.1.
A figure of information networks on the cover of *Dialogues with the Information Society* (1970).

yashi Jun'ichirō—went on to become powerful bureaucrats who worked for the Economic Planning Agency, the Ministry of Construction, and the National Land Agency.[49] Under the aegis of Shimokōbe, several members of Tange Lab including Kurokawa Kishō took part in government-sponsored research activities on the impact of information technologies on urban space. In 1967 Shimokōbe appointed Kurokawa to take part in an information network research group. Three years later, Shimokōbe edited and published *Dialogues with Information Society: Information Networks for Future Japan* (1970) and presented the outcome of a research project commissioned by the Economic Planning Agency. We find Kurokawa's name listed yet again among the participants of this research group. Other researchers included both government officials and corporate representatives from the telecommunications industry.[50] Kurokawa also served as a member of the futurology division of the Japan Techno-Economics Society, an organization that published an official report entitled *Developing a Super-Technological Society: Humans in the Information System* in 1969.[51]

Tange Lab thus had close ties to the proponents of the information society and their government-sponsored futurological research activities at a time when Japan was undergoing massive infrastructural transformations.[52] It is reasonable to assume that Tange Lab's emphasis on communication, information flow, and cybernetics directly paralleled the Japanese government and telecommunication industry's investment in the processes of informatization.[53]

It is within this political climate that these architects paid close attention to "soft" pathways of information, data, and wireless signals in addition to "hard" pathways of transportation and energy infrastructures. This pervasive presence of electric signals and data traffic that formed the invisible informatic membranes of the networked city were seen as both an opportunity and a challenge for architects to radically reimagine urban design (figure 5.1).[54]

CYBERNETIC RESPONSIVE ENVIRONMENTS

The work of Isozaki Arata, who kept a critical distance from the Metabolist group but also shared their interest in a biotechnical conception of the city, participated in this historical shift that I have been calling the cybernetic turn of Japanese architecture.[55] Isozaki's experiments with cybernetic responsive environments and his exploration of the ambient elements of urban design take us closer to the development of networked surveillance as an instrument of urban governance. In particular, I analyze one of the exemplary cases of Isozaki's cybernetic responsive environments—the Festival Plaza at Expo '70—to show how this architectural experiment with cybernetics foreshadowed and paralleled more insidious forms of networked surveillance and policing, which similarly adopted the cybernetic model of control and communication.

Isozaki worked for Tange Lab on several key projects, such as *A Plan for Tokyo, 1960* and Expo '70, the first world's fair held in Japan. If Shimokōbe, Ōbayashi, and Kurokawa represent the bureaucratic face of Tange Lab as a research institution, then Isozaki represents its artistic face. He was deeply involved in the art world,[56] and often collaborated with avant-garde artists, such as Yamaguchi Katsuhiro, active in the fields of multiscreen environments, happenings, intermedia performance, video art, and expanded cinema.[57]

The Festival Plaza was a prototype of Isozaki's cybernetic responsive environment (or "soft architecture," as he puts it), which featured a man-machine interface.[58] Its multimedia setup included two giant robots that allegedly formed a feedback circuit with the mainframe computer in the central control room. The heads of the robots housed secondary control rooms, while their bodies contained built-in sensors responding to changing lights and sounds in the surrounding environment. These sensors would send signals back to the main control room, which in turn modulated the lighting, sound, smoke, and mist machines that constituted the multimedia setup of the Festival Plaza. In theory, these robots were supposed to interject elements of indeterminacy that affected the Festival Plaza's operations.[59] Although the final product fell short of actualizing this interactive system, the idea was still visionary.[60] One could read its architectural design as a precursor to contemporary intelligent buildings and smart cities, which collect ambient data in order to modulate their environments (figure 5.2).

According to Isozaki, what he had in mind was the Mission Control Center at the US National Aeronautics and Space Administration (NASA), which he had visited in 1967 while researching for Expo '70. Recalling the time he first saw the Mission Control Center, Isozaki notes: "It was the time I was writing my essay, 'The Invisible City,' and the Control Center seemed like a perfect model of control and operation, which could handle complex levels of urban design and diverse social phenomena. I thought that if computers could control the Apollo Mission, they should be able to control society. So I decided to turn the Festival Plaza into a miniature version of this operation."[61] Isozaki's evocation of the Mission Control Center as an inspiration for designing the Festival Plaza is suggestive of his embrace of cybernetics. It is also notable that he presents it as a prototype of urban design aimed at social control. Just as the moon, the spacecraft, astronauts, and the operators inside the Mission Control Center back on Earth formed a man-machine system, the participants at the Festival Plaza, the robots, and the control room were supposed to form a cybernetic unit. Developed over two years, from 1967 to 1969, Isozaki's plan for the Festival Plaza emphasized elements of interactivity and feedback. Isozaki and Tsukio Yoshio, a Tange Lab architect and computer programmer who helped design the plaza, envisioned

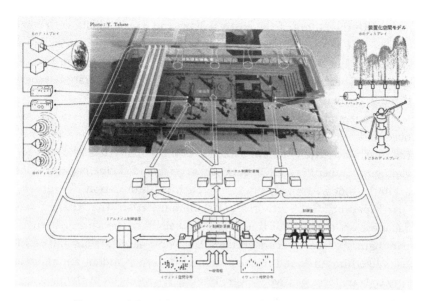

FIGURE 5.2. Diagram of the Festival Plaza from *Kenchiku bunka* (January 1970). Courtesy of Arata Isozaki and Associates.

this computer-controlled space as a type of "environment as a responsive field."[62]

Bridging architecture and computer science, the computerized multimedia setup of the plaza—at least in its ambition—fits the description of a *responsive environment* defined by the computer artist Myron Krueger: an environment "in which a computer perceives the actions of those who enter and responds intelligently through complex visual and auditory displays."[63] Isozaki's design thus paralleled and, in part, anticipated the theorization of responsive, intelligent architecture equipped with artificial intelligence by architects such as Nicholas Negroponte at the MIT Media Lab.[64]

The articulation of art, architecture, and computing also informs other works by Tsukio, who later made his foray into various artificial intelligence and smart city projects while serving as a policy adviser for the Japanese government.[65] Compared to Tsukio, Isozaki's embrace of cybernetics was less technocratic. After his design of the Festival Plaza at Expo '70 and a few other unbuilt projects—such as *Post University Pack* (aka *Computer-Aided City*, 1972)—Isozaki eventually turned away from technology-driven architecture.

This turning away from technology is partly due to his disillusionment with the failure of the Festival Plaza and its complicity with what he saw as oppressive practices of security, policing, and surveillance at the fair. But before this disillusionment hit, he did envision this responsive cybernetic environment as a utopian way to liberate fairgoers through communication, interactivity, and participation.[66]

To understand Isozaki's rather optimistic take on cybernetics, we need to note that the same ideas of communication and interactivity attracted the attention of many Japanese avant-garde artists who were engaging in happenings, environmental art, expanded cinema, and video art in the 1960s. Arguably, buzzwords such as "information," "feedback," "participation," "interactivity," and "communication" that characterize Japanese art criticism of this decade all belong to the same cybernetic paradigm. As Isozaki acknowledges, the avant-garde artists and architects like himself found in the notion of the environment an opportunity to transform passive viewers into "active receivers of the message" sent by the artwork.[67] When transposed to the context of art practice, the cybernetic logic of feedback gained the added participatory connotation of interactivity, resonating with the leftist critique of the unidirectionality of mass media.[68]

Isozaki's turn to cybernetics is in part aided by this general turn toward communication and interactivity by avant-garde artists. For, in the work of Isozaki, we find an interpretation of the environment that departs from the biopolitical and geopolitical connotations of the living sphere, which undergirds Tange and the Metabolists' projects of the same period. Driven by a more phenomenological and semiotic conception of the environment as an ephemeral event where processes of communication, interaction, and feedback occur, his understanding of the environment privileges ambient factors such as light, sound, shadow, and information signals.[69]

Isozaki's interest in the ephemeral dimensions of communication and information infrastructures in the city is also evident in his 1964 essay "Space of Shadows," in which he discusses the importance of the man-machine interface that mediates our experience of the data-saturated urban space. As an example, Isozaki turns to the figure of a pilot who flies an airplane at night. Because of the darkness, the pilot cannot trust his own vision and thus "must rely solely on signals received by flight instruments" in order to navigate the aircraft.[70]

The pilot and the airplane form a man-machine system or servomechanism (like the antiaircraft predictor and gunner Wiener used as the basis of his theory of cybernetics). Isozaki extends this metaphor of the pilot to the daily experience of an urban dweller for whom the city appears as heavily networked with wireless and wired signals.[71] Inversely, the task of contemporary architects becomes how to design urban space without losing sight of these invisible and atmospheric (or "virtual" as he calls it) networks of signals and data.

For Isozaki, architecture's turn toward cybernetics and methods of computer simulations comes naturally out of this understanding of the city as primarily an information environment. Isozaki's emphasis on computer-generated models and simulations as the new basis of urban design is also indicative of the historical moment within which he was writing. Simulation, after all, was the reigning cultural logic of the Cold War era, from game theory to computation.[72] His vision of urban design that privileged signs, codes, and simulated models is clearly reflective of this time.

Isozaki's interest in the primacy of signals and codes is also present in his 1967 essay "The Invisible City," which provides a theoretical framework for his design of the cybernetic environment of the Festival Plaza.[73] The text begins by addressing the inadequacy of using the existing concept of urban space to understand cities such as Los Angeles and Tokyo.[74] The chaotic layout and sprawl of these cities prevents one from seeing their structure in a systematic manner. Lacking grid patterns and landmark structures, the urban space of the contemporary city is no longer representable through spatial coordinates. Instead of landmarks and grids, the city is grasped relationally, that is, by gauging constantly shifting "relations between objects." [75]

Precisely because the experience of space is no longer connected to physical elements, however, the city becomes intelligible only when one pays attention to "an aggregate of various invisible signals and codes: flickering lights, acoustic sounds, telecommunications, traffic, activities, and trajectories of moving objects." In place of measurements, these ephemeral signs, codes, and wireless signals generate haptic sensations. The city dislodged from measurable space thus becomes subjective, relative, environmental—and ambient.[76]

The concept of *ambience*, following the German philosophical tradition of conceptualizing the atmosphere as a subjective experience of attunement, connotes subjective moods, affects, and immersive experiences. It is therefore often associated with the embodied encounter with one's own surroundings. As Paul Roquet writes, the spread of ambient media such as headphones and portable music players help urban dwellers navigate through the hectic rhythm of the city.[77] Ambient factors—such as sound, light, shadow, and wireless signals—need to be perceived as ambient by someone, who increasingly experiences this ambience through the mediation of digital devices. Isozaki's conception of urban design similarly takes this perceptual experience of ambience into consideration.

Isozaki's avid interest in ambient lighting, shadows, and soundscapes also resonated with the concurrent artistic interest in subjective techniques and technologies of biofeedback to exteriorize otherwise imperceptible physiological conditions, such as brainwaves and heart rate. The use of electrical sensors, contact microphones, and EEG (electroencephalogram) headsets was popular at the time, and his close associates, such as Tsukio, were involved in artistic experiments with biofeedback.[78]

Since the 1960s, the cybernetic logic of feedback has been variably combined with neoliberal techniques of the self, including the rise of the use of biometric self-trackers, EEG meditation headsets, and other instruments of quantifying the self in order to monitor, manage, and regulate the body and mind. These embodied experiments with biofeedback that measure and operate through ambient factors have become part of the general practices of social conditioning, medical surveillance, and self-enhancement. However, the earlier artistic experiments with biofeedback held a sense of novelty and optimism. Isozaki's positive outlook on the cybernetic logic of feedback and his investment in embodied experiences of ambient factors oriented around built environments need to be interpreted with this historical context in mind.

In his utopian design of the cybernetic responsive environment in the Festival Plaza, Isozaki attempted, at least in theory, to modulate these ambient elements of the city through the man-machine system of control rooms, robots, and manual operators of lighting, sound, and screens that respond through the constant process of feedback among all the participants in this space. Against Isozaki's expectation, however, the actual operation of the Festival Plaza proved otherwise. While it is called the Festival Plaza, its configuration included the main performance stage and auditorium-style seats for visitors. As he self-critically reflects in his essay, "Technology, Art, and the Establishment" (1972), the Expo organizers and the security team insisted on separating the stage from the visitors, literally preventing them from walking freely across the plaza. The communal sense of the *plaza* had lost its meaning and was turned into an *arena*, which was "carefully controlled, and cunningly administered."[79] In so doing, this cybernetic responsive environment lost its key elements of interactivity and indeterminacy and was left only with programmability.

The sinister counterpart of Isozaki's avant-gardist design of the Festival Plaza as a responsive cybernetic environment is found in the main control room used by the security and surveillance teams who monitored, tracked, and policed the fairgoers. This is not to say that Isozaki's artistic use of cybernetics for operating the Festival Plaza was simply opposed to the non-artistic use of cybernetics for governing the fair. Rather, Isozaki's Festival Plaza still followed a cybernetic vision of governance, which later developed into the practice of smart urbanism and social control.

As Orit Halpern argues in her analysis of South Korea's smart city of Songdo, the cybernetic vision of governance is built on the fantasies of automated monitoring, feedback, and control: "It is a city that is fantasized as being about re-organizing bodies, down to the synaptic level, and reorienting them into global data clouds or populations with other similarly reorganized nervous systems globally." The city deemed "smart" is also imagined as "a self-regulating organism, using crowdsourcing and sensory data to administer the city and limit (in theory) the necessity for human, or governmental intervention."[80] Tange Lab architects—including Isozaki— also shared this vision of the city as a self-regulating living organism.

Tange's writing supports this interpretation of Tange Lab as the forerunner of smart (or intelligent, since the term *intelligence* was used more widely in Japan until the 2000s) urban planning. For instance, he retroactively argued that *A Plan for Tokyo, 1960* was a blueprint for an intelligent city project. The aim of the project presumably was to optimize the transportation and communication capacities of the city of Tokyo. The necessary data to do so were to be gathered by computers. This unfinished project, according to Tange, boldly "imagined that the city itself becomes an *intelligent* city instead of individual buildings becoming intelligent buildings."[81] Similarly, we can read Isozaki's design of the Festival Plaza—for which he took inspiration from the cybernetic man-machine system that connected the Apollo space capsule to NASA's Control Center—as one of the genealogical predecessors of smart urbanism in Japan. What *A Plan for Tokyo, 1960*, the Expo '70 Festival Plaza, and NASA's Apollo Mission Control Center have in common is an organizational optimism and techno-utopianism associated with cybernetics.

The reality of the implementation of this logic, however, is much less utopian. The interior space of a spaceship, for instance, is one of the most

FIGURE 5.3. Expo '70's security team at the Operations Control Center. A still from *Project X: Osaka Banpaku shijō saidai no keibi sakusen*, 2005.

thoroughly monitored and surveilled environments. There is no privacy inside the carefully regulated enclosed climate of the spacecraft, where astronauts are required to constantly wear biometric devices to track their data.[82] Similarly, the Festival Plaza's responsive cybernetic environment had its dystopian analogue in the computerized security system of Expo '70 (figure 5.3).

The Operations Control Center, the security team, and networked electronic devices across the fairgrounds formed another kind of cybernetic environment, an underbelly of the artistic and architectural experiment with cybernetics epitomized by Isozaki's Festival Plaza. This second type of cybernetic environment was centered on the optimization of logistical, administrative, and policing practices that governed the operation of the entire fair. Combined with the disciplinary operations of security guards, this cybernetic environment focused squarely on techniques of social conditioning, which directly targeted the conduct of visitors, who were constantly monitored, tracked, and disciplined.

Commenting on how the fair's organizers came up with new regulations against hosting spontaneous events at the Festival Plaza and thus taking away the element of indeterminacy that he coveted, Isozaki notes that they "employed the soft technology called control through the creations of regulations at this plaza."[83] What Wiener saw as the danger of cybernetics becoming a political technique for controlling the population had become a reality in the security operations at Expo '70.

Urban infrastructures of networked surveillance and security have steadily evolved and have been getting "smarter" since the 1970s. One of the indicators of this change in Japan was a shift in emphasis from older policing techniques of crowd control, which relied on manual patrol and monitoring, to newer digital technologies of crowd control mediated by networked surveillance and cloud computing. This technological shift also corresponded to the growth of the private security, telecommunication, and computer industries.

Cloud computing started with the humble practice of time sharing and networking of computers and terminals. As Vincent Mosco notes, the basic assumption of cloud computing is surprisingly old insofar as it is "an extension of the computer utility concept, once referred to as 'time-sharing,' because usage time on a central computer was shared by multiple users."[85] In Japan, this nascent model of cloud computing and discussions of computer utility took place in the 1960s. Parallel to this shift was another technological change—the spread of closed-circuit television, which changed the practice of urban surveillance. With these two shifts, crowd control practices became cloud-based.[84] And Expo '70 served as a social laboratory for early experiments with this cloud-based crowd control.

While broadcast television became a commercial medium of mass communication, closed-circuit television emerged as an instrument of distant observation and surveillance. From power plants and hospitals to train stations and police headquarters, the panoptic capacity of television was used to monitor, supervise, and regulate the operations and movements of humans and machines. The first successful case of such "industrial television" in Japan was a closed-circuit surveillance system installed inside the control room of the Tōhoku Electric Power Plant in Yanaizu.[86]

By the mid-1960s, the use of cable and wireless television surveillance systems had spread across various Japanese institutions and organizations. The private railway company Keihin Kyūkō, for instance, implemented platform surveillance television in 1962. This rudimentary surveillance system consisted of one television camera and three monitors that assisted the security checkup by train conductors at the Yokohama station.[87] Similar surveillance systems were set up on urban street corners under the banner of crime prevention, and the 1964 Tokyo Olympics officially deployed surveillance cameras for crowd control.[88] The maintenance of security inside control rooms for power plants, at train stations, and on urban streets thus became the mainstay of closed circuit television surveillance in the 1960s. In short, closed-circuit television became an apparatus of social conditioning, whose monitoring power extended from machinery to urban crowds, a function that was fortified in conjunction with networked cloud computing.[89]

To be sure, Expo '70 was not the first world's fair to deploy computers to enforce security and manage crowds. A similar experiment was undertaken at Expo '67 in Montreal. Not surprisingly, the Japanese organizers and architects had paid close attention to this earlier experiment. In 1967 the leading architectural journal *Shinkenchiku*—and its English translation, the *Japan Architect*—published a special issue on Expo '67 that highlighted the exposition's Operations Control Center, located on Île Sainte-Hélène. "For the first time in the history of world expositions, Expo '67 employs a completely computerized management system," the report notes. This report was written by the collective Team Random, a group of young architects (including Tsukio from Tange Lab) and engineers associated with the Institute of Industrial Science at the University of Tokyo. The report goes on to describe the Operations Control Center in detail:

> Also known as the Cybernetics Center, the building is open to the public, though its heart, the control room, is strictly off limits. The centre is in the mid-section of the grounds, at some distance from the Corporation's main office on Cité du Havre. The designers have taken fairly conscious pains to display the computers symbolically in a glass-enclosed building, which is itself moderate in form and scale. The following is how we imagine the control room must look. It contains a large control board (16.5 × 5.4 m) loaded with switches and buttons. In front of the board sit four operators. In the center of the board is a map of the grounds (5.5 × 3.4 m). Monitor television screens ranged on either side flash on-the-spot broadcasts from all over the grounds. In other words, the room is an orthodox equipment space. Should, for instance, a fire break out at La Ronde, in response to contact from the La Ronde control branch, a red light would flash on in the La Ronde section of the master control board.[90]

FIGURE 5.4. Expo Life at Expo '67—Operations and Control, Montréal, Quebec, 1967. Photo © Government of Canada. Reproduced with the permission of the minister of Public Works and Government Services Canada (2012). Source: Library and Archives Canada/Canadian Corporation for the 1967 World Exhibition, fonds/e001096661.

The extraordinary attention paid by Team Random and the *Japan Architect*—two full pages describing the design of the Operations Control Center and its computerized system of management at Expo '67— suggests the interest the Japanese organizers of Expo '70 had in this previous experiment with cybernetic management (figure 5.4).

The contemporaneous response to the Operations Control Center at Expo '67 in Montreal, however, was not devoid of criticism. Writing for the journal *Architectural Review*, Jeremy Baker, a British architect, describes the computerized system of management adopted by Expo '67 organizers as "a form of benevolent despotism." In Baker's analysis, even crisis management appears to be a calculated element of the cybernetic operation of the fair. Noting the efficiency of crowd control undertaken by the Operations Control Center, Baker writes, "Should the situations room see a bottleneck on the site, the gallant Expo Band is ordered into action to siphon off some of the crowd; or if an area of the site looks dull, then a mobile pop group can be driven over there to liven up the proceedings."[91] The management of the fair, in short, relied on blurring the boundary between security operations and entertainment. The two were handled by the same control system.

The confluence of crisis management and entertainment was made literal through the Operations Control Center's status as an attraction itself. As Montreal's city newspaper, the *Gazette*, reported, "Apparatus in the Security Headquarters is so sophisticated that the building has been classified as an exhibit and visitors can watch the emergency equipment at work through an observation window."[92] This elevation of the Operations Control Center to a multimedia spectacle in its own right formed an engineering counterpart to the artistic displays of multiscreen environments housed inside the corporate and national pavilions. The Operations Control Center at Expo '67 thus provided a model for a networked information environment in which the apparatuses of security and control themselves became a source of excitement.

Building on its precursor in Expo '67, the Operations Control Center of Expo '70 went even further in monitoring, tracking, and managing visitors. Housed inside the Operations Control Center were four mainframe Hitachi computers serving NTT's Expo '70 Data Communication System. Hitachi and NTT engineers and programmers described this software as follows: "Programs for data processing at the Expo '70 site are divided into on-line programs, and off-line programs to support the former. The on-line programs consist of two systems, A and B. A processes information on displays and events, on missing children and lost and found articles, and on security arrangements, etc.; system B covers information on arrivals and departures of visitors, the flow of visitors on the fairgrounds, availability of parking spaces, and wait times, etc."[93] The headquarters of the Expo '70 security team also had its own control room connected to the Operations Control Center. There, a flashing map of the exposition grounds was surrounded by dozens of television monitors, videophones, and rows of control panels and switchboards that formed a semicircular information environment.

Although the closed-circuit television system was used for policing purposes at the Tokyo Olympics for the first time, the scale and sophistication of Expo '70 exceeded it. The ubiquity of the closed-circuit television system in Japanese urban spaces has now become the norm, but we find its precursor in the simulated urban environment of Expo '70. This is where the soft technology of social control based on networked operations of policing and surveillance, using the closed-circuit television system, sensors, and computers, was tested on the actual population for the first time.[94] The cost of developing and installing closed-circuit televisions, videophones, laser devices, and computers to create networked security systems at the Expo alone was over $350 million.[95]

The timing of Expo '70, which unfolded against the backdrop of the Cold War geopolitical alliance between Japan and the United States, warrants attention here. This world's fair took place amid mass street protests against the renewal of the Japan-US Security Treaty and the Vietnam War, a war crucially marked by the use of chemical agents including tear gas. Many of these protests led to police using tear gas against the demonstrators. The civilian use of tear gas as an extraordinary technique of policing crowds in Japanese and American cities and the battlefield deployment of the same chemicals as weapons in Vietnam happened at exactly the same time as the emergent technologies of cloud computing and networked surveillance were being developed as ordinary techniques for monitoring and tracking crowds.

Put differently, tear gas and networked surveillance as climatic media are genealogically bound by the transpacific geopolitics of the Cold War. To be sure, tear gas is a chemical substance, and the metaphor of the cloud implied in the systems of networked surveillance is just that—a metaphor. Yet they operate as climatic media of atmospheric control aimed at air-conditioning and social conditioning of crowds. Both are pervasive and atmospheric insofar as tear gas and networked surveillance come together in their capacity to diffuse into the urban environment and enact control upon crowds by virtue of their unique amenability to diffusion. The transmission of chemicals and signals, which define these two types of climatic media, also relies on the medium of air, as their operations often follow the cybernetic logic of biological and informational feedback loops. And their urban applications increased during the Vietnam War.

Given this historical timing, it is not surprising that crowd control at Expo '70 was a top security issue for the government. According to

Osaka Metropolitan Police records, officials expected massive protests against Expo '70 and later gloated that they had prevented sporadic protests from disrupting events during the fair.[96] Memories of the Shinjuku riots of 1968—during which the anti-riot law was invoked and hundreds of youths protesting against the Vietnam War were indiscriminately arrested—were still fresh in the minds of many who were engaged in planning the fair.[97] In this heated political climate, the novel techniques of governance and technologies of surveillance used at Expo '70 found immediate applications outside the fair compound.

In light of such policies, much media hype surrounded the elite Expo '70 security team. The sharp growth of the private security industry during the 1960s contributed to this increased media attention.[98] Also notable are concurrent technological developments, including SECOM's Security Patrol Alarm System (SP Alarm), which used private telephone lines leased from NTT to provide online security services to banks, government buildings, factories, and small businesses, replacing the patrolling services used previously.[99] SECOM's security services piggy-backed on NTT's data communications service. The development of the private security industry clearly benefited from the transformation of the telecom industry in Japan.

This gradual transformation of security businesses from labor-intensive patrolling services to networked communications services, initiated by SECOM, is crucial for our genealogical understanding of networked surveillance as an infrastructural means of atmospheric control. The historical significance of this transition goes beyond the narrow context of the birth of the private security industry. As the name SECOM, which stands for "security" and "communication," indicates, this company branded itself as an electronic security firm that provided home and corporate security systems.

Etymologically, the word *security* derives from the Latin word *securus*, meaning "free from care." SECOM exploited this embedded sense of care in the concept of security and promised to provide "peace of mind." In 1975 the company launched a Computer Security System (CSS), which it boasted as the world's first fully computerized alarm system. In the 1980s, it also tried to brand itself as a multimedia business by marketing its computerized SECOM home security system as "a successful model of new media, since the system allowed customers to receive security services by connecting controllers in their homes to SECOM Control Centers via the existing telecom infrastructure."[100]

During the 1990s the company also expanded its definition of security to include a wide range of technologies, including geographic information service, robotics, and medical services. The SECOM Intelligence Systems Laboratory is currently developing a comprehensive system of home automation ("smart home"), an ambition that is dovetailing with the rise of the Internet of Things. The company continues to market and sell a fingerprint recognition system as a more secure and smarter way of locking and unlocking one's house, along with medical surveillance services targeting elderly residents.[101] Since 2015 the company has offered security drone services, taking to the skies to extend the scope of networked aerial surveillance as a form of atmospheric control. SECOM and other Japanese companies in the private security industry are major participants in the field of smart home design and smart urban infrastructure development.

Fifty years after world's fairs such as Expo '67 and Expo '70 served as intricate laboratories for social and technological experiments, the paradigm of securitization is shifting ever more toward automation, ubiquity, big data, and artificial intelligence. However, as I argue in this chapter, this pervasive environment of automated surveillance systems and cloud-based information networks has genealogical precedents in urban design and architectural experiments, which emerged amid the Cold War geopolitics and the changing strategies of urban governance in the 1960s. Expo '70 was more than a futurological dream and a simulation of the future city. It also functioned as a social laboratory where the avant-garde technocrats, artists, and architects, including Tange Lab architects like Isozaki, projected a techno-utopian image of the cybernetically governed city, paving the way for current experiments with smart urbanism and cloud-based systems of unmanned security and surveillance. The transpacific genealogy of cybernetics and its impact on urban design as an instrument of social conditioning lies at the base of these experiments.

THE FEEDBACK LOOPS OF CLIMATIC MEDIA

In this chapter, I examine the transpacific genealogy of two types of climatic media—tear gas and networked surveillance—while putting emphasis on the latter in order to highlight the impact cybernetics has had on urban design and governance. In order to foreground the transpacific perspective, I attend closely to the formative moments of the Cold War during which the police use of tear gas and networked surveillance became pervasive in Japan and North America.

The political landscape and local contexts of urban governance may differ, but the connection between these two climatic media designed for social conditioning of urban populations remains strong, as governments and tech firms around the world keep investing in smart infrastructures and smart policing initiatives. As shown by Michael Fisch's research on Tokyo's commuter rail network, which runs on artificial intelligence that anticipates frequent suicides as programmed fluctuations of the system in order to respond in a resilient manner, the development of smart infrastructure in Japan has not lost its pace but rather is accelerating.[102] After the 3.11 catastrophe in the Tōhoku region, many municipalities and tech companies began investing in earnest to reconstruct cities that were devastated by the earthquake and tsunami and turn them into prototypes of smart cities. Projects such as Higashimatsushima's "smart disaster prevention eco town," which integrates micro energy grids, smart meters, and other automated systems of surveillance and management into its urban infrastructure, aim to "resiliently" survive the next time a natural or human-made disaster hits the region.[103]

Outside Japan, smart urban infrastructure developments continue to be entangled with street protests and police use of tear gas and networked surveillance as atmospheric instruments of governance. During the pro-democracy protests, for instance, Hong Kong's smart lampposts—equipped with cameras and sensors to collect data about weather and traffic—were toppled by protesters, who suspected that these lampposts were monitoring their movements in the streets.[104] These protesters were swiftly tear-gassed by the riot police. In North America and elsewhere, the relentless and persistent use of tear gas against civilians who gather to protest against police violence appears to be escalating, as indicated by the recent example of the Black Lives Matter movement. These are a handful of examples that indicate that smart urbanism does not in any way decrease law enforcement's reliance on tear gas and other violent methods of social control. The political and material climates of the cities continue to be conditioned, monitored, and managed by the fogs of chemicals and waves of signals that saturate urban atmospheres.

Technologies, however, can break down and machines malfunction all the time. They can be creatively misused and appropriated. The efficacy of these two types of climatic media aimed at social conditioning of urban populations is therefore often only the promise of control, or wishful projection of this promise, onto reality. In many instances, tear gas backfires on the police squads who do not calculate the direction of the wind. Protective gear such as gas and surgical masks are worn by protesters in the streets, who bring leaf blowers to redirect the plume of tear gas. Similarly, computers, cameras, facial recognition software, and microsensor devices often do not perform as intended. Meanwhile, the mining of precious metals and minerals needed to produce sensitive components of these networked surveillance systems are polluting the air, water, and soil. Climatic media interact with one another in a series of ecological and political feedback loops. It is these feedback loops, which undergird atmospheric control as forms of air-conditioning and social conditioning, that this chapter and the preceding chapters have elucidated.

Moving across the Pacific and spanning the decades of the twentieth and twenty-first centuries, this book has traced a transpacific genealogy of technologies of atmospheric control. These technologies function as climatic media that operate as means of air-conditioning and social conditioning. From the invention of cloud-seeding to the dream of solar geoengineering used to reduce the greenhouse effect, and from capsule houses to data centers, I have explored how these technologically mediated experiments with atmospheric control are undergirded by the geopolitically determined thermostatic desire to secure a livable future environment for certain populations while excluding others.

I ended the last chapter with the possible failures of such control. After all, tear gas may backfire with a gust of wind, sensors and security cameras may shut down during a blackout caused by a hurricane or snowstorm, and artificially seeded clouds often do not bring rain to the intended location. Atmospheric phenomena, like people, resist control. The operations of climatic media are indeed contingent on the very elemental, and fundamentally unstable, conditions of the atmosphere they aim to predict, control, and manipulate. Contingency and uncertainty are part of their operations.

Nonetheless, I have focused on the aspirations for control and the projective orientations and experiments of climatic media used primarily as means of designing air-conditioned and climate-controlled shelters, spheres, and habitats in order to trace the bleaker side of their transpacific genealogy. In doing so, I have called attention to the ecological dilemmas—and in some cases political complicity—of the Japanese and American scientists, architects, engineers, and artists who were directly or indirectly involved in the experiments with these climatic media.

By focusing on the narrative of prediction and control, the preceding chapters have deliberately avoided mentioning the more uplifting, elusive, and incalculable sides of climatic engineering. For instance, I have left out discussions about potentially more sustainable and less extractive uses of weather cultivation techniques, such as wind farming and "fog harvesting" that harness energy and moisture in the air. As is evident in the use of the agricultural metaphors of farming and harvesting, these techniques—like cloud seeding—consider weather as a natural resource, yet their aims and effects may not be as drastic or militaristic as planetary geoengineering and steering hurricanes.

Similarly, while I focused on the capsule housing and domed cities of Tange Lab and Metabolist architects and the fog sculpture of Nakaya Fujiko, there are other contemporary architects and artists who take the elemental and meteorological conditions of natural weather as their primary media of experimentation and aesthetic expression, often aiming to directly respond to the ongoing climate crisis by raising critical awareness of forms of ecological injustice. From Latai Taumoepeau, whose performance pieces include being tied to and suspended under blocks of melting ice to draw attention to the plight of the Pacific Islands communities threatened by the rising sea level, to Olafur Eliasson and Néle Azevedo, who similarly use fog and ice in their installations to address the accelerating pace of global warming, contemporary artists and designers across the world have turned to ice, fog, water, wind, heat, and other elemental media to raise public awareness about anthropogenic climate change.[1] By setting up affective encounters with the climate crisis, these works help constitute what Derek McCormack calls "atmospheric publics," in which "the elemental conditions of a meteorological atmosphere become a distributed matter of concern."[2] Instead of simply "explicating" the taken-for-granted background givenness of the atmosphere and its lethal potential (as poison gas, tear gas, and the weaponization of weather have done), they bring to the fore the already altered—and in some cases weaponized—states of the climate that threaten the lives of many.

Unlike the initial moment of atmospheric-explication by poison gas discussed by Sloterdijk, these climate-conscious artistic media explicate the *already-explicated* atmosphere that is constantly air-conditioned, partitioned, and engineered. Not an invention or discovery of the atmosphere as such, these works point instead to the ongoing effects of a previous explication of the atmosphere brought on by modern science and technology. What melting ice makes visible or perceptible as an artistic experiment, for instance, is not the neutral presence of the atmosphere in general, but one that has been engineered and is already explicated by the modern thermostatic desire, which led to the developments of scientific, architectural, military, and policing technologies of controlling the atmosphere and engineering the climate.

Explication of the atmosphere, then, is not a one-time operation. There are multiple types and instances of explication, some of which work as an artistic mode of critique of the effects of preceding explications. What exactly, then, is explication and how does it relate to the act of criticism in general? In closing, I want to briefly touch on the epistemic effect of "explication" and use it to further reflect on the methodological and theoretical stakes of this book's focus on the transpacific genealogy and geopolitics of atmospheric control.

Explication literally means unfolding, and it is the term that Sloterdijk uses to describe the phenomenological disclosure of an otherwise implicit or concealed state of things. For instance, the latent potential of the atmosphere as a medium of distant killing (and not just as a medium of telecommunication) was fully "explicated" or made explicit after the invention of poison gas. This revelation, according to Sloterdijk, caused existential insecurity among many. Yet this insecurity was quickly contained by the inventions of countermeasures such as gas masks and oxygen tanks. Explication of the atmosphere in this regard is not only about insecurity but also about security.

Wearing a gas mask and an oxygen tank on the battlefield is akin to creating a portable air-conditioned shelter around one's body. This gear separates the body from the surrounding zone of contaminated air. As such, explication of the atmosphere is much more than a technological procedure; it is at the core of the generalized mode of technologized existence in modernity. Seeking security and comfort by dwelling inside airconditioned and climate-controlled shelters is, according to Sloterdijk, part of the existential condition of being modern.

Modernity, which he also calls the "age of the background explication," however, is not just about seeking security and comfort. It is also a time when the self-evident givenness of the environment becomes estranged and denatured, and is thrust into the foreground: "In modernity's campaign against the self-evident not only air and the atmosphere, but also culture, art and life have come under an explicative pressure that has radically altered the mode of being specific to these 'givens.'"[3] Put schematically, then, *explication* refers to the phenomenological process of bringing something that had remained in the background of consciousness to the foreground. This process can be applied not only to natural environments, such as Earth's atmosphere, but also to culture and other spheres of human life. As Sloterdijk writes: "To show one's willingness to participate in modernity one is compelled to let oneself be seized by its power of explication over what once discretely under-'lay' everything, that which encompassed and enveloped to form an environment."[4] The key phrase here is *under-lay*, to which I return momentarily.

Thus generalized, the concept of explication stands in for various modes of denaturalization of that which appears to be self-evident, natural, and familiar. Ultimately, then, explication is not too far from the modernist—or more precisely, avant-garde—aesthetic strategies of defamiliarizing the familiar. Not surprisingly, Sloterdijk names surrealism as the exemplary artistic effort of explicating the taken-for-granted norms of Euro-American bourgeois culture. For instance, he highlights the public performance of Salvador Dalí, who donned a deep-sea diving suit in order to symbolize the artist's exploration of the unconscious in the 1930s. The diving suit with its attached oxygen tank, like the gas mask with oxygen tank on the battlefield, is a piece of technical gear meant to separate the air-conditioned interior from the life-threatening exterior. This portable atmospheric bubble ensures a sense of existential security for its wearer, just as the comfort of living a modern bourgeois life does the same for others.[5]

Sloterdijk's formula of explication as both the technoscientific process and the aesthetic process of transforming something that is in the background into the foreground of consciousness is not radically new or critical given its Eurocentrism, but it nonetheless offers a useful framework to think through the similarity between the epistemic act of critique and the phenomenological process of explicating the taken-for-granted background environment. Their core operation is the defamiliarization of the familiar, self-evident, and naturalized background. In the disciplines of humanities, explication is often tied to a method of close textual analysis. One may explicate a text—be it a novel, a film, or a philosophical treatise—by unpacking its implicit meanings, references, and presuppositions. It is an intellectual maneuver that digs under the surface appearance of an object with the aim of disclosing and articulating what may have been implicit at first glance. In that sense, explication is a mode of critique.

This way of reformulating explication as critique allows us to see the broader implications of questioning the taken-for-granted phenomena. While the textually based mode of critique may not seem relevant to studies of non-textual media forms and the materiality of media technologies, I want to suggest otherwise. Explicatory critique is already operative in media studies, especially in the studies of infrastructure. Infrastructure, as many media scholars have argued, is a quintessentially taken-for-granted object, which easily recedes into the background of consciousness in our daily life. To underscore this point, let me take a moment to discuss the operational similarity between *explication* (as an analytical procedure) and *failure* (of media and their infrastructures that instantiate such an analysis).

Infrastructure and environment (including atmosphere) are often compared and equally presented as the invisible ground of modern society. Paul Edwards, for instance, argues that infrastructures constitute "the invisible background" of society. In use since the late nineteenth century, *infrastructure* is a modern military term to designate technical equipment installed as the basis for the necessary operation of a system, an organization, or a society. It literally means a structure that lies below: *under-laid*, to recall Sloterdijk. Infrastructure as the underlying structure or background of the modern society can encompass a wide range of institutions and complex technical objects from telephone lines, railroads, and data centers to dams, sewers, and power plants.

Emphasizing the process of naturalization and the moments of failure, Edwards defines *infrastructure* in the following manner: "Mature technological systems—cars, roads, municipal water supplies, sewers, telephones, railroads, weather forecasting, buildings, even computers in the majority of their uses—reside in a naturalized background, as ordinary and unremarkable to us as trees, daylight, and dirt. Our civilizations fundamentally depend on them, yet we notice them mainly when they fail, which they rarely do. They are the connective tissues and the circulatory systems of modernity. In short, these systems have become infrastructures."[6]

John Durham Peters similarly equates the taken-for-granted presence of the natural environment to the "demure" presence of infrastructure that recedes into the background of everyday perception: "How the taken-for-granted gets constructed in the first place is a classic phenomenological question: how did the water ever become invisible to the fish?" He continues, "Infrastructure is often as hard to see as a light rain through the window."[7] Precisely because of its propensity to recede into the background, sometimes by design, infrastructure, like the environment, is not easy to detect. Its analysis prompts critics to look beyond what appears natural, self-evident, and immediately given to ordinary perception. As he notes, an analysis of both the environment and infrastructure demands the phenomenological questioning of taken-for-granted conditions.

Provocatively, Peters further extends this intellectual maneuver of looking beyond the surface, scrutinizing the obvious, and contemplating the mundane to what he calls the intellectual doctrine of "infrastructuralism." A number of modern canonical thinkers—whose works are characterized by investigations of "the basic, the boring, the mundane, and all the mischievous work done behind the scenes"—fall under this doctrine.[8] His list includes Marx (who revealed labor as an infrastructure of the capitalist economy), Freud (who drew attention to the unconscious as an infrastructure of the human psyche), and Husserl (who interrogated the intentional orientation of human consciousness) among other major figures in biology, sociology, and linguistics. In other words, infrastructuralism for Peters, like explication for Sloterdijk, is a hallmark of a modern European thought that refuses to take for granted the givenness of the surface appearance of phenomena.

On the one hand, to define modernity by this critical gesture of making explicit what appears implicit is valuable. It offers us a vantage point for seeing the terrain of modernity in a telescopic view. On the other hand, it raises the thorny question of the theoretical limits of such a generalization. How, then, might we balance the risk of generalization when we theorize the explication of the background givenness (be it environment or infrastructure) as the defining feature of modernity against the need to analyze historical, material, and site-specific contexts that may resist such generalization? This is one of the questions that has guided me while I was writing this book, and my answer to this lies in my strategy of conducting a geopolitically situated genealogical analysis of climatic media in the transpacific context.

To further reflect on this challenge, we may take a cue from Sara Ahmed's feminist critique of the phenomenological apprehension of an everyday object. She walks us through Husserl's philosophical experiment of bracketing his habituated perception. Taking the writing table as an example, Husserl tries to suspend the immediate impression of the table that is given to him and examine his own act of perception by simultaneously pushing its familiarity into the background and bringing to the fore what has remained in the background of his consciousness.[9] As Ahmed argues, however, his gesture of exploring the background of his perception does not go far enough. For Husserl is concerned only with the background of his habituated perception of this table that appears familiar but not with the historical and material backgrounds of the table itself. These backgrounds that Husserl ignores include the material labor of workers that went into making this table as a commodity, or the housework and other domestic labor that materially and affectively support the social reproduction of Husserl as the white male European philosopher.

To extrapolate from Ahmed and bring us back to the problem of further explicating the background givens, I suggest that this process of explication should not be abstracted from historical and material specificities as well as geopolitical and environmental site-specificities of the "background" and those who perform this act of explication. That means *how* one arrives at the point of explicating the atmosphere matters as much as the act itself. This brings us to the question of power relations. For instance, what matters is not simply that tear gas on urban streets and chemical fogs in the battlefield explicate the atmosphere, reminding us of the existential insecurity posed by such technology. Rather, the geopolitically determined and racialized decision-making to use these weapons by the police and the military as part of social conditioning matters and needs to be interrogated.

Another way to avoid theoretical abstraction is to think what social, material, geopolitical, and historical forces affect and shape instances of atmospheric explication and infrastructural failure: to think not of atmosphere or infrastructure in general, but in their specificities. As Nicole Starosielski and Lisa Parks suggest, "Studying moments of breakdown or failure might be the most appropriate *heuristic* device for infrastructural understanding."[10] Looking at the moment of failure (or explication) offers a heuristic method for analyzing infrastructure (or atmosphere). Focusing on the specific moments and events of failure heuristically—which means strategically—is immensely productive when combined with site-specific approaches to infrastructures that break down. Media scholars such as Brian Larkin and Rahul Mukherjee among others have likewise called attention to the dynamics of social relations and local specificities of infrastructures in places like Nigeria and India.[11]

Similarly, this book has highlighted the genealogical backgrounds and geopolitical contexts of these moments of breakdown and events of failure (such as when regional air-conditioning and the cybernetic environment at Expo '70 failed to meet the designers' utopian aspirations) by focusing on the enduring legacies of Japan's imperialism and its involvement in the Cold War. The explicatory critique of atmospheric control that I developed in the preceding chapters is meant to be grounded in the site-specific and historically specific context in which geopolitics affected and shaped many of the experiments with climatic media in Japan and the United States. It is for this reason that I chose a genealogical method to explicate atmospheric explications.

Genealogy resists the linear narrative of a streamlined history. As a situated method of analysis, which refuses to accept the taken-for-granted existence of a certain practice or idea, a genealogical approach to the past insists on making sense of the present through the historicity of what appears to be obvious, eternal, or natural; this is the position taken by Foucault.[12] It seeks to historicize not only practices and ideas but also analogies and metaphors that have been naturalized and appear to be self-evident, while tracing forgotten or overlooked continuities and discontinuities behind such naturalization. That is, genealogy as a method engages in explication of the obvious or taken-for-granted but does so with its historicity in mind. It is not explication for explication's sake.

As one final example to wrap up this reflection on the genealogical mode of explication, I want to briefly turn my attention to the recent revival of the term *media ecology* within media studies and its methodological affordances and challenges.[13] The analogy of *ecology* is frequently used to analyze complex interactions, systems, and relational networks of media objects, infrastructures, and people. However, media ecology, like atmospheric control, has its own site-specific historicity worth noting.

In North America, the idea of media ecology is often traced back to the foundational work of the mid-twentieth-century media theorists and cyberneticians—such as Marshall McLuhan, Neil Postman, and Gregory Bateson—who used the capacious analogy of "ecology" to analyze the perceptual, cognitive, and affective impact of communication and information technologies. These technologies, they suggested, are not just environmental extensions of human bodies and senses; their interactions with humans form a kind of ecosystem through which both evolve.

As Ursula Heise argues, this conflation of nature and technology through the analogy of media ecology has its roots in the Chicago School of sociologists. This group proposed the idea of "human ecology" to analyze the impact of urban infrastructure such as transportation systems on the social, economic, and demographic transformations of urban neighborhoods in the 1910s and 1920s. These transformations within neighborhoods were studied through the concept of ecological succession of species, such as plant and animal populations in natural habitats, and other analogies drawn from biological science.[14]

At the same time, a similar move to appropriate the language of ecology to understand the increasingly pervasive presence of electronic media was developing in Japan. One of the early proponents of what might be called the media ecological approach to information and communication technologies was Umesao Tadao, a futurologist and cultural anthropologist whose book *An Ecological View of the History of Civilization* (1967) analyzed the historical developments of various civilizations in different geographical and climatic regions. In many ways, his climatic determinism simply repeats that of Watsuji Tetsurō in *Climate and Culture* (1935), which I discussed in the introduction to this book.

Umesao, like the Chicago School sociologist Robert Park, adopted the ecological ideas of autogenic succession and allogenic succession of species within a given habitat to his study of the rise and fall of civilizations.[15] He was a disciple of the prominent scholar Imanishi Kinji, who helped establish the fields of ecology and comparative anthropology in Japan. In the early 1940s, Imanishi led several scientific expeditions (in which Umesao participated) to Japan's colonial and semicolonial territories, including the island of Pohnpei in the western Pacific Ocean. Having studied with Imanishi at Kyoto Imperial University during the same period, Umesao's ecological view of history bears a strong resemblance to Imanishi's theory of "habitat segregation" of multiple species within a given ecological system.[16]

Umesao was also a founding member of the Japanese Association of Futurology, established in 1968 around the time that McLuhan and Postman's ideas of media as environment and ecosystem were attracting attention in North America. Although the notion of environment (*kankyō*) and its affinity with media had already been integrated into the Japanese architectural and artistic discourses on multimedia environments by the 1960s, it was this group of Japanese futurologists, including Umesao, who explicitly drew on the analogies of ecology and ecosystems to talk about the cultural impact of information and communication technology on society.[17]

In 1971, for instance, they held a symposium titled "Problems of an Information Discourse." Collected in the book subtitled *A Challenge from the Information Environment*, papers from the symposium focused on the rising popularity of *information* as a buzzword and explored different methodological approaches to examine its cultural and social impacts.

Using oxygen levels in the air that vary across geographical locations as a handy example, Umesao argued that the uneven distribution of information in postindustrial society can be analyzed as an ecological problem. Information, he suggested, is like the chemical element of oxygen whose density in the atmosphere is unevenly distributed.[18] Following Umesao, the participants of the symposium called for a new mode of cultural analysis which they dubbed "information ecology."[19]

On the other side of the Pacific, ecology also evolved in relation to the transpacific geopolitics of the Cold War—for instance, the ecosystem ecology thinking developed by the American ecologists Howard and Eugene Odum, who worked under the Atomic Energy Commission's directive to study the impact of radioactive fallout after atmospheric nuclear weapons testing in the Marshall Islands. These Pacific islands, as Elizabeth DeLoughrey argues, were ideologically constructed as ecological "isolates," naturally approximating the controlled environment of a laboratory. This fallacy of ecological isolation, amplified by the visual regime of aerial photographs and films that neatly framed island colonies seen from the sky, supposedly helped the US government condone the violence inflicted against Indigenous populations on the islands, who were constructed in advance as "biological isolate" cut off from the mainland United States and therefore fit to serve as specimens for nuclear testing.[20] If Imanishi and Umesao's colonial ecology and media ecology form the Japanese side of the transpacific lineage of ecology as a method, the idea of nuclear ecology and the ecosystem thinking developed by the Odum brothers tells the American side.

Since the 1970s, the finance and tech sectors have also appropriated ecological metaphors and analogies. For instance, today's discourse on smart cities and smart infrastructure relies on the ecological concept of "resilience."[21] Resilience as a biological trait of a living organism is now seen as part of the adaptive evolutionary process of technological infrastructure and has become a transdisciplinary model or general strategy for urban design. Current debates on geoengineering employ this mode of resilient thinking in which smart atmospheric controls applied to buildings and cities are now extended to the planetary scale. For their part, tech companies refer to their product lines and proprietary technologies using the ecosystem metaphor, demonstrating that the concept of "ecosystem" has entered the corporate lexicon.

Given this politically fraught and geopolitically determined genealogy of ecology as a transdisciplinary model of analysis within the humanities and social sciences, it is important that we continue to question what we mean by the term *ecology* when we use it in media studies.[22] Like the multiplicity of elemental philosophies that orient our investigations of elements (including the study of elements and the atmosphere undertaken in this book), there are multiple lineages of ecology, and their presuppositions affect the way we conduct our explicatory critique of media. This is not to refute its efficacy as a method of analysis. Media ecology, like elemental media, has its methodological affordances that should not be ignored. Rather, my point is to be mindful of the historicity of the analogy of ecology itself as we operationalize it in media studies. This is so we can think critically and creatively with the divergences and overlaps of its genealogical lineages, as they intersect with media histories and media infrastructures. Reflexively explicating metaphors, analogies, and methods that may have become too familiar, too self-evident, and thus taken for granted should be part of media studies.

With this historicity in mind, we would do well to continue explicating the atmospheric backgrounds as well as the complex relations and entanglements of events, sites, and actors that shape them. In so doing, we may open up our theoretical investigation of the taken-for-granted presence and assumptions about media and their elements while also reflecting on the legacies of imperialism, colonialism, and ongoing climate change. How the past shapes, haunts, and orients the present should be part of our explicatory critique of media—climatic and otherwise.

INTRODUCTION

1. See news coverage on Sony's "Reon Pocket" wearable air conditioner: "Sony 'kirareru eakon' kaihatsu: Senyō shitagi ni chakusō," *Nihon Nikkei shinbun*, July 22, 2019, https://www.nikkei.com/article/DGXMZo47620540S9A720C1000000/; Matthew Humphries, "Sony's Reon Pocket Is a Wearable Air-Conditioner," *PC Reviews*, July 29, 2019, https://www.pcmag.com/news/369805/sonys-reon-pocket -is-a-wearable-air-conditioner; Ruchi Thukral, "Sony's Wearable, Pocket-Sized Air Conditioner Is Finally Available for Sale!," *Yanko Design*, July 6, 2020, https:// www.yankodesign.com/2020/07/06/sonys-wearable-pocket-sized-air-conditioner -is-finally-available-for-sale/.

2. My use of genealogy as a critical method for making sense of the present is clearly indebted to the work of Michel Foucault. As is evident in the following chapters, I draw in particular on his lecture series, *Security, Territory, and Population: Lectures at the Collège de France, 1977–1978*, trans. Graham Burchell (New York: Palgrave Macmillan, 2007). For more on his take on genealogy, see *Discipline and Punish*, trans. Alan Sheridan (New York: Vintage Books, 1995), and his essays, "What Is Enlightenment?" and "Nietzsche, Genealogy, History," in Paul Rabinow, ed. *The Foucault Reader* (New York: Pantheon, 1984), 32–50, 76–100.

3. Daniel Barber, *Modern Architecture and Climate: Design before Air-Conditioning* (Princeton, NJ: Princeton University Press, 2020), loc. 509, Kindle edition.

4. Peter Sloterdijk, *Terror from the Air*, trans. Amy Patton and Steve Corcoran (Cambridge, MA: MIT Press, 2009), 79.

5. Nick Axel, Daniel A. Barber, Nikolaus Hirsch, and Anton Vidokle, "Editorial: Accumulation," *e-flux: architecture*, accessed August 9, 2019, https://www.e-flux .com/architecture/accumulation/100048/editorial/. Summarizing this primacy of visualization in their definition of "climatic media," the architectural historian Daniel A. Barber writes: "Historically, climatic media within the field of architecture have ranged from technical images of thermal comfort and considerations of solar paths to speculative forms for living in a range of climates and, more recently, the manipulation of false color diagrams in which climatic effects are themselves taken as a space of creativity. In this sense, the coming together of climate and architecture reinforces a positioning of the architect as mediatic agent and opens out to a more general analysis of spatial, material, urbanistic, and climate engaged media production. Artistic practices, methods of resistance

and literary tropes similarly operate across this nexus of aesthetics, space and climate." In his later work, *Modern Architecture and Climate*, Barber expands his discussion of media to include the facade, shades, and other functional components of architecture that mediate indoor and outdoor climates.

6. A number of media scholars have explored the environmental dimension of media. See, for instance, Weihong Bao, *Fiery Cinema: The Emergence of an Affective Medium in China, 1915–1945* (Minneapolis: University of Minnesota Press, 2015); Mark B. N. Hansen, *Feed-Forward: On the Future of Twenty-First-Century Media* (Chicago: University of Chicago Press, 2015); Tung-Hui Hu, *A Prehistory of the Cloud* (Cambridge, MA: MIT Press, 2015); and Antonio Somaini, "Walter Benjamin's Media Theory: The *Medium* and the *Apparat*," *Grey Room* 62 (January 2016): 6–41.

7. John Durham Peters, *The Marvelous Clouds: Toward a Philosophy of Elemental Media* (Chicago: University of Chicago Press, 2016), 165–66.

8. David Gissen, *Manhattan Atmospheres: Architecture, the Interior Environment, and Urban Crisis* (Minneapolis: University of Minnesota Press, 2013), 38.

9. Reyner Banham, *Architecture of the Well-Tempered Environment* (Chicago: University of Chicago Press, 1969).

10. Jiat-Hwee Chang, "Thermal Comfort and Climatic Design in the Tropics: An Historical Critique," *Journal of Architecture* 21, no. 8 (2016): 1171–202; Jiat-Hwee Chang, *A Genealogy of Tropical Architecture: Colonial Networks, Nature and Technoscience* (London: Routledge, 2016).

11. Nicole Starosielski, "Thermocultures of Geological Media," *Cultural Politics* 12, no. 3 (2016): 293–309.

12. See, for instance, Timothy Choy, *Ecologies of Comparison: An Ethnography of Endangerment in Hong Kong* (Durham, NC: Duke University Press, 2011); Douglas Kahn, *Earth Sound Earth Signal* (Berkeley: University of California Press, 2013); Peter Adey, "Air's Affinities: Geopolitics, Chemical Affect and the Force of the Elemental," *Dialogues in Human Geography* 5, no. 1 (2015): 54–75; Cara New Daggett, *The Birth of Energy: Fossil Fuels, Thermodynamics, and the Politics of Work* (Durham, NC: Duke University Press, 2019); and Melody Jue, *Wild Blue Media: Thinking through Seawater* (Durham, NC: Duke University Press, 2020).

13. On these elemental and geological approaches to rethinking media, see Nicole Starosielski, "Thermocultures of Geological Media" and *Media Hot and Cold* (Durham, NC: Duke University Press, 2021); Jussi Parikka, *A Geology of Media* (Minneapolis: University of Minnesota Press, 2015); and Jussi Parikka, "The Alchemic Digital, the Planetary Elemental," in *Subcommunity: Diabolical Togetherness beyond Contemporary Art*, ed. Julieta Aranda, Brian Kuan Wood, and Anton Vidokle, *e-flux journal* (London: Verso, 2017), 341–47. On the environmental impact and logistics of shipping and processing electronic wastes, see Jennifer Gabrys, "Shipping and Receiving: Circuits of Disposal and the 'Social Death' of Electronics," in *Digital Rubbish: A Natural History of Electronics* (Ann Arbor: University of Michigan Press, 2013), 74–98. See also Yuriko Furuhata, "Archipelagic

Archives: Media Geology and the Deep Time of Japan's Settler Colonialism," *Public Culture* 33, no. 3 (forthcoming).

14. Adey, "Air's Affinities," 61. Adey's survey of a wide range of texts that discuss air in relation to geography covers fiction such as Goethe's *Elective Affinities* as well as cultural climatology, science, and political theory including Carl Schmitt's classic works, *Land and Sea* (1942) and *Nomos of the Earth* (1950). Schmitt, he writes, "is explicit in his interest in the geopolitical import of particular kinds of territory which he calls elemental, locating them in the classical form of land (earth), sea (water), air and fire" (68). See also Ben Anderson, "Affective Atmospheres," *Emotion, Space and Society* 2, no. 2 (2009): 77–81; Peter Adey and Ben Anderson, "Anticipation, Materiality, Event: The Icelandic Ash Cloud Disruption and the Security of Mobility," *Mobilities* 6, no. 1 (2011): 11–23; and Derek P. McCormack, *Atmospheric Things: On the Allure of Elemental Envelopment* (Durham, NC: Duke University Press, 2019).

15. Mark Whitehead also uses the Foucauldian framework of "conduct" as a type of discipline to talk about air as part of personal health and hygiene in the United Kingdom in the nineteenth and twentieth centuries. Methodologically, his approach to thinking about "atmospheric government" as a set of "conduct" that combines the public knowledge of atmospheric science with the (neo)liberal personalized "atmospheric self care" responsibilities is resonant with the approach I take toward atmospheric conditioning. See Mark Whitehead, *State, Science and the Skies: Governmentalities of the British Atmosphere* (West Sussex, UK: Wiley-Blackwell, 2009); and Andreas Philippopoulos-Mihalopoulos, *Spatial Justice: Body, Lawscape, Atmosphere* (Oxfordshire, UK: Routledge, 2015).

16. See Philip Kotler, "Atmospherics as a Marketing Tool," *Journal of Retailing* 49, no. 4 (winter 1973–74): 48–64. Peter Sloterdijk connects this marketing use of atmospherics to the architectural form of arcades as a space of commerce: "Let us not forget that today's so-called consumer society was invented in a greenhouse—in the very same glass-canopied, nineteenth-century arcades in which the first generation of 'experience customers' learned to breath the intoxicating scent of an enclosed, interior-world full of commodities." Sloterdijk, *Terror from the Air*, 95–96.

17. Paul Roquet, *Ambient Media: Japanese Atmospheres of Self* (Minneapolis: University of Minnesota Press, 2016), 4–15.

18. In his analysis of the facade as a medium that regulates interior climate before the rise of mechanical air-conditioning, Barber also suggests the multifaceted nature of conditioning. See *Modern Architecture and Climate*, loc. 509 of 9068.

19. My approach is closer to that of Anna Feigenbaum and Anja Kanngieser, who analyze tear gas and sonic warfare as "technologies and techniques for controlling populations" through their relationship with air, which operate as a form of atmospheric policing. Anna Feigenbaum and Anja Kanngieser, "For a Politics of Atmospheric Governance," *Dialogues in Human Geography* 5, no. 1 (2015): 81.

20. "Sonic Science: The High-Frequency Hearing Test," *Scientific American*, May 23, 2013, https://www.scientificamerican.com/article/bring-science-home-high -frequency-hearing/. For more on the policing use of infrasound and sound, see Steve Goodman, *Sonic Warfare: Sound, Affect, and Ecology of Fear* (Cambridge, MA: MIT Press, 2012).

21. Azuma Hiroki reads this strategy by McDonald's through Foucault's concept of governmentality. See Azuma Hiroki, *Hihyō no seishin bunseki: Azuma Hiroki korekushon D* [A psychoanalysis of criticism: Azuma Hiroki collection D] (Tōkyō: Kōdansha, 2007), 351. Azuma notes that his understanding of McDonald's comes from the work of sociologist George Ritzer, *The McDonaldization of Society: An Investigation into the Changing Character of Contemporary Social Life* (Thousand Oaks, CA: Pine Forge Press, 1996).

22. Colin Gordon, "Governmental Rationality: An Introduction," in *The Foucault Effect: Studies in Governmentality*, ed. Graham Burchell, Colin Gordon, and Peter Miller (Chicago: University of Chicago Press, 1991), 1–51; Foucault, *Security, Territory, and Population*, 121.

23. Bernhard Siegert, *Cultural Techniques: Grids, Filters, Doors, and Other Articulations of the Real*, trans. Geoffrey Winthrop-Young (New York: Fordham University Press, 2015), 13–14.

24. Siegert, *Cultural Techniques*, 193.

25. Weihong Bao, "Archaeology of a Medium: The (Agri)Cultural Techniques of a Paddy Film Farm," *boundary 2* 49, no. 1 (forthcoming). See also Bernard Dionysius Geoghegan, "After Kittler: On the Cultural Techniques of Recent Media Theory," *Theory, Culture and Society* 30, no. 6 (2013): 66–82.

26. Andrea Lo, "The Truth behind the Mysterious Holes in Hong Kong's High-Rises," CNN, March 28, 2018, https://www.cnn.com/style/article/hong-kong -skyscrapers-with-holes/index.html; Matthew Keegan, "Hong Kong: The City Still Shaped by Feng Shui," *Guardian*, July 19, 2018, https://www.theguardian.com /cities/2018/jul/19/hong-kong-the-city-still-shaped-by-feng-shui; Department of Architecture, Chinese University of Hong Kong, "Feasibility Study for Establishment of Air Ventilation Assessment System," November 2005, accessed March 9, 2019, https://www.pland.gov.hk/pland_en/p_study/comp_s/avas/papers& reports/final_report.pdf.

27. Peters, *Marvelous Clouds*, 3–4.

28. For more on this speculative and comparative approach to the philosophy of elements, see Yuriko Furuhata, "Of Dragons and Geoengineering: Rethinking Elemental Media," *Media+Environment* 1, no. 1 (2019), https://doi.org/10.1525/001c .10797.

29. Manuela Madeddu and Xiaoqing Zhang, "Harmonious Spaces: The Influence of Feng Shui on Urban Form and Design," *Journal of Urban Design* 22, no. 6 (2017): 709–25; Miyauchi Takahisa, "Kasōkan no juyō katei ni kansuru minzokugaku teki kenkyū oboegaki," *Hikaku minzoku kenkyū* 3 (March 1993): 214–29; Suwa Haruo, *Nihon no fūsui* (Tokyo: Kadokawa sensho, 2018).

30. On European, Chinese, and Japanese cosmological views of meteorological

phenomena before modernity, see Sara J. Schechner, *Comets, Popular Culture, and the Birth of Modern Cosmology* (Princeton, NJ: Princeton University Press, 1997); Qiong Zhang, "From 'Dragonology' to Meteorology: Aristotelian Natural Philosophy and the Beginning of the Decline of the Dragon in China," *Early Science and Medicine* 14, nos. 1–3 (2009): 340–68; and Hayashi Makoto, *Tenmonkata to onmyōdō* [Astronomers and onmyōdō] (Tokyo: Yamakawa shuppan, 2006).

31. Vladimir Jankovic, *Reading the Sky: A Cultural History of English Weather, 1650–1820* (Chicago: University of Chicago Press, 2000), 156 (emphasis in the original). See also Gabrielle Walker, *An Ocean of Air: A Natural History of the Atmosphere* (London: Bloomsbury, 2007).

32. James Rodger Fleming, *Fixing the Sky: The Checkered History of Weather and Climate Control* (New York: Columbia University Press, 2010).

33. China first seeded the clouds to induce artificial rain after it was hit by a severe drought in 1958. Kristine C. Harper, *Make It Rain: State Control of the Atmosphere in Twentieth-Century America* (Chicago: University of Chicago Press, 2017), 162.

34. Clive Hamilton, *Earthmasters: The Dawn of the Age of Climate Engineering* (New Haven, CT: Yale University Press, 2013), 142–43.

35. Higuchi Keiji, *Chikyū kara no hassō* [Ideas that come from Earth] (Tokyo: Asahi bunko, 1991), 26–27.

36. On the history of cybernetics and urban planning in the United States, see Jennifer S. Light, *From Warfare to Welfare: Defense Intellectuals and Urban Problems in Cold War America* (Baltimore, MD: Johns Hopkins University Press, 2003).

37. For more on the history of climate modeling and global data collection, see Paul N. Edwards, *A Vast Machine: Computer Models, Climate Data, and the Politics of Global Warming* (Cambridge, MA: MIT Press, 2010).

38. Oliver Morton, *The Planet Remade: How Geoengineering Could Change the World* (Princeton, NJ: Princeton University Press, 2016), 164.

39. On the genealogy of the environmentally determinist views of race and culture associated with climate, see David N. Livingstone, "Race, Space, and Moral Climatology: Notes toward a Genealogy," *Journal of Historical Geography* 28, no. 2 (2002): 159–80. On the historical development of geography as imperial science, see Gearóid Ó Tuathail, *Critical Geopolitics* (Minneapolis: University of Minnesota Press, 1996).

40. See, for instance, Eric T. Jennings, *Curing the Colonizers: Hydrotherapy, Climatology, and French Colonial Spas* (Durham, NC: Duke University Press, 2006); and Lorenzo Veracini, *Settler Colonialism: A Theoretical Overview* (London: Palgrave Macmillan, 2010).

41. On the historicity of Japan's colonial settlements in Hokkaidō, see Katsuya Hirano, "Settler Colonialism in the Making of Japan's Hokkaidō," in *The Routledge Handbook of the History of Settler Colonialism*, ed. Edward Cavanagh and Lorenzo Veracini (Abingdon, UK: Taylor and Francis, 2016), 351–62. The work of Danika Medak-Saltzman offers an intersectional approach for situating the history of Japanese settler colonialism in relation to Native American and Indigenous

studies. See Danika Medak-Saltzman, "Settler Colonialism and Phantasmagoria: On Asian, Asian Diaspora, and Indigenous Intersections," *Verge: Studies in Global Asias* 5, no. 1 (spring 2019): 39–46.

42. Roquet, *Ambient Media*, 7 (emphasis in the original). Roquet writes: "For Watsuji, being Japanese is not an accident of birth or the result of a historical formation; rather, it is a unilateral collective process of atmospheric subjectivation. Through reference to this totalizing understanding of atmosphere, *Climate and Culture* presents a highly reductive model of environmental determinism, dividing human civilizations into 'Monsoon,' 'Desert,' and 'Meadow' types and positioning Japan against the 'West,' China, and India. The seemingly 'natural' process of climatic attunement serves as a feint for establishing the authority of the nationalist self" (7). On the critique of Watsuji's epistemic reliance on the dichotomy between the East and the West, which undergirds his typological analysis of "Pastoral Europe" and "Monsoon Asia," see Naoki Sakai, "Return to the West/Return to the East: Watsuji Tetsuro's Anthropology and Discussions of Authenticity," *boundary 2* 18, no. 3 (autumn 1991): 157–90. On the Kyoto School's complicity with the state project of imperialism, see Harry Harootunian, *Overcome by Modernity: History, Culture, and Community in Interwar Japan* (Princeton, NJ: Princeton University Press, 2000). According to Harootunian, Watsuji thought culture alone could not provide an adequate explanation for the formation of a national community unless it was supplemented by a consideration of climate and environmental conditions, what he "conceptualized as 'climate and culture' (*fūdo*), which became the basis of a unique mode of analysis" (252).

43. Watsuji Tetsurō, *Fūdo: Ningengaku teki kōsatsu* [Climate and culture: Some humanistic reflections] (Tokyo: Iwanami bunko, 1979), 352.

44. Joseph Masco, "Bad Weather: On Planetary Crisis," *Social Studies of Science* 40, no. 1 (February 2010): 7–40; Elizabeth M. DeLoughrey, "The Myth of Isolates: Ecosystem Ecologies in the Nuclear Pacific," *Cultural Geographies* 20, no. 2 (April 2013): 167–84.

45. Jairus Victor Grove, *Savage Ecology: War and Geopolitics at the End of the World* (Durham, NC: Duke University Press, 2019), 38–39.

46. For more on the critical "transpacific" approach to studying flows of people, culture, and capital across the Pacific Ocean, see Viet Thanh Nguyen and Janet Hoskins, "Introduction: Transpacific Studies; Critical Perspectives on an Emerging Field," in *Transpacific Studies: Framing an Emerging Field*, ed. Janet Hoskins and Viet Thanh Nguyen (Honolulu: University of Hawai'i Press, 2014), 1–38.

47. Lisa Yoneyama, "Toward a Decolonial Genealogy of the Transpacific," *American Quarterly* 69, no. 3 (September 2017): 473.

CHAPTER 1: **Outdoor Weather**
An earlier version of chapter 1 appeared as "The Fog Medium: Visualizing and Engineering the Atmosphere" in *Screening Genealogies: From Optical Device to Environmental Medium*, ed. Craig Buckley, Rüdiger Campe, and Francesco Casetti (Amsterdam: Amsterdam University Press, 2019).

1. Nakaya Fujiko, "Kūki to mizu" [Air and water], in special issue on Expo '70, *Bijutsu techō* [Art notebook] (July 1970): 106.

2. Jennifer Holt and Patrick Vonderau, "'Where the Internet Lives': Data Centers as Cloud Infrastructure," in Parks and Starosielski, *Signal Traffic*, 82. On the ecological footprint of data centers, see also Mél Hogan, "Facebook Data Storage Centers as the Archive's Underbelly," *Television and New Media* 16, no. 1 (2015): 3–18, https://doi.org/10.1177/1527476413509415.

3. Holt and Vonderau, "'Where the Internet Lives,'" 83. See also Alix Johnson, "Data Centers as Infrastructural In-Betweens: Expanding Connections and Enduring Marginalities in Iceland," *American Ethnologist* 46, no. 1 (February 2019): 75–88; and Hogan, "Facebook Data Storage Centers," 3–18.

4. Will Calvert, "Kyocera to Build Snow-Cooled Data Center, Fully Powered by Renewable Energy," Data Center Dynamics, April 5, 2019, https://www.data centerdynamics.com/news/kyocera-build-snow-cooled-data-center-fully -powered-renewable-energy/; "WDC (howaito dēta sentā) kōsō," accessed August 8, 2019, http://www.city.bibai.hokkaido.jp/jyumin/docs/2015090100125/.

5. See Sloterdijk, *Terror from the Air*.

6. An affinity between the fog sculpture and media is present in John Durham Peters's passing comment; artworks like fog and mist installations befittingly belong to "an age of poison gas, cloud seeding, and geoengineering." Peters, *Marvelous Clouds*, 255.

7. Quoted in Carolyn Marvin, *When Old Technologies Were New: Thinking about Electric Communication in the Late Nineteenth Century* (Oxford: Oxford University Press, 1988), 184.

8. Erkki Huhtamo, "The Sky Is (Not) the Limit: Envisioning the Ultimate Public Media Display," *Journal of Visual Culture* 8, no. 3 (2009): 335.

9. Colin Williamson, *Hidden in Plain Sight: An Archaeology of Magic and the Cinema* (New Brunswick, NJ: Rutgers University Press, 2015), 107.

10. Francesco Casetti, *The Lumière Galaxy: Seven Key Words for the Cinema to Come* (New York: Columbia University Press, 2015), 93.

11. Scott MacDonald, *A Critical Cinema 2: Interviews with Independent Filmmakers* (Berkeley: University of California Press, 1992), 164.

12. Matsumoto Toshio writes: "I had a desire to project onto something that was not a [regular] screen. . . . First, I imagined this work as a projection onto a gaseous body." Printed program for "Cross Talk/Intermedia," Tokyo, February 1969, n.p.

13. Roger Reynolds, *Cross Talk Intermedia I*, newsletter of the Institute of Current World Affairs, May 10, 1969, accessed March 18, 2017, http://www.icwa.org /wp-content/uploads/2015/11/PR-20.pdf. For more on "Cross Talk/Intermedia," see Yuriko Furuhata, *Cinema of Actuality: Avant-Garde Filmmaking in the Season of Image Politics* (Durham, NC: Duke University Press, 2013); and Miryam Sas, "By Other Hands: Environment and Apparatus in 1960s Intermedia," in *The Oxford Handbook of Japanese Cinema*, ed. Miyao Daisuke (Oxford: Oxford University Press, 2014), 383–415.

14. Julian Ross, "Beyond the Frame: Intermedia and Expanded Cinema in 1960–1970s Japan" (PhD diss., University of Leeds, 2014), 139–46.

15. Shuzo Azuchi Gulliver, "Flying Focus," in *Ekusupandeddo shinema saikō/ Japanese Expanded Cinema Reconsidered*, exhibition catalog (Tokyo: Tokyo Shashin Bijutsukan, 2017), 71. For more on Gulliver's work, see Ross, *Beyond the Frame*.

16. McCormack, *Atmospheric Things*, 68.

17. Inge Hinterwaldner, "Parallel Lines as Tools for Making Turbulence Visible," *Representations* 124, no. 1 (fall 2013): 1–42.

18. Marta Braun, *Picturing Time: The Work of Etienne-Jules Marey (1830–1904)* (Chicago: University of Chicago Press, 1992), 217. Some critics have compared Nakaya Fujiko's fog sculpture to Marey's smoke photographs. Anne-Marie Duguet, for instance, notes that, although Nakaya's primary objective is aesthetic, her creative process relies on rigorous scientific protocols of observation and experimentation. See Anne-Marie Duguet, "Naturally Artificial," in *Fujiko Nakaya: Fog, Kiri, Brouillard* (Paris: Éditions Anarchive, 2012), 35.

19. Peter Galison, *Image and Logic: A Material Culture of Microphysics* (Chicago: University of Chicago Press, 1997), 75. *Mimetic experimentation* is a term Galison uses to describe a series of scientific "attempt[s] to reproduce natural physical phenomena, with all their complexity, in the laboratory."

20. The art critic Okazaki Kenjirō suggests that Nakaya Fujiko's keen interest in the observation of the structure and metamorphic process of fog formation comes from her father Ukichirō's devotion to the scientific analysis of the principles of snow crystallization. See Okazaki Kenjirō, "The Lucid, Unclouded Fog— The Movement of Bright and Swinging Water Particles," in *Kiri no teikō/Resistance of Fog: Nakaya Fujiko ten* (Tokyo: Firumu Āto, 2019), 106–21.

21. Sloterdijk, *Terror from the Air*, 57.

22. Fleming, *Fixing the Sky*, 6.

23. "Fog Wiped Out by Chemical Spray," *Popular Science*, October 1934, 39. Houghton's research on pressure nozzles is also mentioned by Nakaya Fujiko. See Nakaya Fujiko, "Making of 'Fog' or Low-Hanging Stratus Cloud," in Billy Klüver, Julie Martin, and Barbara Rose, eds., *Pavilion: Experiments in Art and Technology* (New York: E. P. Dutton, 1972), 220.

24. Fleming, *Fixing the Sky*, 6.

25. Higashi Akira, *Yuki to kōri no kagakusha Nakaya Ukichirō* [Snow and ice scientist Nakaya Ukichirō] (Sapporo: Hokkaidō daigaku tosho kankōkai, 1997), 70–96.

26. Sugiyama Shigeo, *Nakaya Ukichirō: Hito no yaku ni tatsu kenkyū o seyo* [Nakaya Ukichirō: Do the research that helps people] (Tokyo: Mineruva shobō, 2015), 84.

27. Machimura Takashi, *Kaihatsu shugi no kōzō to shinsei* [The structure and disposition of developmentalism] (Tokyo: Ocha no mizu shobō, 2011), 45.

28. Kobayashi Hideo, "Teion Kenkyūjo o meguru gunji kenkyū" [Military research around the Institute of Low Temperature Science], *Kokumin no kagaku* [Science of the National Citizens], March 1955, 21–22. Nakaya defended his involvement in military research as "a necessary evil" and upheld his ideal of engaging in "useful" basic research that served the common good. See Nakaya

Ukichirō, "Gunji kenkyū to wa nanika" [What is military research?], *Hokudai kikan* [Hokkaidō University Quarterly], January 1955, 28.

29. Sugiyama, *Nakaya Ukichirō*, 155.

30. Nakaya Ukichirō poetically called these snowflakes falling from the sky "letters from heaven."

31. Nakaya Ukichirō, *Yuki* [Snow] (Tokyo: Iwanami bunko, 1994), 148–49.

32. Higashi, *Yuki to kōri no kagakusha Nakaya Ukichirō*, 162–63.

33. Sugiyama, *Nakaya Ukichirō*, 174.

34. Kristine C. Harper and Ronald E. Doel, "Environmental Diplomacy in the Cold War: Weather Control, the United States, and India, 1966–1967," in *Environmental Histories of the Cold War*, ed. J. R. McNeill and Corinna R. Unger (Cambridge: Cambridge University Press, 2010), 118. See also Fleming, *Fixing the Sky*.

35. Fleming, *Fixing the Sky*, 150.

36. Howard T. Orville, "Weather Made to Order?," *Collier's* magazine, May 28, 1954, 26.

37. Orville, "Weather Made to Order?," 26. For more on this article by Orville and his role in the governmental discourse of weather modification, see Fleming, *Fixing the Sky*, 174–76.

38. Orville, "Weather Made to Order?," 29.

39. Harper and Doel, "Environmental Diplomacy in the Cold War," 130.

40. On the use of digital computers and other electronic communications devices during the Vietnam War, see Paul N. Edwards, *The Closed World: Computers and the Politics of Discourse in Cold War America* (Cambridge, MA: MIT Press, 1996), 137–38.

41. Citing a 1996 study by the US Air Force titled "Weather as a Force Multiplier: Owning the Weather in 2025," Sloterdijk lists possible means of weather control: "Based on current projections, the range of weather weapons will include: the maintaining or hindering of vision in air space; the increasing or decreasing the troops' comfort levels (i.e., their morale); thunderstorm enhancement and modification; rainfall prevention over enemy territories and the inducing of artificial drought; the intercepting and blocking of enemy communication; and preventing the enemy from performing analogous weather activities." Sloterdijk, *Terror from the Air*, 64.

42. Terada Kazuhiko and Sakagami Tsutomu, "Jinkō kōu no kenkyū" [Research on aritificial rain], *Kaishō to kishō* [Oceanic weather and weather] 6, no. 2–4 (December 1954): 1–3. See also Yoshimoto Hideyuki, "Denki jigyō to jinkō kōu" [The electric power industry and artificial rain], *Denryoku* [Electric power] 46, no. 5 (May 1962): 12–21.

43. Harper and Doel, "Environmental Diplomacy in the Cold War," 119.

44. Tsuchiya Iwao, "Kishō seigyo, Kikō kaizō" [Weather control and climate engineering], *Kishō kenkyū nōto* [Meteorological research notes] 104 (June 1970): 213.

45. Sloterdijk, *Terror from the Air*, 79.

46. Sloterdijk, *Terror from the Air*, 79.

47. As Eduardo Mendieta puts it, all technology, for Sloterdijk, is primordially

"space-originating technology." Eduardo Mendieta, "A Letter on Überhumanismus," in *Sloterdijk Now*, ed. Stuart Elden (Cambridge: Polity, 2012), 73.

48. Strictly speaking, E.A.T. (Experiments in Art and Technology) as a group was formally established after the success of "9 Evenings." Notably, Nakaya also served as the coordinator for E.A.T.'s Tokyo Headquarters. For more on the history of E.A.T., see the 2003 exhibition catalog *E.A.T.—The Story of Experiments in Art and Technology* (Tokyo: NTT InterCommunication Center, 2003).

49. Randall Packer, "The Pepsi Pavilion: Laboratory for Social Experimentation," in *Future Cinema: The Cinematic Imaginary after Film*, ed. Jeffrey Shaw and Peter Weibel (Cambridge, MA: MIT Press, 2003), 146.

50. Billy Klüver, "The Pavilion," in Klüver, Martin, and Rose, *Pavilion*, ix–xvi. See also Billy Klüver, "Atarashii taiken no ba: Pepshi kan no 'ikita kankyō,'" trans. Nakaya Fujiko, *Bijutsu techō* [Art notebook] (July 1970): 94–108.

51. Nakaya Fujiko writes: "Constantly changing atmosphere acted as a mold; the Fog sculpture was given its form instantaneously by the physical condition of its environment." Nakaya Fujiko, "Making of 'Fog' or Low-Hanging Stratus Cloud," 207.

52. Nilo Lindgren, "Into the Collaboration," in Klüver, Martin, and Rose, *Pavilion*, 23.

53. Nakaya Fujiko, "Making of 'Fog' or Low-Hanging Stratus Cloud," 209.

54. Bill Viola, "Music for Fog Sculpture Event by Fujiko Nakaya, Kawaji Onsen, Japan, 1980," in *Fujiko Nakaya: Fog, Kiri, Brouillard* (Paris: Éditions Anarchive, 2012), 150.

55. Sloterdijk, *Terror from the Air*, 47.

56. Nakaya Fujiko, "Making of 'Fog' or Low-Hanging Stratus Cloud," 220.

57. Nakaya Fujiko writes: "The area around the Pavilion was open except for the southwest side where it was backed up by a small hill; there were no other obstacles nearby, such as tall buildings or trees to serve as windbreaks." Nakaya, "Making of 'Fog' or Low-Hanging Stratus Cloud," 208.

58. I am thinking in particular of debates around Rosalind Krauss's seminal 1979 essay "Sculpture in the Expanded Field," *October* 8 (spring 1979): 30–44. For its enduring relevance to the fields of sculpture, architecture, and conceptual art, see *Retracing the Expanded Field: Encounters between Art and Architecture*, ed. Spyros Papapetros and Julian Rose (Cambridge, MA: MIT Press, 2014).

59. Peters, *Marvelous Clouds*, 3.

60. Peters, *Marvelous Clouds*, 3. On the nexus between the concepts of milieu and media, see also Melody Jue, "Vampire Squid Media," *Grey Room* 57 (fall 2014): 82–105.

61. Klüver, "Pavilion," xii.

62. "Data Center Uses MeeFog System," Mee Industries Inc., accessed April 5, 2019, http://www.meefog.com/case-studies-post/data-center/data-center-uses-meefog-system-keep-operating-heat-wave/.

63. "Facebook Uses MeeFog System to Achieve Free Cooling in Datacenter,"

Mee Industries Inc., accessed September 25, 2020, http://www.meefog.com /case-studies-post/data-center/facebook/.

64. Hansen, *Feed-Forward*, 5. Marked by anticipatory temporality, these atmospheric media, he argues, have reconfigured the relationship between humans and their environments.

65. Peters, *Marvelous Clouds*, 332.

66. Nakaya Ukichirō, "Yuki wa shigen de aru" [Snow is a resource], accessed August 8, 2019, https://www.aozora.gr.jp/cards/001569/files/57313_59463.html.

67. See Ozaki Tetsuya, "Nakaya Fujiko + dNA: MU," *ART iT*, accessed August 24, 2019, http://www.art-it.asia/u/admin_exrev/HsLPfgloEvCVG1oBUwXu/.

68. Hu, *Prehistory of the Cloud*, 81.

CHAPTER 2: **Indoor Weather**

1. In her geological analysis of media and thermocultures, from the manipulation of temperature used in mineral extraction to the use of air-conditioning at data centers, Starosielski writes, for instance, "After media is extracted, assembled, and circulated, thermal manipulation makes preservation possible—chilled in data centers and archives. Whether via furnaces or air-conditioners, ductwork or cables, the manipulation of heat is critical to the transformation of the earth's raw materials into media and to maintaining those materials *as* media." See Starosielski, "Thermocultures of Geological Media," 294.

2. Phu Hoang, "Can You Believe the Weather We're Having? The Politics of the Weather Report," in *Climates: Architecture and the Planetary Imaginary*, ed. James Graham (Zurich: Lars Müller, 2016), 257.

3. "Hitachi Room Air Conditioner 'Stainless Clean Shirokuma-kun' New E Series/W Series/G Series Products to Include 'Frost Wash' Technology," accessed May 29, 2018, http://www.jci-hitachi.com/about/news/20180427news.

4. Andreas Philippopoulos-Mihalopoulos similarly argues against this view of the air's indivisibility. Citing the military use of air, he writes, "No longer unlimited, air is now understood as *rupture*: air as control, manipulation, compulsive desiring, communal identities and spatial partitioning. Air traverses freely everything we know and care for; yet it is also put in the service of ruptured atmospherics." See Andreas Philippopoulos-Mihalopoulos, "Withdrawing from Atmosphere: An Ontology of Air Partitioning and Affective Engineering," *Environment and Planning D: Society and Space* 34, no. 1 (February 2016): 153, https://doi.org/10.1177/0263775815600443.

5. Willis Carrier, on the website of Carrier Corporation, accessed May 23, 2018, https://www.carrier.com/container-refrigeration/en/worldwide/about-carrier /willis-carrier/.

6. Banham, *Architecture of the Well-Tempered Environment*, 172.

7. Wendy Hui Kyong Chun, *Programmed Visions: Software and Memory* (Cambridge, MA: MIT Press, 2011), 29.

8. Kristine C. Harper, *Weather by the Numbers: The Genesis of Modern Meteorol-*

ogy (Cambridge, MA: MIT Press, 2008), 1 (emphasis in the original). However, skilled human forecasters are still needed to supplement numerical models. See Edwards, *Vast Machine*, 132.

9. Edwards, *Vast Machine*, 112.

10. Edwards, *Vast Machine*, 136.

11. I am borrowing the term *pampering* here from Sloterdijk, who uses it to discuss the psychophysical condition of living in the self-enclosed modern capitalist world. See Peter Sloterdijk, *In the World Interior of Capital: For a Philosophy of Globalization*, trans. Wieland Hoban (Cambridge: Polity, 2013), 212–22.

12. Edwards, *Vast Machine*, 114.

13. Furukawa Takehiko, *Kishōchō monogatari: Tenki yohō kara jishin, tsunami, kazan made* [The tale of the Japan Meteorological Agency: From weather forecasting to earthquakes, tsunamis, and volcanos] (Tokyo: Chūkō shinsho, 2015), 8–9, 41–44.

14. Harper and Doel, "Environmental Diplomacy in the Cold War," 115.

15. Furukawa Takehiko, *Hito to gijutsu de kataru tenki yohōshi: Sūchi yohō o hiraita 'kin'iro no kagi'* [A history of weather forecasting focusing on people and technology: 'A golden key' to the development of numerical weather prediction] (Tokyo: Tokyo daigaku shuppankai, 2012), 129.

16. Edwards, *Vast Machine*, 154; Furukawa, *Hito to gijutsu de kataru tenki yohōshi*, 254–55.

17. Edwards, *Vast Machine*, 158; Furukawa, *Hito to gijutsu de kataru tenki yohōshi*, 252.

18. Kasahara worked on general circulation models used for forecasting the weather and simulating the climate. Furukawa, *Hito to gijutsu de kataru tenki yohōshi*, 259; Edwards, *Vast Machine*, 148.

19. Furukawa, *Hito to gijutsu de kataru tenki yohōshi*, 198–200.

20. Furukawa, *Hito to gijutsu de kataru tenki yohōshi*, 207.

21. Furukawa, *Hito to gijutsu de kataru tenki yohōshi*, 181–84.

22. For more on humans who played the role of embodied thermostats, see Starosielski, *Media Hot and Cold*.

23. Furukawa, *Hito to gijutsu de kataru tenki yohōshi*, 214.

24. In this passage and in what follows I argue that weather control is itself a form of producing weather.

25. Rem Koolhaas and Hans Ulrich Obrist, eds., *Project Japan: Metabolism Talks . . .* (Cologne: Taschen, 2011), 47.

26. Yatsuka Hajime, "Kikigatari chōsa: Tange Kenkyūshitsu no āban dezain 1960–70" [An oral history: Tange Lab's urban design 1960–70], in *Tange Kenzō o kataru: Shoki kara 1970 nendai ni made no kiseki* [Speaking of Tange Kenzō: A trajectory from the early years to the 1970s], ed. Maki Fumihiko and Kamiya Kōji (Tokyo: Kajima shuppankai, 2013), 197.

27. Kaya Tolon, "Future Studies: A New Social Science Rooted in Cold War Strategic Thinking," in *Cold War Social Science: Knowledge Production, Liberal Democ-*

racy, and Human Nature, ed. Mark Solovey and Hamilton Cravens (New York: Palgrave Macmillan, 2012), 51.

28. William O. Gardner, "The 1970 Osaka Expo and/as Science Fiction," *Review of Japanese Culture and Society* 23 (December 2011): 29. See also William O. Gardner, *The Metabolist Imagination: Visions of the City in Postwar Japanese Architecture and Science Fiction* (Minneapolis: University of Minnesota Press, 2020).

29. Hayashi Yūjirō, *Jōhōka shakai: Hādo na shakai kara sofuto na shakai e* [The information society: From a hard society to a soft society] (Tokyo: Kōdansha, 1969).

30. At the planning stage, they advocated that "the molding of the expo environment must not be carried out by conservative bureaucrats, but rather planners should give cutting-edge artists and architects free rein to realize innovative visions." See Gardner, "1970 Osaka Expo and/as Science Fiction," 30. While the critical take on the future by this study group sometimes collided with the conservative bureaucracy, their members nonetheless had close ties to the central government. Their version of futurology was ultimately in sync with the governmental initiatives to expand and strengthen Japan's industrial sectors. The publication of a book, *Miraigaku no teishō* [A proposal for futurology] (Tokyo: Nihon seisan honbu, 1967), ed. Umesao, Katō, Kawazoe, Komatsu, and Hayashi, is a good example. Based on the special issue of *Energy*, a corporate PR magazine for the oil company Esso, it was published by the Japan Productivity Center, a governmental think tank.

31. Kōyama Ken'ichi, *Miraigaku nyūmon* [Introduction to futurology] (Tokyo: Ushio shinsho, 1967), 27.

32. Kōyama Ken'ichi, "21 seiki no sekkei: Sousa kanō na mirai" [The design for the 21st century: The manipulable future], *Ushio* [Tide] (February 1967): 127.

33. Kōyama, *Miraigaku nyūmon*, 80.

34. Martin Heidegger, *What Is a Thing?*, trans. W. B. Barton and V. Deutsch (South Bend, IN: Gateway Editions, 1967), 75–76.

35. Martin Heidegger, *Basic Writings*, ed. David Farrell Krell (New York: Harper Collins, 1993), 291.

36. The foreseeable, predictable, and calculable future as a territory and an extractive resource is opposed to the temporal openness of the unknowable future. These two distinct ways of conceiving the future is similar to the difference between "firmative speculation" and "affirmative speculation," as analyzed by Bishnupriya Ghosh and Bhaskar Sarkar. They write: "While affirmative speculation is more invested in exploring the fullness of possibilities without being circumscribed by narrow teleologies and short-term returns, the more opportunistic practices of 'firmative speculation' seek to privatize the commons, capitalize on every prospect, and close off many future possibilities to develop the few pathways with the highest pecuniary yields" (5). See "Media and Risk: An Introduction," in *The Routledge Companion to Media and Risk*, ed. Bishnupriya Ghosh and Bhaskar Sarkar (New York: Routledge, 2020), 1–24.

37. Tolon, "Future Studies," 48.

38. Edwards, *Closed World*, 14.

39. Yamada Gaku and Tsukio Yoshio, two architects responsible for most of the programming tasks at Tange Lab, were the first programmers to theorize the relevance of computer simulations for architecture and urban planning in Japan. Tsukio Yoshio, "Toshi keikaku no tame no gengo taikei: URTRAN" [A language system for urban planning: URTRAN], *Computopia* (February 1969): 109–14; Yatsuka Hajime, *Metaborizumu nekusasu* [Metabolism nexus] (Tokyo: Ohmsha, 2011), 378–79.

40. Tange Kenzō and Kawazoe Noboru, "Nihon bankoku hakurankai no motarasu mono" [What Japan's World's Fair can bring], *Shin kenchiku* [New architecture] (May 1970): 151. For more on Tange Lab, see Yuriko Furuhata, "Architecture as Atmospheric Media: Tange Lab and Cybernetics," in Steinberg and Zahlten, *Media Theory in Japan*, 52–79.

41. Mizutani Akihiro, "Tange Kenzō kenkyūshitsu no konpyūta riyō no saihyōka to sono kon'nichi teki igi ni tsuite" [A reevaluation of Tange Lab's use of digital computers and its contemporary significance], *Nihon kenchiku gakkai kankyō kei ronbun shū* [The Architectural Institute of Japan's collection of research papers on the environment] 81, no. 735 (May 2016): 487–94.

42. Tessa Morris-Suzuki, *Beyond Computopia: Information, Automation and Democracy in Japan* (London: Kegan Paul International, 1988), 20.

43. Takeda Haruhito, *Nihon no jōhō tsūshin sangyō shi: Futatsu no sekai kara hitotsu no sekai e* [A history of Japan's information and communication industry: From two worlds to a single world] (Tokyo: Yuhikaku, 2011), 88.

44. Hirata Keiichirō, preface to *Konpyūta hakusho* [White Paper on computers], Nihon denshi keisan kaihatsu kyōkai [Japan Association for development of digital computers] (Tokyo: Nihon denshi keisan kaihatsu kyōkai, 1965), n.p.

45. Stafford Beer, *Management Science: The Business Use of Operations Research* (New York: Doubleday, 1968).

46. Nihon denshi keisan kaihatsu kyōkai, *Konpyūta hakusho: MIS to konpyūta ūtiriti no shindōkō* [White Paper on the computer: New directions in MIS and computer utilities] (Tokyo: Nihon denshi keisan kaihatsu kyōkai, 1968).

47. Masuda Yoneji, *Konpyūtopia: Konpyūta ga tsukuru shinjidai* [Computopia: A new era built by computers] (Tokyo: Daiyamondo sha, 1967), 139.

48. Masuda Yoneji, *The Information Society as Post-Industrial Society* (Tokyo: Institute for the Information Society, 1980), 147.

49. Chalmers Johnson, *MITI and the Japanese Miracle: The Growth of Industrial Policy, 1925–1975* (Stanford, CA: Stanford University Press, 1982).

50. Marie Anchordoguy, *Computers, Inc.: Japan's Challenge to IBM* (Cambridge, MA: Harvard University Press, 1989).

51. Alfred D. Chandler Jr., *Inventing the Electronic Century: The Epic Story of the Consumer Electronics and Computer Industries* (New York: Free Press, 2001), 189.

52. Anchordoguy, *Computers, Inc.*, 23. By the early 1980s, however, the American elephant was taking the challenge of Japanese mosquitoes seriously. The fear of a Japanese takeover of the American market was particularly strong in the 1980s

and 1990s. We can discern this sentiment in Hollywood films and the press coverage of the IBM Spy Incident, an industrial espionage incident for which executives of Hitachi were arrested after the FBI's sting operation revealed that they had conspired to steal trade secrets to build peripherals interoperable with IBM computers in 1982. See Jeff Gerth, "Japanese Executives charged in I.B.M. Theft Case," *New York Times*, June 23, 1982.

53. Katagata Zenji, *Nihon IBM no keiei: Seichō yōin no tetteiteki kenkyū* [The management of IBM Japan: A complete study of its growth factors] (Tokyo: Nihon jitsugyō shuppansha, 1969); Taniguchi Yūji, "IBM teikoku no sekai senryaku to Nihon" [The world strategies of the IBM empire and Japan], *Keizai hyōron* [Economic review] (June 1971): 174–82; Takeda Haruhito, *Nihon no jōhō tsūshin sangyō shi*, 79.

54. John Harwood, *The Interface: IBM and the Transformation of Corporate Design, 1945–1976* (Minneapolis: University of Minnesota Press, 2011), 9.

55. Chandler, *Inventing the Electronic Century*, 190.

56. Shimoda Hirotsugu, *Tsūshin kakumei to Denden kōsha* [The telecommunication revolution and the Nippon Telegraph and Telephone Public Corporation] (Tokyo: Mainichi shinbunsha, 1981), 61.

57. Nihon Denshin Denwa Kōsha, *Nihon bankokuhaku to Denden kōsha* [Japan's World's Fair and the Nippon Telegraph and Telephone Public Corporation] (Osaka: Nihon Denshin Denwa Kōsha, 1970), 111.

58. Kitahara Yasusada, *Terekomu kakumei: Denden kōsha no INS kōsō o kataru* [A telecommunication revolution: Narrating the Nippon Telegraph and Telephone Public Corporation's vision of INS] (Tokyo: Tokuma shoten, 1983), 71–73, 117.

59. Fred Turner, *From Counterculture to Cyberculture: Stewart Brand, the Whole Earth Network, and the Rise of Digital Utopianism* (Chicago: University of Chicago Press, 2006), 33–34.

60. David Graeber, *The Utopia of Rules: On Technology, Stupidity, and the Secret Joys of Bureaucracy* (New York: Melville House, 2015), 156–58.

61. Matei Calinescu, *Five Faces of Modernity: Modernism, Avant-Garde, Decadence, Kitsch, Postmodernism* (Durham, NC: Duke University Press, 1987); Armand Mattelart, *The Invention of Communication*, trans. Susan Emanuel (Minneapolis: University of Minnesota Press, 1996).

62. This lineage of the technocratic avant-garde, moreover, also runs through the American context of futurology, which is preceded by the prewar American technocracy movement. Similarly, the Japanese technocratic avant-garde lineage goes back to the wartime technocratic movement of the 1930s and 1940s. To discuss the political connections between these two technocracy movements and their pragmatic utopianism as precursors to the postwar development of futurology in both countries, however, is beyond the scope of this book. Notably, Daniel Bell called Saint-Simon "the father of technocracy" whose vision had "begun to bear fruit" with postindustrialization in the 1960s and 1970s. Like Masuda, he too declared the arrival of the postindustrial "technocratic age" as one that is characterized by the collective "orientation to the future." Daniel Bell, *The Com-*

ing of the Post-Industrial Society: A Venture in Social Forecasting (New York: Basic Books, 1973), 348.

63. Graeber, *Utopia of Rules*, 164.

64. Ojima Toshio, "Banpaku kaijō no jinkō kankyō: Chiiki reibō to sono riyō keikaku" [The World's Fair's artificial environment: Regional air-conditioning and plans for its use], *Shinkenchiku* [New architecture] 45, no. 8 (August 1970): 284.

65. Ojima Toshio, "Chiiki reibō keikaku" [Plans for regional air-conditioning], *Kenchiku zasshi* [Architecture magazine] 85, no. 1021 (March 1970): 228.

66. Ojima Toshio, "Jinkō kikō to ningen: Jinrui no han'ei ni machi ukeru kurepasu" [Artificial climate and humans: The pitfalls of humanity's prosperity], *U.D.C.* 628.8.02 (November 1965): 751; Nomura Takeshi and Ojima Toshio, "Chiiki reidanbō to dōmudo spēsu e no tenbō" [An outlook on regional air-conditioning and domed spaces], *Shinkenchiku* [New architecture] 45, no. 8 (August 1970): 233–40.

67. Buckminster Fuller, *Utopia or Oblivion* (Zurich: Lars Müller, 2008), 431.

68. Nomura and Ojima, "Chiiki reidanbō to dōmudo supēsu e no tenbō," 239.

69. Ojima, "Banpaku kaijō no jinkō kankyō," 284.

70. Lloyd Treinish, "Deep Thunder Now Hyper-Local on a Global Scale," IBM, June 15, 2016, https://www.ibm.com/blogs/research/2016/06/deep-thunder-now-hyper-local-global/.

71. "Deep Thunder: Icons of Progress," IBM, accessed May 20, 2018, http://www-03.ibm.com/ibm/history/ibm100/us/en/icons/deepthunder/. Michael D. Holmes, program director of Insight Cloud Services Marketing at the Weather Company, stated that "the Weather Company, an IBM company, is using data science, analytics, and machine learning to help tens of millions of people make more informed, confident decisions every day." Michael D. Holmes, "Driving the World's Most Accurate Weather Forecasts," IBM, December 21, 2016, https://www.ibm.com/blogs/think/2016/12/accurate-weather-forecasts/.

72. "Deep Thunder: Icons of Progress."

73. "Kigyō muke no kishō jōhō teikyō sābisu o kaishi" [The start of the weather information service for businesses], IBM, March 13, 2017, https://www-03.ibm.com/press/jp/ja/pressrelease/51820.wss.

74. "'Kurashi kamera' tanjō sutōrī" [An origin story of Life Camera], Hitachi Applications, Inc., accessed June 27, 2018, https://kadenfan.hitachi.co.jp/ra/camera/hamada.html.

75. "Development of Image-Analysis Technology with AI for Real-Time People-Detection and Tracking," news release, Hitachi Applications, Inc., March 27, 2017, http://www.hitachi.com/New/cnews/month/2017/03/170327.html.

76. What I call the neoliberal practice of customization resonates with the neoliberal technique of self-attunement through the atmospheric mediation of music, which Paul Roquet analyzes in *Ambient Media*.

77. Bernhard Siegert, "(Not) in Place: The Grid, or Cultural Techniques of Ruling Spaces," in *Cultural Techniques: Grids, Filters, Doors, and Other Articulations of*

the Real, trans. Geoffrey Winthrop-Young (New York: Fordham University Press, 2015), 115.

78. Melinda Cooper, "Turbulent Worlds: Financial Markets and Environmental Crisis," *Theory, Culture and Society* 27, no. 2–3 (2010): 167–90; Orit Halpern, "Hopeful Resilience," *e-flux: architecture*, accessed June 27, 2018, http://www.e-flux.com /architecture/accumulation/96421/hopeful-resilience/.

79. Orit Halpern, Robert Mitchell, and Bernard Dionysius Geoghegan, "The Smartness Mandate: Notes toward a Critique," *Grey Room* 68 (summer 2017): 124.

CHAPTER 3: **To the Greenhouse**

Sections of chapter 3 have appeared in my chapter "Tange Lab and Biopolitics: From Geopolitics of the Sphere to the Nervous System of the Nation" in *Beyond Imperial Aesthetics: Theories of Art and Politics in Japan*, ed. Steve Choe and Mayumo Inoue (Hong Kong: University of Hong Kong Press, 2019); my chapter "Architecture as Atmospheric Media: Tange Lab and Cybernetics" in *Media Theory in Japan*, ed. Marc Steinberg and Alexander Zahlten (Durham, NC: Duke University Press, 2017); and my article "Multimedia Environments and Security Operations: Expo '70 as a Laboratory of Governance," in *Grey Room* 54 (winter 2014): 56–79.

1. Franklin Foer, "Jeff Bezos's Master Plan," *Atlantic*, November 2019, https:// www.theatlantic.com/magazine/archive/2019/11/what-jeff-bezos-wants/598363/.

2. Lorene Edwards Forkner, "Humans and Horticulture, Plants and Productivity, Inspiration and (Lots of!) Irrigation Convene inside Amazon's Spheres," *Seattle Times*, March 13, 2019, https://www.seattletimes.com/pacific-nw-magazine/ humans-and-horticulture-plants-and-productivity-inspiration-and-lots-of -irrigation-convene-inside-amazons-spheres/. See also Sarah Anne Lloyd, "Inside the Amazon Spheres: The Plants, the Architecture, and a Transforming City," *Seattle Curbed*, January 30, 2018, https://seattle.curbed.com/2018/1/30/16947838 /amazon-spheres-seattle-architecture-photos; and Amazon's The Spheres website, accessed December 23, 2019, https://www.seattlespheres.com/the-plants.

3. Gissen, *Manhattan Atmospheres*, 67–68.

4. Lucile H. Brockway, *Science and Colonial Expansion: The Role of the British Royal Botanical Gardens* (New Haven, CT: Yale University Press, 2002); Ian Jared Miller, *The Nature of the Beasts: Empire and Exhibition at the Tokyo Imperial Zoo* (Berkeley: University of California Press, 2013).

5. Siegert, *Cultural Techniques*, 9 (emphasis in the original).

6. "In the greenhouse," Sloterdijk writes, "the Europeans began a series of far-reaching experiments concerning the botanical, climatic and cultural implications of globalization." Peter Sloterdijk, *Foams, Spheres Volume III: Plural Spherology*, trans. Wieland Hoban (Cambridge, MA: MIT Press, 2016), 320. See also Peter Sloterdijk, *Bubbles, Spheres Volume I: Microspherology* (Cambridge, MA: MIT Press, 2011); and Peter Sloterdijk, *Globes, Spheres Volume II: Macrospherology* (Cambridge, MA: MIT Press, 2014).

7. Sloterdijk's uncritical stance toward European colonial voyages is evident, for instance, in the following reference to Columbus: "The offensive string of

early globalization knowledge lay in the Magellanic views of the true extension of the oceans and their acknowledgment as the true world media. That the *oceans* are the carriers of global affairs, and thus the natural media of unrestricted capital flow, is the message of all messages in the period between Columbus, the hero of the maritime medium, and Lindbergh, the pioneer of the age of the air medium—a message the grounded Europeans fought for centuries with their will to provincialism." See Sloterdijk, *In the World Interior of Capital*, 43.

8. Miranda Nieboer and Craig William McCormack, "Under Geodesic Skies: A Cultural Perspective on the Former South Pole Dome and Geodesic Domes in Outer Space," *Polar Journal* 7, no. 2 (2017): 351–73.

9. Yatsuka Hajime, "Hon tenrankai no kōsei: 'Metaborizumu nekusasu' to iu 'kindai no chōkoku'" [The trajectory of this exhibit: An overcoming of modernity called the "metabolism nexus"], in Hirose et al., *Metaborizumu no mirai toshi ten* [Metabolism, the city of the future: Dreams and visions of reconstruction in postwar and present-day Japan] (Tokyo: Shinkenchikusha, 2011), 12. Most notably, Hokkaidō as well as Okinawa remained as prefectures of postwar Japan and thus part of its territory.

10. Toyokawa Saikaku, "Kanreichi kyojūkenkyū to nankyoku Shōwa kichi: Asada Takashi no kapuseru kenchikuron" [Research on cold climate housing and the Shōwa Station in Antarctica: Asada Takashi's capsule architecture], in Hirose et al., *Metaborizumu no mirai toshi ten*, 235.

11. Zhongjie Lin, *Kenzo Tange and the Metabolist Movement: Urban Utopias of Modern Japan* (London: Routledge, 2010), 1.

12. To use the expression of Rem Koolhaas and Hans Ulrich Obrist, "If there is no ground to build on, Metabolism will adapt to build its own ground." Koolhaas and Obrist, *Project Japan*, 186.

13. Isozaki Arata, *Kenchiku no kaitai* [Dismantling architecture] (Tokyo: Bijutsu shuppansha, 1975), 366.

14. This was an unrealized project, though some of its elements are preserved in his postwar design of the Hiroshima Peace Memorial Park. On the connection between these two projects, see Lisa Yoneyama, *Hiroshima Traces: Time, Space, and the Dialectics of Memory* (Berkeley: University of California Press, 1999); and Hyunjung Cho, "Hiroshima Peace Memorial Park and the Making of Japanese Postwar Architecture," *Journal of Architectural Education* 66, no. 1 (2012): 72–83. Around the same time that Tange's design won the competition, the architecture journal *Kenchiku zasshi* generated a survey of future architectural styles for the Greater East Asia Co-Prosperity Sphere, soliciting responses from architects working on the mainland and occupied territories. In his youth, Tange seemed to have fully aligned himself with the expansionist propaganda of the Japanese Empire. His answers to the questionnaire leave little ambiguity. He urged architects to have confidence in the tradition and the future of the Japanese race (*nihon minzoku*) and contended that the realization of the Greater East Asia Co-Prosperity Sphere was an inevitable necessity. See also Isozaki Arata, "Tange

Kenzō no 'kenchiku=toshi=kokka' kyōdōtai to shite no Nihon" [Japan as the "architectural=urban=state" community in Tange Kenzō], in *Isozaki Arata kenchiku ronshū 1: Sanshu sareta modanizumu: "Nihon" to iu mondai kikō* [Collected architectural essays of Isozaki Arata volume 1: Disseminated modernism: The problematic called "Japan"], ed. Yokote Yoshihiro (Tokyo: Iwanami shoten, 2013), 176; and Yatsuka Hajime, *Shisō to shite no Nihon kindai kenchiku* [Modern Japanese architecture as thought] (Tokyo: Iwanami shoten, 2005), 485. On Isozaki's critique of Tange's commitment to the nation and its modernist reinvention of Japaneseness, see also Isozaki Arata, *Kenchiku ni okeru "Nihon teki na mono"* ["Japaneseness" in architecture] (Tokyo: Shinchōsha, 2003). Both Isozaki and Yatsuka compare Tange's embrace of modernism based on the Japanese architectural tradition to the predicament of Japanese literati expressed at the 1942 symposium, "Overcoming Modernity."

15. Asada Takashi, "Nihon kokumin kenchiku yōshiki," as cited in Toyokawa Saikaku, *Tange Kenzō to toshi* [Tange Kenzō and cities] (Tokyo: Kajima shuppan, 2017), 107.

16. Toyokawa Saikaku, *Gunzō to shite Tange kenkyūshitsu: Sengo Nihon kenchiku toshi shi no meinsutoriimu* [The Tange Lab as a group: The mainstream of postwar Japanese architecture and the history of urban design] (Tokyo: Ohmsha, 2012), 49, 79–85. See also Hyunjung Cho, "Competing Futures: War Narratives in Postwar Japanese Architecture, 1945–1970" (PhD diss., University of Southern California, 2011). Tange's postwar preoccupation with the statistical studies of population density, economic productivity, and transportation infrastructure started with research he undertook at the University of Tokyo while studying with architects such as Takayama Eika and Kishida Hideto.

17. Toyokawa, "Kanreichi kyojūkenkyū to nankyoku Shōwa kichi," 35–36. On Asada's Antarctica project, see also Sasahara Katsu, *Asada Takashi: Tsukuranai kenchikuka, Nihon hatsu no toshi purannā* [Asada Takashi: Japan's first urban planner and an architect who does not build] (Tokyo: Ohmsha, 2014), 33.

18. Toyokawa, "Kanreichi kyojūkenkyū to nankyoku Shōwa kichi," 235.

19. Yatsuka, *Metaborizumu nekusasu*, 18. Yatsuka also traces this concept back to wartime geopolitics in his book *Shisō to shite no Nihon kindai kenchiku*. This attempt to draw close connections between postwar and wartime architecture around the notion of the habitable environment is not the purview of Yatsuka alone. For instance, the art historian Sawaragi Noi has also noted that the wartime discourse on the environment (*kankyō*) was an important precursor to the postwar popularization of the term by Asada Takashi, and Isozaki Arata—one of Tange Lab's graduates—has long held a critical stance against Tange's political commitment to nation building and his collaboration with the wartime regime. See Sawaragi Noi, *Sensō to banpaku* [War and the World's Fair] (Tokyo: Bijutsu shuppansha, 2005); Isozaki, "Tange Kenzō no 'kenchiku=toshi=kokka' kyōdōtai to shite no Nihon," 173–202. It is worth noting that Yatsuka studied with Tange and worked with Isozaki. For further reading on the relation between the postwar notion of the environment and architecture, see Yuriko Furuhata, "Multi-

media Environments and Security Operations: Expo '70 as a Laboratory of Governance," *Grey Room* 54 (winter 2014): 56–79.

20. While applauding Ratzel's organicist theory of the state, Watsuji criticizes his understanding of "life" as only biological, not subjective (or existential). Watsuji, *Fūdo*, 353.

21. Thomas Lemke, *Biopolitics: An Advanced Introduction* (New York: New York University Press, 2011), 12–13.

22. Roberto Esposito, *Bios: Biopolitics and Philosophy* (Minneapolis: University of Minnesota Press, 2008), 16–17.

23. Yamamuro Shin'ichi, "Kokumin teikoku: Nihon no keisei to kūkan chi" [The nationalist empire: The formation of Japan and its spatial knowledge], in *"Teikoku" Nihon no gakuchi: Kūkan keisei to sekai ninshiki* [Imperial Japan's learning: The formation of space and the cognition of the world], ed. Yamamuro Shin'ichi (Tokyo: Iwanami shoten, 2006), 51–53. See also Takeuchi Keiichi, "Japanese Geopolitics in the 1930s and 1940s," in *Geopolitical Traditions: Critical Histories of a Century of Geopolitical Thought*, ed. David Atkinson and Klaus Dodds (London: Routledge, 2000), 72–92.

24. Takeuchi, "Japanese Geopolitics in the 1930s and 1940s," 64.

25. On the 1940 list of countries and territories to be included in the Greater East Asia Co-Prosperity Sphere, see Yamamoto Yūzō, *"Dai tōa kyōei ken" keizai shi kenkyū* [A study of the economic history of the Greater East Asia Co-Prosperity Sphere](Tokyo: Nagoya daigaku shuppankai, 2011), 72.

26. Yamamuro, "Kokumin teikoku," 63.

27. The history of Japanese architecture in the first four decades of the twentieth century cannot be narrated without accounting for the contributions made by architects who worked on urban projects in colonial cities and occupied territories in Asia. Famed architects such as Sano Toshikata, Maekawa Kunio, Sakakura Junzō, Ishikawa Hideaki, Uchida Yoshikazu, and Takayama Eika were all involved at one time or another in projects in cities such as Datong, Shanghai, and Xinjing. See Lin, *Kenzo Tange and the Metabolist Movement*, 48; and Koolhaas and Obrist, *Project Japan*, 29. On the specific involvement of architects in Manchuria, see also Koshizawa Akira, *Manshūkoku no shuto keikaku* [Planning the capital city of Manchuria] (Tokyo: Nihon keizai hyōron sha, 1988); and Nakajima Naoto et al., *Toshi keikakuka Ishikawa Hideaki: Toshi kenkyū no kiseki* [Urban planner Ishikawa Hideaki: A trajectory of urban studies] (Tokyo: Kajima shuppan, 2009).

28. Louise Young, *Japan's Total Empire: Manchuria and the Culture of Wartime Imperialism* (Berkeley: University of California Press, 1998), 291.

29. Young, *Japan's Total Empire*, 242, 245.

30. Yatsuka, *Metaborizumu nekusasu*, 19.

31. Kobayashi Hideo, *"Manshū" no rekishi* [A history of Manchuria] (Tokyo: Kōdansha gendai shinsho, 2008), 41–42. On the activities of the South Manchurian Railway Company's research department (Mantetsu chōsabu), see also Kobayashi Hideo, *Mantetsu chōsabu: "Ganso shinku tanku" no tanjō to hōkai* [The

research department of the South Manchurian Railway Company: The birth and fall of "the original think tank"] (Tokyo: Heibonsha, 2005).

32. Nakaya Ukichirō, "Manshū tsūshin" [Letters from Manchuria], in *Nakaya Ukichirō kikō shū: Arasuka no hyōga* [A travelogue of Nakaya Ukichirō: Glaciers in Alaska] (Tokyo: Iwanami bunko, 2002), 49.

33. According to Mark R. Peattie, "It accepted without reservation the notion that not only did 'biological laws' determine the course of human institutions but also that there were 'biological'—that is, racial—differences in the political capacities of various peoples. It thus assumed, on the one hand, the separate evolution of races according to their inherent capacities or incapacities to modernize and, on the other hand, the moral right of 'superior' races to dominate and guide the destinies of 'lesser' peoples." Mark R. Peattie, "The Japanese Colonial Empire, 1895–1945," in *The Cambridge History of Japan*, vol. 6, *The Twentieth Century*, ed. John Whitney Hall (Cambridge: Cambridge University Press, 1988), 238.

34. Karube Tadashi, "Teikoku no rinri: Gotō Shinpei ni okeru risō shugi" [An ethics of empire: The idealism of Gotō Shinpei], in *Jidai no senkakusha: Gotō Shinpei, 1857–1929* [The Pioneer of the era: Gotō Shinpei], ed. Mikuriya Takashi (Tokyo: Fujiwara shoten, 2004), 81. The original title of Gotō's book in Japanese is *Kokka eisei genri*.

35. Foucault, *Security, Territory, Population*, in Rabinow, *Foucault Reader*, 339.

36. Foucault, *Security, Territory, Population*, in Rabinow, *Foucault Reader*, 367.

37. Ruth Rogaski, *Hygienic Modernity: Meanings of Health and Disease in Treaty-Port China* (Berkeley: University of California Press, 2004), 153.

38. Karube, "Teikoku no rinri," 81 (emphasis mine). The original Japanese words are "race" (*minzoku*), "vital desire" (*seimei yoku*), and "expansionist desire" (*bōchō yoku*); the original Japanese title of his book is *Nihon bōchōron*.

39. Gotō Shinpei, *Seiden: Gotō Shinpei, Mantetsu jidai 1906–1908* [The authentic biography: Gotō Shinpei, the Manchurian railroad period 1906–1908], vol. 4 (Tokyo: Fujiwara shoten, 2005), 149.

40. Azuma Hideki, *Tokyo no toshi keikakuka: Takayama Eika* [The urban planner of Tokyo: Takayama Eika] (Tokyo: Kajima shuppan, 2010), 141; Yatsuka, *Shisō to shite no Nihon kindai kenchiku*, 445. Tange was not only familiar with the planning of the city of Datong in Manchuria, designed by Takayama and Uchida Yoshibumi under the supervision of Uchida Yoshikazu, but he also worked on Sakakura's 1939 Nanhu housing project in Xinjing, the new capital of Manchuria.

41. Descriptions of Tange's work as postmodern appear in broad discussions of postwar Japanese architecture. See, for instance, Steven Best and Douglas Kellner, *The Postmodern Turn* (New York: Guilford Press, 1997), 188.

42. Yuriko Furuhata, "Architecture as Atmospheric Media, 52–79.

43. Tange Kenzō, *Nihon rettō no shōraizō: 21 seiki e no kenchiku* [The future of the Japanese archipelago: Architecture for the 21st century] (Tokyo: Kōdansha, 1966), 169.

44. Tange, *Nihon rettō no shōraizō*, 173.

45. Tange Kenzō, "A Plan for Tokyo, 1960: Toward a Structural Reorganization," in *Architecture Culture 1943–1968: A Documentary Anthology*, ed. Joan Ockman (New York: Columbia Books of Architecture, 1993), 330.

46. Tange, *Nihon rettō no shōraizō*, 168.

47. Mark Wigley, "Network Fever," in *New Media, Old Media: A History and Theory Reader*, ed. Wendy Hui Kyong Chun and Thomas Keenan (London: Routledge, 2006), 387.

48. Tange, *Nihon rettō no shōraizō*, 33. Tange's description of the communication revolution or the "second industrial revolution" resonates with and anticipates the discourse on electric media propelled by the likes of Marshall McLuhan in the 1960s. He writes, for instance, that the second industrial revolution is characterized by "an extension of the human nervous system" through the means of new information and communication technologies. Unlike the first industrial revolution, which extended the manual capacity of the human body, the second industrial revolution extends the cognitive capacity of the human nervous system.

49. Katharine Anderson, *Predicting the Weather: Victorians and the Science of Meteorology* (Chicago: University of Chicago Press, 2005), 187. Anderson writes: "By the 1850s, the analogy between the nervous system and the telegraph was sufficiently established that the comparison operated as readily in the other direction: mental acts were like telegraphy, but telegraphy was also like mental acts." See also Elizabeth Green Musselman, *Nervous Conditions: Science and the Body Politic in Early Industrial Britain* (Albany: State University of New York Press, 2006).

50. Matsuda Hiroyuki, *Meiji denshin denwa monogatari: Jōhō tsūshin shakai no "gen fūkei"* [The tale of telegraphy and telephone in the Meiji era: The "original landscape" of the telecommunication society] (Tokyo: Nihon keizai hyōronsha, 2001), 70.

51. Daqing Yang, *Technology of Empire: Telecommunications and Japanese Expansionism in Asia, 1883–1945* (Cambridge, MA: Harvard University Asia Center, 2010), 15.

52. Yang, *Technology of Empire*, 11.

53. Yang, *Technology of Empire*, 44.

54. On the history of Japan's telecommunications infrastructure and imperial propaganda, see Ariyama Teruo, *Jōhō haken to teikoku Nihon II: Tsūshin gijutsu no kakudai to senden sen* [The information hegemony and Imperial Japan II: The expansion of telecommunication technology and the propaganda war] (Tokyo: Yoshikawa Kōbunkan, 2013).

55. Nakaya Ukichirō, "Manshū tsūshin," 41–46.

56. The Japanese name for the Continental Science Institute is Tairiku kagakuin. Nakaya Ukichirō succeeded in creating artificial snowflakes before the establishment of the Institute of Low Temperature Science in 1940. Where Nakaya created the artificial snowflake (or "snow crystal") in 1936 is where the Low Temperature Laboratory was built in 1936. See the Nakaya Ukichirō Foundation website: https://nakayafoundation.or.jp/.

57. Toyokawa Saikaku, *Tange Kenzō to toshi*, 107–8.

58. Toyokawa Saikaku, *Tange Kenzō to toshi*, 110–12.

59. Sasahara Katsu, *Asada Takashi*, 40–41.

60. David Crowley, "Looking Down on Spaceship Earth: Cold War Landscapes," in David Crowley and Jane Pavitt, *Cold War Modern: Design 1945–1970* (London: V&A, 2008), 257–58.

61. Foer, "Jeff Bezos's Master Plan."

62. Foer, "Jeff Bezos's Master Plan," 257. Following Crowley, Hyunjung Cho calls Metabolist megastructures and capsules "survival architecture." See Cho, "Competing Futures," 208.

63. Crowley, "Looking Down on Spaceship Earth," 257.

64. Foer, "Jeff Bezos's Master Plan."

65. Asian settlements in Hawai'i are by no means homogeneous and its power dynamics differ across ethnic and national communities and historical periods. See, for instance, *Asian Settler Colonialism: From Local Governance to the Habits of Everyday Life in Hawai'i*, ed. Candace Fujikane and Jonathan Y. Okamura (Honolulu: University of Hawai'i Press, 2008).

66. As Derek Woods argues in his critique of the Anthropocene discourse, however, the human is not a scalable concept. Similarly, I would suggest that we regard atmospheric control not necessarily as scalable in reality, but as a fantasy that persists to this day because of the thermostatic desire that propels it. This imagined scalability of atmospheric control also marks the contemporary discourse on terraforming extraterrestrial territories, as in the case of space settlements. Derek Woods, "Scale Critique for the Anthropocene," *Minnesota Review* 83, no. 1 (2014): 133–42.

CHAPTER 4: **Spaceship Earth**

1. Simone Jeska, *Transparent Plastics: Design and Technology* (Basel: Birkhäuser, 2008), 12; Whitney Moon, "Environmental Wind-Baggery," *e-flux architecture*, accessed July 3, 2019, https://www.e-flux.com/architecture/structural-instability /208703/environmental-wind-baggery/.

2. Hyunjung Cho compares Metabolist capsules, including Asada's Antarctica housing, to underground fallout shelters and spaceships that protect astronauts from the hostile exterior environment. Cho writes, "Given that the capsule is a survival mechanism as well as an exhibitionist house, its logic is analogous to that of the home fallout shelter, which was popular in the US at the height of the Cold War. I would consider the capsule, a fortified domestic space attached to a high-rise megastructure, as an underground bomb shelter *in reverse*" (emphasis in the original). See Cho, "Competing Futures," 207.

3. Referencing Engels's *Dialectics of Nature*, in which he argues that the fundamental mode of existence of life is metabolism, Kawazoe notes that they chose this term because it would be legible to Euro-Americans. Commenting on Kawazoe's explanation of metabolism and linking it to John Bellamy Foster's discussion of the metabolic rift, Hyunjung Cho writes: "Kawazoe has made it clear that the concept of metabolism derived from Marx and Engels' ideas about the material exchange between nature and humans, the fundamental relationship between external conditions and human society. Marx and Engels employed the

term 'metabolism' in their key publications including *Capital* to suggest a dialectical interaction between nature and society. As the sociologist John Bellamy
Foster has pointed out, Marx and Engels relied on the concept of metabolism to
criticize humankind's alienation from nature and the ecological crisis caused by
capitalism and to restore the relationship between nature and human society to
its rightful form through socialism." See Kawazoe Noboru, "Metaborisuto tachi
to mananda toki to ima," in Ōtaka Masato and Kawazoe Noboru, *Metaborizumu
to Metaborisuto tachi* [Metabolism and the Metabolists] (Tokyo: Bijutsu shuppansha, 2005), 15; Cho, "Competing Futures, 194–95.

4. Brett Clark and Richard York, "Carbon Metabolism: Climate Change and the
Biospheric Rift," *Theory and Society* 34, no. 4 (August 2005): 391–428; John Bellamy Foster, Brett Clark, and Richard York, *The Ecological Rift: Capitalism's War
on the Earth* (New York: Monthly Review Press, 2010); McKenzie Wark, *Molecular
Red: Theory for the Anthropocene* (London: Verso, 2015); Jason W. Moore, "Transcending the Metabolic Rift: A Theory of Crises in the Capitalist World-Ecology,"
Journal of Peasant Studies 1, no. 38 (2011): 1–46.

5. Koolhaas and Obrist, *Project Japan*, 486.

6. Hirose Mami, Sasaki Hitomi, Maeda Naotake, Tagomori Miho, Tamayama
Ami, and Yoshida Yuri, eds. *Metaborizum no mirai toshi ten: Sengo Nihon, ima yomigaeru fukkō no yume to bijon* [Metabolism, the city of the future: Dreams and
visions of reconstruction in postwar and present-day Japan] (Tokyo: Shinkenchikusha, 2011), 156.

7. Heather Davis, "Life and Death in the Anthropocene: A Short History of Plastic," in *Art in the Anthropocene: Encounters among Aesthetics, Politics, Environments
and Epistemologies*, ed. Heather Davis and Etienne Turpin (London: Open Humanities Press, 2015), 349. See also Heather Davis, *Plastic Matter* (Durham, NC: Duke
University Press, 2022).

8. Kamiya Kōji, "Ōyane" [Large roof], *Shinkenchiku* [New architecture] 45, no. 5
(May 1970): 171; Nakawada Minami and Atmosphere Ltd., *Expo '70: Kyōgaku Osaka
hakurankai no subete* [Expo '70: Everything about the marvelous World's Fair in
Osaka] (Tokyo: Daiyamondo sha, 2005), 59. Also, Kurokawa's Capsule House is
like an all-plastic prefabricated "bath module" (or *yunitto basu*), which is a combination of bathtub, toilet, and sink in one modular unit. Japan developed it for
Hotel New Otani anticipating foreign visitors coming to the Tokyo Olympics. It is
often made of fiber-reinforced plastics.

9. Kawazoe Noboru, "Metaborisuto tachi to mananda toki to ima" [What I
learned from the Metabolists then and now], in Ōtaka and Kawazoe, *Metaborizumu to Metaborisutotachi*, 16.

10. Kawazoe, "Metaborisuto tachi to mananda toki to ima," 15.

11. Foster, Clark, and York, *Ecological Rift*, 241–42. John Bellamy Foster and
Paul Burkett also argue over how Marx borrowed the dialectical pair of the concepts of "organic" and "inorganic" from Hegel. The concept of organic is etymologically associated with the Greek term *organon* ("tools"), hence Hegel aligned
the realm of human consciousness with the organic. Foster and Burkett write:

"The organism (particularly the animal organism), in other words, comes to stand for subjectivity and self-dependence—that is, for rational life connected to the life of the spirit within nature. Here, animate species are the means by which the spirit discovers itself in nature and overcomes its estrangement" (410). See John Bellamy Foster and Paul Burkett, "The Dialectic of Organic/Inorganic Relations: Marx and the Hegelian Philosophy of Nature," *Organization and Environment* 13, no. 4 (December 2000): 403–25.

12. John Bellamy Foster, "Marx's Theory of Metabolic Rift: Classical Foundations for Environmental Sociology," *American Journal of Sociology* 105, no. 2 (September 1999): 382.

13. Foster, "Marx's Theory of Metabolic Rift," 370.

14. Foster, "Marx's Theory of Metabolic Rift," 381.

15. Foster, "Marx's Theory of Metabolic Rift," 379.

16. Karl Marx, *Capital: A Critique of Political Economy*, ed. Frederick Engels, trans. Samuel Moore and Edward Aveling (Moscow: Progress, accessed July 12, 2019), https://www.marxists.org/archive/marx/works/1867-c1/ch27.htm.

17. John Bellamy Foster and Paul Burkett, *Marx and the Earth: An Anti-Critique* (Chicago: Haymarket Books, 2017), 23–25.

18. Brett L. Walker, *Toxic Archipelago: A History of Industrial Disease in Japan* (Seattle: University of Washington Press, 2010), 156. I draw much of the following account of chemical fertilizer from Walker's research on the environmental history of Japanese industrial disease.

19. Kankyōshō, *Kankyō Junkan gata shakai hakusho* [White Paper on the environmentally conscious recycling society] (Tokyo: Nikkei insatsu, 2008), 70–71. As Vaclav Smil notes, "Nitrogen content of human wastes also varies considerably with the quality of average diets." Vaclav Smil, *Enriching the Earth: Fritz Haber, Carl Bosch, and the Transformation of World Food Production* (Cambridge, MA: MIT Press, 2001), 27.

20. Quoted in Brett Clark and Stefano B. Longo, "Land-Sea Ecological Rifts," *Monthly Review: An Independent Socialist Magazine*, July 1, 2018, https://monthlyreview.org/2018/07/01/land-sea-ecological-rifts/.

21. B. L. Walker, *Toxic Archipelago*, 157. The use of synthetic nitrogen fertilizer dramatically increased in Japan in the first half of the twentieth century. By 1950, Japan, along with Europe and North America, consumed 95 percent of all nitrogen fertilizer in the world. Smil, *Enriching the Earth*, 142.

22. Ikeda Shūichi, "Shōwa 10 nendai no Tokyo ni okeru shinyō shori" [The treatment of human waste in Tokyo during the second decade of the Shōwa era], in *Toire: Haisetsu no kūkan kara miru Nihon no bunka to rekishi* [The toilet: Japanese culture and history seen from the space of excretion], ed. Shinyō Gesui Kenkyūkai (Tokyo: Mineruva shobō, 2016), 142–47.

23. B. L. Walker, *Toxic Archipelago*, 158.

24. B. L. Walker, *Toxic Archipelago*, 160.

25. Mikio Sumiya, *A History of Japanese Trade and Industry Policy* (Oxford: Oxford University Press, 2001), 322.

26. Mark Tilton, *Restrained Trade: Cartels in Japan's Basic Materials Industries* (Ithaca, NY: Cornell University Press, 1996), 127.

27. B. L. Walker, *Toxic Archipelago*, 208.

28. B. L. Walker, *Toxic Archipelago*, 209.

29. Nakaya Fujiko, among many Japanese artists and filmmakers, critically dealt with this notorious case of industrial pollution in her video artwork, *Friends of Minamata Victims—Video Diary* (1971–72).

30. Masazumi Harada, "Minamata Disease: Methylmercury Poisoning in Japan Caused by Environmental Pollution," *Critical Reviews in Toxicology* 25, no. 1 (1995): 4.

31. B. L. Walker, *Toxic Archipelago*, 19.

32. Cho, "Competing Futures," 211.

33. Sasahara Katsu, *Asada Takashi*, 40–44.

34. Kurokawa Kishō, *Metaborizumu no hassō* [Ideas of Metabolism] (Kyoto: Hakuba shuppan, 1972), 286–87.

35. Kurokawa Kishō, "Watashi no sumitai megaroporisu" [The megalopolis where I want to live], in *Metaborizumu no hassō*, 256–57.

36. Cho, "Competing Futures," 216; Koolhaas and Obrist, *Project Japan*, 388.

37. Kenneth Boulding, "The Economics of the Coming Spaceship Earth," in *Environmental Quality in a Growing Economy*, ed. H. Jarrett (Baltimore, MD: published for Resources for the Future by Johns Hopkins University Press, 1966), 3–14; Donella H. Meadows, Dennis L. Meadows, Jørgen Randers, and William W. Behrens III, *The Limits to Growth* (New York: Potomac Associates, 1972).

38. Robert Scott, *Kenneth Boulding: A Voice Crying in the Wilderness* (New York: Palgrave Macmillan, 2014), 92.

39. Boulding, "Economics of the Coming Spaceship Earth," 7–9.

40. Kurokawa, *Metaborizumu no hassō*, 309.

41. Kurokawa, *Metaborizumu no hassō*, 310.

42. For more on this history of Toyota's "just-in-time" production, also known as the "kanban system," see Marc Steinberg, "Management's Mediations: The Case of Toyotism," *Media and Management* by Rutvica Andrijasevic, Julie Yujie Chen, Melissa Gregg, and Marc Steinberg (Minneapolis: University of Minnesota Press, 2021), 1–30.

43. Deborah Cowen, *The Deadly Life of Logistics: Mapping Violence in Global Trade* (Minneapolis: University of Minnesota Press, 2014), 35. Coined by the British cybernetician Stafford Beer, the idea of "management cybernetics" influenced economic experiments and managerial theories across the world, including the utopian vision of the Chilean government under the leadership of Salvador Allende. See Eden Medina, *Cybernetic Revolutionaries: Technology and Politics in Allende's Chile* (Cambridge, MA: MIT Press, 2011).

44. Cowen, *Deadly Life of Logistics*, 40.

45. David Marutschke, *Continuous Improvement Strategies: Japanese Convenience Store Systems* (Basingstoke, UK: Palgrave Macmillan, 2012).

46. Kurokawa, *Metaborizumu no hassō*, 309.

47. "Life maintains a dynamic balance through the cycle of the birth of new

cells and the death of old cells. Halting this cycle means death. The cessation of blood flow due to cardio-respiratory arrest also means death. The same can be said about the ecosystem of the earth, whose equilibrium is maintained by the climatic cycle and food chain of living organisms." Kurokawa Kishō, "Metaborizumu to kyōsei no shisō" [The Metabolist idea of symbiosis], in Ōtaka and Kawazoe, *Metaborizumu to Metaborisuto tachi*, 222.

48. Kurokawa, "Metaborizumu to kyōsei no shisō," 223.

49. Kurokawa, "Metaborizumu to kyōsei no shisō," 224.

50. The Marxist-Leninist revolutionary politics of the Japanese Red Army, for instance, brought a collaboration among Japanese activists and Palestinian activists, especially those affiliated with the Popular Front for the Liberation of Palestine. For more on the media activist network between Japan and the Middle East, especially the legacy of militant cinema, see Yuriko Furuhata, *Cinema of Actuality*.

51. Koolhaas and Obrist, *Project Japan*, 598.

52. Koolhaas and Obrist, *Project Japan*, 599.

53. Koolhaas and Obrist, *Project Japan*, 606.

54. Tange Kenzō, *Ippon no enpitsu kara* (Tokyo: Nihon tosho sentā, 1997), 121.

55. Tange, *Ippon no enpitsu kara*, 117–48.

56. Koolhaas and Obrist, *Project Japan*, 622–26.

57. Kurokawa Kishō, *Shin kyōsei no shisō* [A renewed idea of symbiosis] (Tokyo: Tokuma shoten, 1996), 579.

58. Paul J. Crutzen, "Albedo Enhancement by Stratospheric Sulfur Injections: A Contribution to Resolve a Policy Dilemma?," *Climate Change* 77, no. 3–4 (2006): 211–19.

59. Fleming, *Fixing the Sky*, 253–55. See also Hamilton, *Earthmasters*; and "Geoengineering the Planet? More Scientists Now Say It Must Be an Option," *Yale Environment 360*, May 29, 2019, https://e360. yale.edu/features/geoengineer-the -planet-more-scientists-now-say-it-must-be-an-option.

60. Hamilton, *Earthmasters*, 15–16. Hamilton is referencing the situation that Paul Crutzen has called a Catch-22. See also Crutzen, "Albedo Enhancement by Stratospheric Sulfur Injections," 211.

CHAPTER 5: **Cloud Control**

Sections of chapter 5 have appeared in my chapter "Tange Lab and Biopolitics: From Geopolitics of the Sphere to the Nervous System of the Nation" in *Beyond Imperial Aesthetics: Theories of Art and Politics in Japan*, ed. Steve Choe and Mayumo Inoue (Hong Kong: University of Hong Kong Press, 2019); my chapter "Architecture as Atmospheric Media: Tange Lab and Cybernetics" in *Media Theory in Japan*, ed. Marc Steinberg and Alexander Zahlten (Durham, NC: Duke University Press, 2017); and my article "Multimedia Environments and Security Operations: Expo '70 as a Laboratory of Governance," in *Grey Room* 54 (winter 2014): 56–79.

1. As Lisa Parks suggests in her analysis of vertical aerial surveillance and drone warfare, the atmospheric mediation of wireless signals through airwaves invites an atmospheric approach to study these practices. Invoking the concept of

"cultural atmospherics" used by geographers and anthropologists, Parks writes: "The concept of *cultural atmospherics* is invoked in a literal and figurative sense, literally to account for the way that cultural practices such as audiovisual communication move through (or beyond) the atmosphere in the process of their production, distribution, and/or, reception, and figuratively, to account for the potential of such processes to generate affects and sensations, modulate moods, reorder lifeworlds, and alter everyday spaces." See Lisa Parks, *Rethinking Media Coverage: Vertical Mediation and the War on Terror* (New York: Routledge, 2018), 14.

2. As Kelly Gates notes, one of the first computerized facial recognition experiments took place at Expo '70 at the Nippon Electric Company's exhibition "Computer Physiognomy" at its pavilion. Kelly A. Gates, *Our Biometric Future: Facial Recognition Technology and the Culture of Surveillance* (New York: New York University Press, 2011), 25–26.

3. Anna Feigenbaum, *Tear Gas: From the Battlefields of World War I to the Streets of Today* (London: Verso, 2017), 181.

4. Feigenbaum, *Tear Gas*, 30.

5. Edwards, *Closed World*, 141.

6. "Sairui gasu de demo tai o ou keikan tai" [Riot police chasing the protestors with tear gas]. *Asahi shinbun* [Asahi newspaper], May 2, 1952.

7. "Keibō to sairui gasu to Sasebo" [Batons, tear gas, and Sasebo]. *Asahi shinbun* [Asahi newspaper], January 17, 1968.

8. "Gin bura mo namida nagara" [Walking around Ginza in tears], *Asahi shinbun* [Asahi newspaper], April 29, 1969.

9. McLuhan owes his idea of electronic media as a prosthetic extension of the human nervous system to his encounters with architects, especially Buckminster Fuller. Wigley, "Network Fever," 377.

10. Wigley, "Network Fever," 377–78.

11. Wigley, "Network Fever," 387.

12. Reinhold Martin, *The Organizational Complex: Architecture, Media, and Corporate Space* (Cambridge, MA: MIT Press, 2003), 21.

13. Tange Kenzō, *Nihon rettō no shōraizō*, 32–43. According to Yatsuka Hajime, Tange's book was inspired in part by the French geographer Jean Gottmann's *Megalopolis* (1961). Tange most likely learned of Gottmann's work from the urban sociologist Isomura Ei'ichi, who had learned of his work from the urban planner Kevin Lynch. From his visiting professorship at MIT, Tange knew Lynch, whose book *Image of the City* (1960) he cotranslated into Japanese in 1968. See Yatsuka Hajime, *Metaborizumu Nekusasu*, 321.

14. McLuhan had a prominent presence in Japan, just as he did in North America. Following the 1967 translation of *Understanding Media: The Extensions of Man* (1964), Japan underwent what some call a "McLuhan boom." As Marc Steinberg argues, McLuhan's aphorisms and ideas were channeled and widely disseminated through public intellectuals such as Takemura Ken'ichi, who introduced McLuhan to the advertising and marketing industries. See Marc Steinberg, "McLuhan as Prescription Drug: Actionable Theory and Advertising Industries," in

Steinberg and Zahlten, *Media Theory in Japan*, 131–50. We can also glimpse the extent of McLuhan's popularity in the discursive milieu of art and architecture criticism of the late 1960s. For example, the January 1968 issue of the architecture journal *SD* (Space design) published a special feature section titled "A Tactile Approach to the Environment." Two prominent art critics of the time—Tōno Yoshiaki and Nakahara Yūsuke—contributed essays to the issue and discussed McLuhan's claims about the resurgence of the tactile sense in *Understanding Media*. Tōno Yoshiaki, "Shokkakuteki to iu koto" [On being tactile], *SD* 38 (January 1968): 6–8; Nakahara Yūsuke, "Shokkaku no fukken" [A Revival of tactility], *SD* 38 (January 1968): 33–36, 48.

15. Kitagawa Toshio, "Saibanetikusu no kōsei genri" [Principles of cybernetics], in *Saibanetikusu: Kyōkai ryōiki to shite no kōsatsu* [Reflections on cybernetics as an interdisciplinary field], ed. Kitagawa Toshio (Tokyo: Misuzu shobō, 1953), 1–3.

16. Kitagawa Toshio, *Tōkei kagaku no sanjū nen: Waga shi waga tomo* [Thirty years of statistical science: My teachers and friends] (Tokyo: Kyōritsu shuppan, 1969), 93.

17. Kitagawa, *Tōkei kagaku no sanjū nen*, 100.

18. "Saibanetikusu o megutte" [On cybernetics], *Shinbun kenkyū* [Newspaper studies] (January 1954): 16–21.

19. Correspondence from George Olcott to Ikehara Shikao, March 7, 1955, MC-0022, box 14, folder 211, Norbert Wiener Papers, Institute Archives and Special Collections, Massachusetts Institute of Technology, Cambridge, MA (hereafter cited as Norbert Wiener Papers). The American Embassy offered to pay him a per diem during his two weeks' stay in Japan, during which Wiener gave lectures in major cities, including Tokyo and Osaka. The same year, 1956, scholars also witnessed a plethora of publications on cybernetics, including books by Japanese academics who attempted to explain cybernetics, and the Japanese translations of mathematicians and computer scientists such as Georges-Théodule Gilbaud and Edmund Berkeley.

20. Peter Galison, "The Ontology of the Enemy: Norbert Wiener and the Cybernetic Vision," *Critical Inquiry* 21, no. 1 (autumn 1994): 228–66. See also Orit Halpern's nuanced take on Galison's analysis of Wiener in *Beautiful Data: A History of Vision and Reason since 1945* (Durham, NC: Duke University Press, 2014), 44.

21. Correspondence from V. Bush to Norbert Wiener, June 12, 1935, MC-0022, box 15, folder 42, Norbert Wiener Papers.

22. Ronald R. Kline, *The Cybernetics Moment: Or Why We Call Our Age the Information Age* (Baltimore, MD: Johns Hopkins University Press, 2015), 19.

23. Correspondence from V. Bush to Norbert Wiener, June 12, 1935, MC-0022, box 15, folder 42, Norbert Wiener Papers.

24. Correspondence from V. Bush to Norbert Wiener, June 12, 1935, MC-0022, box 15, folder 42, Norbert Wiener Papers.

25. Correspondence from Ikehara Shikao to Norbert Wiener, July 24, 1939, MC-0022, box 3, folder 54, Norbert Wiener Papers.

26. Galison, "Ontology of the Enemy," 229.

27. Kline, *Cybernetics Moment*, 21.

28. Galison, "Ontology of the Enemy," 253.

29. Correspondence from Ikehara opens his letter with the following sentence: "It is indeed my privilege to send you my ever grateful compliments. I am alive today though I was machine-gunned and bombed turning a few of my hair[s] white." Ikehara Shikao to Norbert Wiener, November 29, 1945, MC-0022, box 4, folder 69, Norbert Wiener Papers. Ikehara's letters to Wiener stopped after 1943 and resumed in 1945, after Japan's unconditional surrender.

30. Correspondence from Ikehara Shikao to Norbert Wiener, July 1, 1950, MC-0022, box 8, folder 121, Norbert Wiener Papers.

31. Correspondence from Ikehara Shikao to Norbert Wiener, July 1, 1950, MC-0022, box 8, folder 121, Norbert Wiener Papers.

32. Correspondence from Norbert Wiener to Ikehara Shikao, April 5, 1955, MC-0022, box 14, folder 211, Norbert Wiener Papers.

33. In *The Human Use of Human Beings*, Wiener comments on the potential misuse of cybernetics. Elaborating on the idea of "the *machine à governer*" that the French reviewer of his book painted as a dystopian future of the automated decision-making machine ruling over the humans, Wiener argues that "the *machine à governer* of Père Dubarle is not frightening because of any danger that it may achieve autonomous control over humanity." The real danger, according to Wiener, lies not in the machines, but in the humans, especially in the conduct of politicians who "may attempt to control their populations by means not of machines themselves but through political techniques as narrow and indifferent to human possibility as if they had, in fact, been conceived mechanically." It is this possibility of cybernetics as a political technique of government driven by the instrumental rationality of control that he warns against. Turning to the Cold War deployment of game theory as an example, Wiener writes: "But even without the state machine of Père Dubarle we are already developing new concepts of war, of economic conflict, and of propaganda on the basis of von Neumann's *Theory of Games*, which is itself a communicational theory, as the developments of the 1950s have already shown. This theory of games, as I have said in the earlier chapter, contributes to the theory of language, but there are in existence government agencies bent on applying it to military and quasi-military aggressive and defensive purposes." Norbert Wiener, *The Human Use of Human Beings: Cybernetics and Society* (Boston, MA: De Capo Press, 1954), 181.

34. Norbert Wiener, *Cybernetics or Control of Communication in the Animal and the Machine* (New York: John Wiley, 1948), 19.

35. Tange, *Nihon rettō no shōraizō*, 34–35.

36. Tange's cybernetic turn can be seen as part of an epistemic paradigm, which Reinhold Martin has called the "organizational complex."

37. Tange, *Nihon rettō no shōraizō*, 42.

38. Martin, *Organizational Complex*, 57–61.

39. Tange, *Nihon rettō no shōraizō*, 41–42.

40. Martin, *Organizational Complex*, 8–9.

41. For more on information society discourse and its promoters, see Yuriko Furuhata, "Architecture as Atmospheric Media," 52–79.

42. Keizai shingikai jōhō kenkyū iinkai [The Committee for the Economic Council for Information Studies], *Nihon no Jōhōka shakai: Sono bijon to kadai* [Japan's information society: Its vision and challenges] (Tokyo: Daiyamondo sha, 1969), 5. The original Japanese term for the committee is Keizai shingikai jōhō kenkyū iinkai.

43. Hayashi Shūji, *Ryūtsū kakumei: Seihin, keiro, oyobi shōhisha* [A revolution in distribution: Products, pathways, and consumers] (Tokyo: Chūō kōron shinsho, 1962).

44. For more on this, see Morris-Suzuki, *Beyond Computopia*, chapters 4–6.

45. Katherine Hayles, "Cybernetics," in *Critical Terms for Media Studies*, ed. W. J. T. Mitchell and Mark B. N. Hansen (Chicago: University of Chicago Press, 2010), 145 (emphasis in the original).

46. Toyokawa Saikaku, "The Core System and Social Scale: Design Methodology at the Tange Laboratory," trans. Watanabe Hiroshi, in *Kenzō Tange: Architecture for the World*, ed. Seng Kuan and Yukio Lippit (Zurich: Lars Müller and the president and fellows of Harvard College, 2012), 25.

47. Michel Foucault, *The Birth of Biopolitics: Lectures at the Collège de France, 1978–1979*, trans. Graham Burchell (New York: Palgrave Macmillan, 2008), 13.

48. In spite of the ostensible purge of war criminals during the occupation period, many of the governmental institutions—such as the Economic Planning Agency, which undertook state-led planning and development projects—either preserved or welcomed back wartime technocrats. Some politicians and bureaucrats who were imprisoned as class-A war criminals, such as the media tycoon Shōriki Matsutarō, were brought back on the center stage of the postwar reconstruction by the United States during the Cold War. On the legacy of Shōriki as a CIA informant, see Arima Tetsuo, *Kōshite Terebi wa hajimatta: Senryō, reisen, saigunbi no hazama de* [This is how television started: Between the Occupation, the Cold War, and remilitarization] (Tokyo: Mineruva shobō, 2013), 144–45.

49. The original Japanese name is Zenkoku Sōgō Kaihatsu Keikaku. Toyokawa Saikaku, *Gunzō to shite no Tange Kenkyūshitsu*, 44. On Tange Lab's impact on social and economic policies, see also Toyokawa, "Core System and Social Scale," 15–28. Shimokōbe's and Ōbayashi's research on industrial productivity had a direct impact on the Comprehensive National Development Plan launched by the Economic Planning Agency in 1962, around the same time that the futurologist Umesao Tadao's essay on the information industry and a book on the logistics revolution by Hayashi Shūji, another futurologist, were published.

50. In 1972 Kurokawa also published *The Future of Information Archipelago Japan*, a book that echoed the title of Tange's 1965 essay, "The Future of the Japanese Archipelago." See Shimokōbe Atsushi, ed., *Jōhōshakai to no taiwa: Mirai Nihon no jōhō nettowaaku* [Dialogues with information society: Information networks for future Japan] (Tokyo: Tōyō Keizai Shinhōsha, 1970), iii. See also Koolhaas and Obrist, *Project Japan*, 638; and Kurokawa Kishō, *Jōhō rettō Nihon no shōrai* [The future of information archipelago Japan] (Tokyo: Dai san bunmei sha, 1972), 1–2.

51. See Hayashi Yūjirō and Kagaku Gijutsu to Keizai no Kai, eds., *Chō gijutsu shakai e no tenkai: Jōhōka shisutemu no ningen* [Developing a supertechnological society: Humans in the information system] (Tokyo: Daiyamondo sha, 1969).

52. Yatsuka, *Metaborizumu nekusasu*, 320.

53. Toyokawa, *Gunzō to shite no Tange kenkyūshitsu*, 314.

54. Kurokawa, for instance, attributes his interest in the biological system of data processing to the architect's need to respond to the demands of the time: "I became interested in the vital mechanism, especially in the living organism's information systems since I predicted that the informational *soft* component of the human environment—namely, communication, transportation, and energy—rather than its *hard* component would become more prominent in the future." Kurokawa, *Jōhō rettō Nihon no shōrai*, 2 (emphasis mine).

55. Isozaki often describes the difference between his view of urban design and that of the Metabolist group as a difference between the image of "ruin" and the image of utopia. On his discussion of the future city as a ruin, see Isozaki Arata, "Haikyo ron" [On ruins], in *Kigō no umi ni ukabu "shima"* [Islands in the sea of signs] (Tokyo: Iwanami shoten, 2013), 24–40.

56. Isozaki participated in landmark art exhibitions, including *Shikisai to kūkan ten* [Color and space, 1966); *Kūkan kara kankyō e ten* (From space to environment, 1966); and the Fourteenth Milan Triennale (1968). He also worked as an exhibition space designer for *Okamoto Tarō ten* (Okamoto Tarō exhibition, 1964).

57. Isozaki Arata, "Aatisuto-Aakitekuto no jidai: Osaka banpaku nosōzōryoku o hokan shita aato shin" [The era of an artist-architect: Art scenes that supplemented the imagination of the World's Fair in Osaka], interview with Arata Isozaki, by Yasuko Imura, Yuriko Furuhata, and Shigeru Matsui, *Tokyo Geijutsu Daigaku Eizōkenkyū Kiyō* (October 2012): 36–80.

58. In his essay "Sofuto aakitekuchua," published in *Kenchiku bunka* in 1970, Isozaki Atelier described the computer-programmed cybernetic environment of the Festival Plaza as "soft architecture," a phrase he borrowed from Warren Brodey's work. See Warren M. Brodey, "The Design of Intelligent Environment: Soft Architecture," *Landscape* 17, no. 1 (autumn 1967): 8–12.

59. Isozaki Atelier, "Sofuto aakitekuchua: Ōtōba to shite no kankyō" [Soft architecture: The environment as a response field], *Kenchiku bunka* [Architectural culture] 279 (January 1970): 73. The model for this tightly networked two-way communication environment was the Mission Control Center at NASA, which he had visited in 1967. See Isozaki Arata and Hino Naohiko, "Taaning pointo: Kūkan kara kankyō e" [Turning point: From space to environment] *10+1* 48 (2007): 203.

60. While the published materials on the Festival Plaza, such as the article "Sofuto ākitekuchua" in *Kenchiku bunka* (1970), indicate that the robots were responsive, Tsukio Yoshio notes that the plaza's computerized system of control was imperfect and did not actualize the original plan of creating a fully interactive environment. Tsukio Yoshio in discussion with the author and Matsui Shigeru on November 12, 2015.

61. Isozaki and Hino, "Taaning pointo," 203.

62. The original Japanese words for this phrase are *ōtōba to shite no kankyō*.

63. Myron W. Krueger, "Responsive Environments," in *The New Media Reader*, ed. Noah Wardrip-Fruin and Nick Monfront (Cambridge, MA: MIT Press, 2003), 379.

64. For more information on Negroponte's and Krueger's work, see Nicholas Negroponte, *Soft Architecture Machines* (Cambridge, MA: MIT Press, 1976); and Krueger, "Responsive Environments," 379–89.

65. Tsukio Yoshio wrote and edited books such as *Business Environments for the Information Age* (1987), *Cyber-Technology* (1990), and *A Mechanism for the IT Revolution* (2000).

66. In his turn away from monumental architecture, Isozaki found company with the younger generation of architects, such as Archigram, an avant-garde architecture group whose works he helped introduce to Japan. Written around the same time as Expo '70, for instance, he ends the essay "Archigram Group: Architecture Reduced to Information" with the following observation: "Things like the audio-visual helmet, portable minimal environments, and Enviro-pill are fashionable concerns of many young architects including Hans Hollein, who are engaged in the informatized situation today. No doubt that this is indicative of the phenomenon of dismantlement [of architecture], but for those architects who willingly embarked on an exploration of the liminal territory, the label 'architect' is no longer needed. What is a profession that emerges after this departure? This is a question I ask myself, as I too have wandered and arrived at the same spot. This is also the question commonly shared by many young architects including Archigram and others around it." Isozaki Arata, "Ākiguramu gurūpu: Jōhō ni kangen sareta kenchiku" [Archigram: Architecture reduced to information], *Bijutsu techō* [Art notebook] 324 (February 1970): 177.

67. Isozaki Arata and Tōno Yoshiaki, "'Kankyō' ni tsuite" [On 'environment'], in "Kūkan kara kankyō e" [From space to environment], special issue, *Bijutsu Techō* [Art notebook] 275 (November 1966): 100.

68. Throughout the 1960s, the construction of multimedia installations and environmental artwork that allowed interactive and participatory experience through feedback loops became the locus of experimentation among artists as well as architects in Japan. The use of video was particularly important for creating feedback loops. See Sas, "By Other Hands," 383–415; David Joselit, *Feedback: Television against Democracy* (Cambridge, MA: MIT Press, 2007); and Fred Turner, *The Democratic Surround: Multimedia and American Liberalism from World War II to the Psychedelic Sixties* (Berkeley: University of California Press, 2014). Crucial to this collective investment in interactivity and participation by avant-garde artists was the postwar reception of American communication theory along with cybernetics. For more on the Japanese reception of communication theory, see Furuhata, "Architecture as Atmospheric Media."

69. Isozaki Arata, "Toshi dezain no hōhō" [Methods of urban design], in Isozaki, *Kūkan e* [To space], 106; Isozaki Arata, "Invisible City," in *Architecture Cul-*

ture, 1943–1968: A Documentary Anthology, ed. Joan Ockman (New York: Columbia Books of Architecture, 1993), 405.

70. Isozaki Arata, "Yami no kūkan" [Space of darkness], in Isozaki, *Kūkan e* [To space], 151.

71. Isozaki Arata, "Yami no kūkan," 151.

72. Edwards, *Closed World*, 14. The era of simulation also signaled for Jean Baudrillard the end of the modernist order of mechanical reproduction. Writing around the same time as Isozaki, Baudrillard argued that the simulation of models—rather than serial products, which belonged to the second order of simulacra—ushered in the third order of simulacra that corresponded to the proliferation of codes. See Jean Baudrillard, *Symbolic Exchange and Death* (London: SAGE Publications, 1993), 56.

73. Isozaki Arata and Hino Naohiko, "*Kūkan e*; Omatsuri Hiroba, *Nihon no toshi kūkan*: 1960 nen dai ni okeru toshiron no hōhō o megutte" [To space, the Festival Plaza, and Japan's urban space: On the methods of urban theory from the 1960s], 10+1 45 (2006): 187–97.

74. Isozaki Arata, "Mienai toshi" [The invisible city], in Isozaki, *Kūkan e* [To space], 374. My translation. This first section of the essay has not been translated into English, though the second half has been translated under the same title, "Invisible City." See Isozaki, "Invisible City," 403–97.

75. Isozaki, "Mienai toshi," 378.

76. Isozaki, "Mienai toshi," 381.

77. Roquet, *Ambient Media*, 9–10. For more on the German concept of *Stimmung* ("mood" or "attunement"), which plays a central role in the German philosophical approach to atmosphere and ambience, see also Hans Ulrich Gumbrecht, *Atmosphere, Mood, Stimmung: On a Hidden Potential of Literature*, trans. Erik Butler (Stanford, CA: Stanford University Press, 2011).

78. "Biogode Purosesu happyōkai yori," *Japan Interior Design* 5, no. 47 (1967): 9.

79. Isozaki Arata, "Tekunorojī, geijutsu, taisei" [Technology, art, and the establishment], in *Isozaki Arata kenchiku ronshū 1*, 224.

80. Halpern, *Beautiful Data*, 4–5.

81. Tange Kenzō, *Ippon no enpitsu kara*, 211 (emphasis mine). He continues: "The dominant understanding [of urban planning] from the 1920s to the 1960s was functionalist, that is, the idea that space is there to serve a particular function. However, what we need in our informatized society [*jōhōka shakai*] is a structural understanding that space is a site of communication, which connects different functions. Before, space was regarded separate from things; rather, now relations between things develop because there is space" (211). This argument is reminiscent of Isozaki's own analysis of Tange and his approaches to urban planning.

82. Nicholas de Monchaux, *Spacesuit: Fashioning Apollo* (Cambridge, MA: MIT Press, 2011), 289.

83. Isozaki, "Tekunorojī, geijutsu, taisei," 224.

84. I borrow the phrase *cloud control* from the title of Seb Franklin's essay on

cloud computing and apply it to the cloud-based crowd control practice. See Seb Franklin, "Cloud Control, or the Network as Medium," *Cultural Politics* 8, no. 3 (2012): 443–64.

85. Vincent Mosco, *To the Cloud: Big Data in a Turbulent World* (Boulder, CO: Paradigm, 2014), 18.

86. Terebijon gijutsushi henshū iinkai, *Terebijon gijutsu shi* [A history of television technology] (Tokyo: Terebijon gakkai, 1971), 324.

87. "Hōmu ni kanshi terebi" [Surveillance cameras on the platform] *Asahi shinbun* [Asahi newspaper], October 16, 1962, 15.

88. "Kenka no genba kyacchi" [Catching the moment of fighting], *Asahi shinbun* [Asahi newspaper], February 15, 1962, 7.

89. Historically, regulatory mechanisms of security that target the population developed alongside, and worked in correlation with, disciplinary mechanisms that target individual conduct. The apparatus of closed-circuit television used for surveillance operates at both levels simultaneously—as an apparatus for managing individuals and organizing multiplicities alongside other techniques and mechanisms. More than the disciplinary effects, here I am especially interested in the articulation of the panoptic function of television with urban security.

90. Team Random, "The General Plan," *Japan Architect* 133 (August 1967): 34.

91. Jeremy Baker, "Expo and the Future City," *Architectural Review* 142, no. 846 (1967): 152–53.

92. Terry Haig, "Elaborate Security System Designed to Protect Visitors at Expo," *Montreal Gazette*, April 28, 1967.

93. Noguchi Akimasa et al., "Bankokuhaku dēta tsūshin shisutemu shori puroguram" [The World's Fair's data communication system's processing program], in special issue on Expo '70, *Hitachi Hyōron* [Hitachi review] (1970): 70.

94. In addition to this technological setup for policing, ground security operations performed at Expo '70 deserve our attention as they helped develop new tactics and techniques for crowd control. The most salient case is "Operation Buffalo" (Baffarō sakusen), a military-inspired crowd control strategy that was specifically designed to prevent a possible stampede. For more on this, see Furuhata, "Multimedia Environments and Security Operations," 56–79.

95. Hashizume Shinya, ed., *Expo '70: Pabirion; Osaka Banpaku kōshiki memoriaru gaido* [Expo '70 pavilions: Official memorial guide for Osaka Expo] (Tokyo: Heibonsha, 2010), 105.

96. Osakafu keisatsu honbu [Osaka police headquarters], ed., *Nihon bankoku hakuran kai no keisatsu kiroku* [Police records for Japan's World's Fair] (Osaka: Naniwa Insatsu, 1971), 28. Immediately after Expo '70, Isozaki also criticized the negative effects that the excessive presence of security guards had on the Festival Plaza, which failed to serve as a space of spontaneous communication for visitors. See Isozaki Arata, "Tekunorojii, geijutsu, taisei" [Technology, art, and the establishment], in *Geijutsu no susume* [Recommendations for art], ed. Tōno Yoshiaki (Tokyo: Chikuma shobō, 1972), 161.

97. On the Shinjuku riots on Antiwar Day (October 21) and other mass protests

that took place in 1968, see Mainichi shinbunsha, *1968 nen gurafitii* [Graffiti of 1968] (Tokyo: Mainichi shinbunsha, 2010), 319.

98. Nihon Keibihoshō (now known as SECOM), the first private security service company in Japan, and now its largest, was established in 1962. The Tokyo Olympics Organizing Committee hired the company to guard the Olympic Village during the 1964 Tokyo Olympics. Media attention around its success helped spur the growth of the industry. By the mid-1970s, more than 1,900 private security firms were operating in Japan. Tanaka Tomohito, *Keibigyō no shakaigaku* [The sociology of the security-guard business] (Tokyo: Akashi shoten, 2009), 54.

99. H. T. Shimazaki, *Vision in Japanese Entrepreneurship: The Evolution of a Security Enterprise* (London: Routledge, 1992), 73–75.

100. "Milestones," SECOM, accessed July 16, 2016, http://www.secom.co.jp /english/corporate/vision/history.html.

101. SECOM home security, accessed August 4, 2020, https://www.secom.co.jp /homesecurity/goods/idf.html.

102. Following Gilbert Simondon, Michael Fisch analyzes the model of emergence used in the East Japan Railway Company's "Autonomous Decentralized Transport Operation Control System," which anticipates and responds to frequent suicides on Tokyo's commuter trains. See Michael Fisch, *An Anthropology of the Machine: Tokyo's Commuter Train Network* (Chicago: University of Chicago Press, 2018).

103. Impress Smart Grid Newsletter Editorial Department, "VPP Maikuro guriddo de jitsugen suru 'Higashimatsushima shi sumāto bousai eko taun,'" Impress Smart Grid Forum, accessed August 4, 2020, https://sgforum.impress.co.jp /article/3589.

104. Eli Binder, "Hong Kong Protesters Spy a New Enemy: Lampposts," *Wall Street Journal*, August 30, 2019.

CONCLUSION: **Explicating the Backgrounds**

1. For more on the works of Latai Taumoepeau and Olafur Eliasson, see Janine Randerson, *Weather as Medium: Toward a Meteorological Art* (Cambridge, MA: MIT Press, 2018).

2. McCormack, *Atmospheric Things*, 210.

3. Sloterdijk, *Terror from the Air*, 107.

4. Sloterdijk, *Terror from the Air*, 50.

5. Sloterdijk, *Terror from the Air*, 79.

6. Paul N. Edwards, "Infrastructure and Modernity: Force, Time, and Social Organization in the History of Sociotechnical Systems," in *Modernity and Technology*, ed. Thomas J. Misa, Philip Brey, and Andrew Feenberg (Cambridge, MA: MIT Press, 2003), 185.

7. Peters, *Marvelous Clouds*, 35.

8. Peters, *Marvelous Clouds*, 33.

9. Ahmed writes, "Husserl's approach to the background as what is 'unseen' in its 'thereness' or 'familiarity' allows us to consider how the familiar takes shape

by being unnoticed." Sara Ahmed, "Orientations Matter," in *New Materialisms: Ontology, Agency, and Politics*, ed. Diana Coole and Samantha Frost (Durham, NC: Duke University Press, 2010), 240.

10. Lisa Parks and Nicole Starosielski, introduction to Parks and Starosielski, *Signal Traffic*, 13 (emphasis mine).

11. See, for instance, Brian Larkin, *Signal and Noise: Media, Infrastructure, and Urban Culture in Nigeria* (Durham, NC: Duke University Press, 2000); Nicole Starosielski, *The Undersea Network* (Durham, NC: Duke University Press, 2015); Rahul Mukherjee, *Radiant Infrastructures: Media, Environment, and Cultures of Uncertainty* (Durham, NC: Duke University Press, 2020); and Joshua Neves, *Underglobalization: Beijing's Media Urbanism and the Chimera of Legitimacy* (Durham, NC: Duke University Press, 2020).

12. Foucault, "Nietzsche, Genealogy, History," 76–100.

13. The philosophical work of Félix Guattari, who draws on the work of Gregory Bateson in order to extend the idea of ecology to the realms of socioeconomic conditions and human subjectivity in *The Three Ecologies* (*Les trois écologies*, Paris: Édition Galilée, 1989) (English trans., London: Bloomsbury, 2005) is also important in this context. See also Matthew Fuller, *Media Ecologies: Materialist Energies in Art and Technoculture* (Cambridge, MA: MIT Press, 2005); and Thomas Lamarre, *The Anime Ecology: A Genealogy of Television, Animation, and Game Media* (Minneapolis: University of Minnesota Press, 2018). Within Japanese studies, Alexander Zahlten and Franz Prichard also use the notion of media ecology to highlight the connections, circulations, and distributions of multiple media forms in their analyses of Japanese film, literature, and media. See Alexander Zahlten, *The End of Japanese Cinema: Industrial Genres, National Times, and Media Ecologies* (Durham, NC: Duke University Press, 2017); and Franz Prichard, *Residual Futures: The Urban Ecologies of Literary and Visual Media of 1960s and 1970s Japan* (New York: Columbia University Press, 2019).

14. Ursula Heise, "Unnatural Ecologies: The Metaphor of the Environment in Media Theory," *Configurations* 10, no. 1 (winter 2002): 149–68.

15. Umesao Tadao, *Bunmei no seitaishi kan* [An ecological view of the history of civilization] (Tokyo: Chūōkōronsha, 1967). The original essays were published in the journal *Chūō kōron* (Central Review) in 1957. Predating the spread of the American ecosystem ecology thinking, which Howard and Eugene Odum developed through their analysis of the ecological impact of nuclear radiation in the Pacific Islands, Umesao's understanding of ecology drew on the earlier work of Imanishi Kinji and the American ecologist Frederic Clements.

16. Instead of privileging competition and natural selection as the basis of evolution, Imanishi argued for peaceful cohabitation and coevolution of different species based on their subjective responses to their given environments. This is why Imanishi's theory is often called anti-Darwinian. For more on Imanishi's view of symbiosis and habitat segregation, see Imanishi Kinji, *A Japanese View of Nature: The World of Living Things*, trans. Pamela J. Asquith, Heita Kawakatsu, Shusuke Yagi, and Hiroyuki Takasaki (London: Routledge, 2002).

17. For more on the Japanese discourse on the term *environment* (*kankyō*), see Furuhata, "Multimedia Environments and Security Operations," 56–79.

18. Katō Hidetoshi, Komatsu Sakyō, Umesao Tadao, Hayashi Yūjirō, and Kawazoe Noboru, "Jōhōron no kadai" [Challenges of the information theory], in *Gendai ni ikiru: Jōhō kankyō kara no chosen* [Living in the contemporary time: Challenges from the information environment], ed. Katō Hidetoshi (Tokyo: Tōyō keizai hinhōsha, 1971), 253.

19. Katō Hidetoshi et al., "Jōhōron no kadai," 253, 259–60. Unrelated to Umesao's group's conceptualization of information ecology, the concept of "information ecology" is used by the anthropologists Bonnie Nardi and Vicki O'Day to describe social interactions among people mediated by technology in a particular local environment. Their examples of information ecologies include a library, a hospital intensive care unit, and a self-service copy shop. Bonnie A. Nardi and Vicki L. O'Day, *Information Ecologies: Using Technology with Heart* (Cambridge, MA: MIT Press, 1999), 49.

20. DeLoughrey, "Myth of Isolates," 167–84.

21. Resilience means "the capacity of a system to change in periods of intense external perturbation and thus to persist over longer time periods." Halpern, Mitchell, and Geoghegan, "Smartness Mandate," 122. On the historical connection between the concept of the ecosystem and resilience, see also Thomas Pringle, "The Ecosystem Is an Apparatus: From Machinic Ecology to the Politics of Resilience," in *Machine*, by Thomas Pringle, Gertrude Koch, and Bernard Stiegler (Minneapolis: University of Minnesota Press, 2019), 49–103.

22. For the analysis of the use of the concept of ecosystem and the metaphor of "platform" applied to digital media industries, see Marc Steinberg, *The Platform Economy: How Japan Transformed the Consumer Internet* (Minneapolis: University of Minnesota Press, 2019), 138.

Adey, Peter. "Air's Affinities: Geopolitics, Chemical Affect and the Force of the Elemental." *Dialogues in Human Geography* 5, no. 1 (2015): 54–75.

Adey, Peter, and Ben Anderson. "Anticipation, Materiality, Event: The Icelandic Ash Cloud Disruption and the Security of Mobility." *Mobilities* 6, no. 1 (2011): 11–23.

Ahmed, Sara. "Orientations Matter." In *New Materialisms: Ontology, Agency, and Politics*, edited by Diana Coole and Samantha Frost, 234–57. Durham, NC: Duke University Press, 2010.

Anchordoguy, Marie. *Computers, Inc.: Japan's Challenge to IBM*. Cambridge, MA: Harvard University Press, 1989.

Anderson, Ben. "Affective Atmospheres." *Emotion, Space and Society* 2, no. 2 (2009): 77–81.

Anderson, Katharine. *Predicting the Weather: Victorians and the Science of Meteorology*. Chicago: University of Chicago Press, 2005.

Arima Tetsuo. *Kōshite Terebi wa hajimatta: Senryō, reisen, saigunbi no hazama de* [This is how television started: Between the Occupation, the Cold War, and remilitarization]. Tokyo: Mineruva shobō, 2013.

Ariyama Teruo. *Jōhō haken to teikoku Nihon II: Tsūshin gijutsu no kakudai to senden sen* [The information hegemony and Imperial Japan II: The expansion of telecommunication technology and the propaganda war]. Tokyo: Yoshikawa Kōbunkan, 2013.

Axel, Nick, Daniel A. Barber, Nikolaus Hirsch, and Anton Vidokle. "Editorial: Accumulation." *e-flux: architecture*. Accessed August 9, 2019. https://www.e-flux.com/architecture/accumulation/100048/editorial/.

Azuma, Hideki. *Tokyo no toshi keikakuka: Takayama Eika* [The urban planner of Tokyo: Takayama Eika]. Tokyo: Kajima shuppan, 2010.

Azuma Hiroki. *Hihyō no seishin bunseki: Azuma Hiroki korekushon D* [A psychoanalysis of criticism: Azuma Hiroki collection D]. Tōkyō: Kōdansha, 2007.

Baker, Jeremy. "Expo and the Future City." *Architectural Review* 142, no. 846 (1967): 152–53.

Banham, Reyner. *The Architecture of the Well-Tempered Environment*. Chicago: University of Chicago Press, 1969.

Bao, Weihong. "Archaeology of a Medium: The (Agri)Cultural Techniques of a Paddy Film Farm." *boundary 2* 49, no. 1 (forthcoming 2022).

Bao, Weihong. *Fiery Cinema: The Emergence of an Affective Medium in China, 1915–1945*. Minneapolis: University of Minnesota Press, 2015.

Barber, Daniel A. *Modern Architecture and Climate: Design before Air-Conditioning*. Princeton, NJ: Princeton University Press, 2020. Kindle edition.

Baudrillard, Jean. *Symbolic Exchange and Death*. London: SAGE Publications, 1993.

Beer, Stafford. *Management Science: The Business Use of Operations Research*. New York: Doubleday, 1968.

Bell, Daniel. *The Coming of the Post-Industrial Society: A Venture in Social Forecasting*. New York: Basic Books, 1973.

Best, Steven, and Douglas Kellner. *The Postmodern Turn*. New York: Guilford Press, 1997.

"Biogode Purosesu happyōkai yori." *Japan Interior Design* 5, no. 47 (1967): 9.

Boulding, Kenneth. "The Economics of the Coming Spaceship Earth." In *Environmental Quality in a Growing Economy*, edited by H. Jarrett, 1–14. Baltimore, MD: published for Resources for the Future by Johns Hopkins University Press, 1966.

Braun, Marta. *Picturing Time: The Work of Etienne-Jules Marey (1830–1904)*. Chicago: University of Chicago Press, 1992.

Brockway, Lucile H. *Science and Colonial Expansion: The Role of the British Royal Botanical Gardens*. New Haven, CT: Yale University Press, 2002.

Brodey, Warren M. "The Design of Intelligent Environment: Soft Architecture." *Landscape* 17, no. 1 (autumn 1967): 8–12.

Calinescu, Matei. *Five Faces of Modernity: Modernism, Avant-Garde, Decadence, Kitsch, Postmodernism*. Durham, NC: Duke University Press, 1987.

Calvert, Will. "Kyocera to Build Snow-Cooled Data Center, Fully Powered by Renewable Energy." Data Center Dynamics. April 5, 2019. https://www.data centerdynamics.com/news/kyocera-build-snow-cooled-data-center-fully -powered-renewable-energy/.

Carrier Corporation. Accessed May 23, 2018. https://www.carrier.com /container-refrigeration/en/worldwide/about-carrier/willis-carrier/.

Casetti, Francesco. *The Lumière Galaxy: Seven Key Words for the Cinema to Come*. New York: Columbia University Press, 2015.

Chandler, Alfred D., Jr. *Inventing the Electronic Century: The Epic Story of the Consumer Electronics and Computer Industries*. New York: Free Press, 2001.

Chang, Jiat-Hwee. *A Genealogy of Tropical Architecture: Colonial Networks, Nature and Technoscience*. London: Routledge, 2016.

Chang, Jiat-Hwee. "Thermal Comfort and Climatic Design in the Tropics: An Historical Critique." *Journal of Architecture* 21, no. 8 (2016): 1171–202.

Cho, Hyunjung. "Competing Futures: War Narratives in Postwar Japanese Architecture 1945–1970." PhD diss., University of Southern California, 2011.

Cho, Hyunjung. "Hiroshima Peace Memorial Park and the Making of Japanese Postwar Architecture." *Journal of Architectural Education* 66, no. 1 (2012): 72–83.

Choy, Timothy. *Ecologies of Comparison: An Ethnography of Endangerment in Hong Kong*. Durham, NC: Duke University Press, 2011.

Chun, Wendy Hui Kyong. *Programmed Visions: Software and Memory*. Cambridge, MA: MIT Press, 2011.

Clark, Brett, and Richard York. "Carbon Metabolism: Climate Change, and the Biospheric Rift." *Theory and Society* 34, no. 4 (August 2005): 391–428.

Clark, Brett, and Stefano B. Longo. "Land-Sea Ecological Rifts." *Monthly Review: An Independent Socialist Magazine*, July 1, 2018. https://monthlyreview.org/2018/07/01/land-sea-ecological-rifts/.

Cooper, Melinda. "Turbulent Worlds: Financial Markets and Environmental Crisis." *Theory, Culture and Society* 27, no. 2–3 (2010): 167–90.

Cowen, Deborah. *The Deadly Life of Logistics: Mapping Violence in Global Trade*. Minneapolis: University of Minnesota Press, 2014.

Crowley, David. "Looking Down on Spaceship Earth: Cold War Landscapes." In David Crowley and Jane Pavitt, *Cold War Modern: Design 1945–1970*, 249–67. London: V&A, 2008.

Crutzen, Paul J. "Albedo Enhancement by Stratospheric Sulfur Injections: A Contribution to Resolve a Policy Dilemma?" *Climate Change* 77, no. 3–4 (2006): 211–19.

Daggett, Cara New. *The Birth of Energy: Fossil Fuels, Thermodynamics, and the Politics of Work*. Durham, NC: Duke University Press, 2019.

"Data Center Uses MeeFog System." Mee Industries Inc. Accessed April 5, 2019. http://www.meefog.com/case-studies-post/data-center/data-center-uses-meefog-system-keep-operating-heat-wave/.

Davis, Heather. "Life and Death in the Anthropocene: A Short History of Plastic." In *Art in the Anthropocene: Encounters among Aesthetics, Politics, Environments and Epistemologies*, edited by Heather Davis and Etienne Turpin, 347–58. London: Open Humanities Press, 2015.

Davis, Heather. *Plastic Matter*. Durham, NC: Duke University Press, 2022.

"Deep Thunder: Icons of Progress." IBM. Accessed May 20, 2018. http://www-03.ibm.com/ibm/history/ibm100/us/en/icons/deepthunder/.

DeLoughrey, Elizabeth M. "The Myth of Isolates: Ecosystem Ecologies in the Nuclear Pacific." *Cultural Geographies* 20, no. 2 (April 2013): 167–84.

de Monchaux, Nicholas. *Spacesuit: Fashioning Apollo*. Cambridge, MA: MIT Press, 2011.

Department of Architecture, Chinese University of Hong Kong. "Feasibility Study for Establishment of Air Ventilation Assessment System." November 2005. Accessed March 9, 2019. https://www.pland.gov.hk/pland_en/p_study/comp_s/avas/papers&reports/final_report.pdf.

"Development of Image-Analysis Technology with AI for Real-Time People-Detection and Tracking." News release. Hitachi Applications, Inc. March 27, 2017. http://www.hitachi.com/New/cnews/month/2017/03/170327.html.

Duguet, Anne-Marie. "Naturally Artificial." In *Fujiko Nakaya: Fog, Kiri, Brouillard*, 20–48. Paris: Éditions Anarchive, 2012.

E.A.T.—The Story of Experiments in Art and Technology. Tokyo: NTT InterCommunication Center, 2003. Exhibition catalog.

Edwards, Paul N. *The Closed World: Computers and the Politics of Discourse in Cold War America*. Cambridge, MA: MIT Press, 1996.

Edwards, Paul N. "Infrastructure and Modernity: Force, Time, and Social Organization in the History of Sociotechnical Systems." In *Modernity and Technology*, edited by Thomas J. Misa, Philip Brey, and Andrew Feenberg, 185–225. Cambridge, MA: MIT Press, 2003.

Edwards, Paul N. *A Vast Machine: Computer Models, Climate Data, and the Politics of Global Warming*. Cambridge, MA: MIT Press, 2013.

Esposito, Roberto. *Bios: Biopolitics and Philosophy*. Minneapolis: University of Minnesota Press, 2008.

"Facebook Uses MeeFog System to Achieve Free Cooling in Datacenter." Mee Industries Inc. Accessed September 25, 2020. http://www.meefog.com/case -studies-post/data-center/facebook/.

Feigenbaum, Anna. *Tear Gas: From the Battlefields of World War I to the Streets of Today*. London: Verso, 2017.

Feigenbaum, Anna, and Anja Kanngieser. "For a Politics of Atmospheric Governance." *Dialogues in Human Geography* 5, no. 1 (2015): 80–84.

Fisch, Michael. *An Anthropology of the Machine: Tokyo's Commuter Train Network*. Chicago: University of Chicago Press, 2018.

Fleming, James Rodger. *Fixing the Sky: The Checkered History of Weather and Climate Control*. New York: Columbia University Press, 2010.

Foer, Franklin. "Jeff Bezos's Master Plan." *Atlantic*, November 2019. https://www .theatlantic.com/magazine/archive/2019/11/what-jeff-bezos-wants/598363/.

"Fog Wiped Out by Chemical Spray." *Popular Science*, October 1934.

Foster, John Bellamy. "Marx's Theory of Metabolic Rift: Classical Foundations for Environmental Sociology." *American Journal of Sociology* 105, no. 2 (September 1999): 366–405.

Foster, John Bellamy, and Paul Burkett. "The Dialectic of Organic/Inorganic Relations: Marx and the Hegelian Philosophy of Nature." *Organization and Environment* 13, no. 4 (December 2000): 403–25.

Foster, John Bellamy, and Paul Burkett. *Marx and the Earth: An Anti-Critique*. Chicago: Haymarket Books, 2017.

Foster, John Bellamy, Brett Clark, and Richard York. *The Ecological Rift: Capitalism's War on the Earth*. New York: Monthly Review Press, 2010.

Foucault, Michel. *The Birth of Biopolitics: Lectures at the Collège de France, 1978–1979*. Translated by Graham Burchell. New York: Palgrave Macmillan, 2008.

Foucault, Michel. *Discipline and Punish*. Translated by Alan Sheridan. New York: Vintage Books, 1995.

Foucault, Michel. "Nietzsche, Genealogy, History." In Rabinow, *Foucault Reader*, 76–100.

Foucault, Michel. *Security, Territory, and Population: Lectures at the Collège de France, 1977–1978*. Translated by Graham Burchell. New York: Palgrave Macmillan, 2007.

Foucault, Michel. "What Is Enlightenment?" In Rabinow, *Foucault Reader*, 32–50.

Franklin, Seb. "Cloud Control, or the Network as Medium." *Cultural Politics* 8, no. 3 (2012): 443–64.

Fujikane, Candace, and Jonathan Y. Okamura, eds. *Asian Settler Colonialism: From Local Governance to the Habits of Everyday Life in Hawai'i*. Honolulu: University of Hawai'i Press, 2008.

Fujikane, Candace. *Mapping Abundance for a Planetary Future: Kanaka Maoli and Critical Settler Cartographies in Hawai'i*. Durham, NC: Duke University Press, 2021.

Fuller, Buckminster. *Utopia or Oblivion*. Zurich: Lars Müller, 2008.

Fuller, Matthew. *Media Ecologies: Materialist Energies in Art and Technoculture*. Cambridge, MA: MIT Press, 2005.

Furuhata, Yuriko. "Architecture as Atmospheric Media: Tange Lab and Cybernetics." In Steinberg and Zahlten, *Media Theory in Japan*, 52–79.

Furuhata, Yuriko. *Cinema of Actuality: Avant-Garde Filmmaking in the Season of Image Politics*. Durham, NC: Duke University Press, 2013.

Furuhata, Yuriko. "Multimedia Environments and Security Operations: Expo '70 as a Laboratory of Governance." *Grey Room* 54 (winter 2014): 56–79.

Furuhata, Yuriko. "Of Dragons and Geoengineering: Rethinking Elemental Media." *Media+Environment* 1, no. 1 (2019). https://doi.org/10.1525/001c.10797.

Furuhata, Yuriko. "Archipelagic Archives: Media Geology and the Deep Time of Japan's Settler Colonialism." *Public Culture* 33, no. 3 (forthcoming 2021).

Furukawa Takehiko. *Hito to gijutsu de kataru tenki yohōshi: Sūchi yohō o hiraita 'kin'iro no kagi'* [A history of weather forecasting focusing on people and technology: "A golden key" to the development of numerical weather prediction]. Tokyo: Tokyo daigaku shuppankai, 2012.

Furukawa Takehiko. *Kishōchō monogatari: Tenki yohō kara jishin, tsunami, kazan made* [The tale of the Japan Meteorological Agency: From weather forecasting to earthquakes, tsunamis, and volcanos]. Tokyo: Chūkō shinsho, 2015.

Gabrys, Jennifer. "Shipping and Receiving: Circuits of Disposal and the 'Social Death' of Electronics." In *Digital Rubbish: A Natural History of Electronics*, 74–98. Ann Arbor: University of Michigan Press, 2013.

Galison, Peter. *Image and Logic: A Material Culture of Microphysics*. Chicago: University of Chicago Press, 1997.

Galison, Peter. "The Ontology of the Enemy: Norbert Wiener and the Cybernetic Vision." *Critical Inquiry* 21, no. 1 (autumn 1994): 228–66.

Gardner, William O. "The 1970 Osaka Expo and/as Science Fiction." *Review of Japanese Culture and Society* 23 (December 2011): 26–43.

Gardner, William O. *The Metabolist Imagination: Visions of the City in Postwar Japanese Architecture and Science Fiction*. Minneapolis: University of Minnesota Press, 2020.

Gates, Kelly A. *Our Biometric Future: Facial Recognition Technology and the Culture of Surveillance*. New York: New York University Press, 2011.

"Geoengineering the Planet? More Scientists Now Say It Must Be an Option." *Yale Environment 360*, May 29, 2019. https://e360.yale.edu/features /geoengineer-the-planet-more-scientists-now-say-it-must-be-an-option.

Geoghegan, Bernard Dionysius. "After Kittler: On the Cultural Techniques of Recent German Media Theory." *Theory, Culture and Society* 30, no. 6 (2013): 66–82.

Ghosh, Bishnupriya, and Bhaskar Sarkar. "Media and Risk: An Introduction." In *The Routledge Companion to Media and Risk*, edited by Bishnupriya Ghosh and Bhaskar Sarkar, 1–24. New York: Routledge, 2020.

Gissen, David. *Manhattan Atmospheres: Architecture, the Interior Environment, and Urban Crisis*. Minneapolis: University of Minnesota Press, 2013.

Goodman, Steve. *Sonic Warfare: Sound, Affect, and Ecology of Fear*. Cambridge, MA: MIT Press, 2012.

Gordon, Colin. "Governmental Rationality: An Introduction." In *The Foucault Effect: Studies in Governmentality*, edited by Graham Burchell, Colin Gordon, and Peter Miller, 1–51. Chicago: University of Chicago Press, 1991.

Gotō Shinpei. *Seiden: Gotō Shinpei, Mantetsu jidai 1906–1908* [The authentic biography: Gotō Shinpei, the Manchurian railroad period 1906–1908]. Vol. 4. Tokyo: Fujiwara shoten, 2005.

Graeber, David. *The Utopia of Rules: On Technology, Stupidity, and the Secret Joys of Bureaucracy*. New York: Melville House, 2015.

Grove, Jairus Victor. *Savage Ecology: War and Geopolitics at the End of the World*. Durham, NC: Duke University Press, 2019.

Guattari, Félix. *Les trois écologies*. Paris: Édition Galilée, 1989.

Guattari, Félix. *The Three Ecologies*. London: Bloomsbury, 2005.

Gulliver, Shuzo Azuchi. "Flying Focus." In *Ekusupandeddo shinema saikō/Japanese Expanded Cinema Reconsidered*. Tokyo: Tokyo Shashin Bijutsukan, 2017. Exhibition catalog.

Gumbrecht, Hans Ulrich. *Atmosphere, Mood, Stimmung: On a Hidden Potential of Literature*. Translated by Erik Butler. Stanford, CA: Stanford University Press, 2011.

Halpern, Orit. *Beautiful Data: A History of Vision and Reason since 1945*. Durham, NC: Duke University Press, 2014.

Halpern, Orit. "Hopeful Resilience." *e-flux: architecture*. Accessed June 27, 2018. http://www.e-flux.com/architecture/accumulation/96421/hopeful-resilience/.

Halpern, Orit, Robert Mitchell, and Bernard Dionysius Geoghegan. "The Smartness Mandate: Notes toward a Critique." *Grey Room* 68 (summer 2017): 106–29.

Hamilton, Clive. *Earthmasters: The Dawn of the Age of Climate Engineering*. New Haven, CT: Yale University Press, 2013.

Hansen, Mark B. N. *Feed-Forward: On the Future of Twenty-First-Century Media*. Chicago: University of Chicago Press, 2015.

Harada, Masazumi. "Minamata Disease: Methylmercury Poisoning in Japan Caused by Environmental Pollution." *Critical Reviews in Toxicology* 25, no. 1 (1995): 1–24.

Harootunian, Harry. *Overcome by Modernity: History, Culture, and Community in Interwar Japan*. Princeton, NJ: Princeton University Press, 2000.

Harper, Kristine C. *Make It Rain: State Control of the Atmosphere in Twentieth-Century America*. Chicago: University of Chicago Press, 2017.

Harper, Kristine C. *Weather by the Numbers: The Genesis of Modern Meteorology.* Cambridge, MA: MIT Press, 2008.

Harper, Kristine C., and Ronald E. Doel. "Environmental Diplomacy in the Cold War: Weather Control, the United States, and India, 1966–1967." In *Environmental Histories of the Cold War,* edited by J. R. McNeill and Corinna R. Unger, 115–37. Cambridge: Cambridge University Press, 2010.

Harwood, John. *The Interface: IBM and the Transformation of Corporate Design, 1945–1976.* Minneapolis: University of Minnesota Press, 2011.

Hashizume Shinya, ed. *Expo '70: Pabirion; Osaka Banpaku kōshiki memoriaru gaido* [Expo '70 pavilions: Official memorial guide for Osaka Expo]. Tokyo: Heibonsha, 2010.

Hayashi Makoto. *Tenmonkata to onmyōdō* [Astronomers and onmyōdō]. Tokyo: Yamakawa shuppan, 2006.

Hayashi Shūji. *Ryūtsū kakumei: Seihin, keiro, oyobi shōhisha* [A revolution in distribution: Products, pathways, and consumers]. Tokyo: Chūō kōron shinsho, 1962.

Hayashi Yūjirō. *Jōhōka shakai: hādo na shakai kara sofuto na shakai e* [The information society: From a hard society to a soft society]. Tokyo: Kōdansha, 1969.

Hayashi Yūjirō, and Kagaku Gijutsu to Keizai no Kai, eds. *Chō gijutsu shakai e no tenkai: Jōhōka shisutemu no ningen* [Developing a supertechnological society: Humans in the information system]. Tokyo: Daiyamondo sha, 1969.

Hayles, Katherine. "Cybernetics." In *Critical Terms for Media Studies.* Edited by W. J. T. Mitchell and Mark B. N. Hansen. Chicago: University of Chicago Press, 2010.

Heidegger, Martin. *Basic Writings.* Edited by David Farrell Krell. New York: HarperCollins, 1993.

Heidegger, Martin. *What Is a Thing?* Translated by W. B. Barton and V. Deutsch. South Bend, IN: Gateway Editions, 1967.

Heise, Ursula. "Unnatural Ecologies: The Metaphor of the Environment in Media Theory." *Configurations* 10, no. 1 (winter 2002): 149–68.

Higashi Akira. *Yuki to kōri no kagakusha Nakaya Ukichirō* [Snow and ice scientist Nakaya Ukichirō]. Sapporo: Hokkaidō daigaku tosho kankōkai, 1997.

Higuchi Keiji. *Chikyū kara no hassō* [Ideas that come from Earth]. Tokyo: Asahi bunko, 1991.

Hinterwaldner, Inge. "Parallel Lines as Tools for Making Turbulence Visible." *Representations* 124, no. 1 (fall 2013): 1–42.

Hirano, Katsuya. "Settler Colonialism in the Making of Japan's Hokkaidō." In *The Routledge Handbook of the History of Settler Colonialism,* edited by Edward Cavanagh and Lorenzo Veracini, 351–62. Abingdon, UK: Taylor and Francis, 2016.

Hirata Keiichirō. Preface to *Konpyūta hakusho* [White Paper on computers] edited by Nihon Denshi Keisan Kaihatsu Kyōkai [Japan Association for Development of Digital Computers]. Tokyo: Nihon denshi keisan kaihatsu kyōkai, 1965.

Hirose Mami, Sasaki Hitomi, Maeda Naotake, Tagomori Miho, Tamayama Ami, and Yoshida Yuri, eds. *Metaborizumu no mirai toshi ten: Sengo Nihon, ima yomigaeru fukkō no yume to bijon* [Metabolism, the city of the future: Dreams and visions of reconstruction in postwar and present-day Japan]. Tokyo: Shinkenchikusha, 2011. Exhibition catalog.

"Hitachi Room Air Conditioner 'Stainless Clean Shirokuma-kun' New E Series/ W Series/G Series Products to Include 'Frost Wash' Technology." April 27, 2018. http://www.jci-hitachi.com/about/news/20180427news.

Hoang, Phu. "Can You Believe the Weather We're Having? The Politics of the Weather Report." In *Climates: Architecture and the Planetary Imaginary*, edited by James Graham, 252–60. Zurich: Lars Müller, 2016.

Hogan, Mél. "Facebook Data Storage Centers as the Archive's Underbelly." *Television and New Media* 16, no. 1 (2015): 3–18. https://doi.org/10.1177/1527476 413509415.

Holmes, Michael D. "Driving the World's Most Accurate Weather Forecasts." IBM. December 21, 2016. https://www.ibm.com/blogs/think/2016/12/accurate -weather-forecasts/.

Holt, Jennifer, and Patrick Vonderau. "'Where the Internet Lives': Data Centers as Cloud Infrastructure." In Parks and Starosielski, *Signal Traffic*, 71–93.

Hu, Tung-Hui. *A Prehistory of the Cloud*. Cambridge, MA: MIT Press, 2015.

Huhtamo, Erkki. "The Sky Is (Not) the Limit: Envisioning the Ultimate Public Media Display." *Journal of Visual Culture* 8, no. 3 (2009): 329–48.

Humphries, Matthew. "Sony's Reon Pocket Is a Wearable Air-Conditioner." *PC Reviews*, July 29, 2019.

Ikeda Shūichi. "Shōwa 10 nendai no Tokyo ni okeru shinyō shori" [The treatment of human waste in Tokyo during the second decade of the Shōwa era]. In *Toire: Haisetsu no kūkan kara miru Nihon no bunka to rekishi* [The toilet: Japanese culture and history seen from the space of excretion], edited by Shinyō Gesui Kenkyūkai, 142–47. Tokyo: Mineruva shobō, 2016.

Imanishi, Kinji. *A Japanese View of Nature: The World of Living Things*. Translated by Pamela J. Asquith, Heita Kawakatsu, Shusuke Yagi, and Hiroyuki Takasaki. London: Routledge, 2002.

Impress Smart Grid Newsletter Editorial Department. "VPP Maikuro guriddo de jitsugen suru 'Higashimatsushima shi sumāto bousai eko taun.'" Impress Smart Grid Forum. Accessed August 4, 2020. https://sgforum.impress.co.jp /article/3589.

Isozaki Arata. "Aatisuto-Aakitekuto no jidai: Osaka banpaku no sōzōryoku o hokan shita aato shin" [The era of an artist-architect: Art scenes that supplemented the imagination of the world's fair in Osaka]. Interview by Yasuko Imura, Yuriko Furuhata, and Shigeru Matsui. *Tokyo Geijutsu Daigaku Eizōkenkyū Kiyō* (October 2012): 36–80.

Isozaki Arata. "Ākiguramu gurūpu: Jōhō ni kangen sareta kenchiku" [Archigram: Architecture reduced to information]. *Bijutsu techō* [Art notebook] 324 (February 1970): 173–77.

Isozaki Arata. "Haikyo ron" [On ruins]. In *Kigō no umi ni ukabu "shima"* [Islands in the sea of signs], 24–40. Tokyo: Iwanami shoten, 2013.

Isozaki Arata. "Invisible City." In *Architecture Culture, 1943–1968: A Documentary Anthology*, edited by Joan Ockman, 403–97. New York: Columbia Books of Architecture, 1993.

Isozaki Arata. *Kenchiku ni okeru 'Nihon teki na mono'* ["Japaneseness" in architecture]. Tokyo: Shinchōsha, 2003.

Isozaki Arata. *Kenchiku no kaitai* [Dismantling architecture]. Tokyo: Bijutsu shuppansha, 1975.

Isozaki Arata. *Kūkan e* [To space]. Tokyo: Kajima shuppankai, 1997.

Isozaki Arata. "Mienai toshi" [The invisible city]. In Isozaki, *Kūkan e* [To space], 370–94.

Isozaki Arata. "Tange Kenzō no 'kenchiku=toshi=kokka' kyōdōtai to shite no Nihon" [Japan as the "architectural=urban=state" community in Tange Kenzō]. In *Isozaki Arata kenchiku ronshū 1: Sanshu sareta modanizumu: 'Nihon' to iu mondai kikō* [Collected architectural essays of Isozaki Arata volume 1: Disseminated modernism: The problematic called "Japan"], edited by Yokote Yoshihiro, 173–202. Tokyo: Iwanami shoten, 2013.

Isozaki Arata. "Tekunorojīi, geijutsu, taisei" [Technology, art, and the establishment]. In *Geijutsu no susume* [Recommendations for art], edited by Tōno Yoshiaki, 127–70. Tokyo: Chikuma shobō, 1972.

Isozaki Arata. "Tekunorojīi, geijutsu, taisei" [Technology, art, and the establishment]. In *Isozaki Arata kenchiku ronshū 1: Sanshu sareta modanizumu* [Collected architectural essays of Isozaki Arata volume 1: Disseminated modernism: The problematic called "Japan"], edited by Yokote Yoshihiro, 215–25. Tokyo: Iwanami shoten, 2013.

Isozaki Arata. "Toshi dezain no hōhō" [Methods of urban design]. In Isozaki, *Kūkan e* [To space], 88–121.

Isozaki Arata. "Yami no kūkan" [Space of darkness]. In Isozaki, *Kūkan e* [To space], 136–54.

Isozaki Arata and Hino Naohiko. "*Kūkan e*, Omatsuri Hiroba, *Nihon no toshi kūkan*: 1960 nen dai ni okeru toshiron no hōhō o megutte" [To space, the Festival Plaza, and Japan's urban space: On the methods of urban theory from the 1960s]. *10+1* 45 (2006): 187–97.

Isozaki Arata and Hino Naohiko. "Taaning pointo: Kūkan kara kankyō e" [Turning point: From space to environment]. *10+1* 48 (2007): 193–205.

Isozaki Arata and Tōno Yoshiaki. "'Kankyō' ni tsuite" [On 'environment']. In "Kūkan kara kankyō" [From space to environment]. Special issue, *Bijutsu Techō* [Art notebook] 275 (November 1966): 91–105.

Isozaki Atelier. "Sofuto aakitekuchua: Ōtōba to shite no kankyō" [Soft architecture: The environment as a response field]. *Kenchiku bunka* [Architectural culture] 279 (January 1970): 73–78.

Jankovic, Vladimir. *Reading the Sky: A Cultural History of English Weather, 1650–1820*. Chicago: University of Chicago Press, 2000.

Jennings, Eric T. *Curing the Colonizers: Hydrotherapy, Climatology, and French Colonial Spas*. Durham, NC: Duke University Press, 2006.

Jeska, Simone. *Transparent Plastics: Design and Technology*. Basel: Birkhäuser, 2008.

Johnson, Alix. "Data Centers as Infrastructural In-Betweens: Expanding Connections and Enduring Marginalities in Iceland." *American Ethnologist* 46, no. 1 (2019): 74–88.

Johnson, Chalmers. MITI *and the Japanese Miracle: The Growth of Industrial Policy, 1925–1975*. Stanford, CA: Stanford University Press, 1982.

Joselit, David. *Feedback: Television against Democracy*. Cambridge, MA: MIT Press, 2007.

Jue, Melody. "Vampire Squid Media." *Grey Room* 57 (fall 2014): 82–105.

Jue, Melody. *Wild Blue Media: Thinking through Seawater*. Durham, NC: Duke University Press, 2020.

Kahn, Douglas. *Earth Sound Earth Signal*. Berkeley: University of California Press, 2013.

Kamiya Kōji. "Ōyane" [Large roof]. *Shinkenchiku* [New architecture] 45, no. 5 (May 1970): 165–72.

Kankyōshō. *Kankyō Junkan gata shakai hakusho* [White Paper on the environmentally conscious recycling society]. Tokyo: Nikkei insatsu, 2008.

Karube Tadashi. "Teikoku no rinri: Gotō Shinpei ni okeru risō shugi" [An ethics of empire: The idealism of Gotō Shinpei]. In *Jidai no senkakusha: Gotō Shinpei, 1857–1929* [The pioneer of the era: Gotō Shinpei], edited by Mikuriya Takashi, 79–86. Tokyo: Fujiwara shoten, 2004.

Katagata Zenji. *Nihon IBM no keiei: Seichō yōin no tetteiteki kenkyū* [The management of IBM Japan: A complete study of its growth factors]. Tokyo: Nihon jitsugyō shuppansha, 1969.

Katō Hidetoshi, Komatsu Sakyō, Umesao Tadao, Hayashi Yūjirō, and Kawazoe Noboru. "Jōhōron no kadai" [Challenges of the information theory]. In *Gendai ni ikiru: Jōhō kankyō kara no chosen* [Living in the contemporary time: Challenges from the information environment], edited by Katō Hidetoshi, 219–87. Tokyo: Tōyō keizai hinhōsha, 1971.

Kawazoe Noboru. "Metaborisuto tachi to mananda toki to ima" [What I learned from the Metabolists then and now]. In Ōtaka and Kawazoe, *Metaborizumu to Metaborisuto tachi* [Metabolism and the Metabolists], 9–41. Tokyo: Bijutsu shuppan, 2005.

Keizai shingikai jōhō kenkyū iinkai [The Committee for the Economic Council for Information Studies]. *Nihon no Jōhōka shakai: Sono bijon to kadai* [Japan's information society: Its vision and challenges]. Tokyo: Daiyamondo sha, 1969.

"Kigyō muke no kishō jōhō teikyō sābisu o kaishi" [The start of the weather information service for businesses]. IBM. March 13, 2017. https://www-03.ibm.com/press/jp/ja/pressrelease/51820.wss.

Kitagawa Toshio. "Saibanetikusu no kōsei genri" [Principles of cybernetics]. In *Saibanetikusu: Kyōkai ryōiki to shite no kōsatsu* [Reflections on cybernetics as an interdisciplinary field], edited by Kitagawa Toshio, 1–25. Tokyo: Misuzu shobō, 1953.

Kitagawa Toshio. *Tōkei kagaku no sanjū nen: Waga shi waga tomo* [Thirty years of statistical science: My teachers and friends]. Tokyo: Kyōritsu shuppan, 1969.

Kitahara Yasusada. *Terekomu kakumei: Denden kōsha no INS kōsō o kataru* [A telecommunication revolution: Narrating the Nippon Telegraph and Telephone Public Corporation's vision of INS]. Tokyo: Tokuma shoten, 1983.

Kline, Ronald R. *The Cybernetics Moment: Or Why We Call Our Age the Information Age*. Baltimore, MD: Johns Hopkins University Press, 2015.

Klüver, Billy. "Atarashii taiken no ba: Pepshi kan no 'ikita kankyō'" [A place for novel experiences: Pepsi Pavilion's 'living environment']. Translated by Nakaya Fujiko. *Bijutsu techō* [Art notebook] (July 1970): 94–108.

Klüver, Billy. "The Pavilion." In Klüver, Martin, and Rose, *Pavilion*, ix–xvi.

Klüver, Billy, Julie Martin, and Barbara Rose, eds. *Pavilion: Experiments in Art and Technology*. New York: E. P. Dutton, 1972.

Kobayashi Hideo. *'Manshū' no rekishi* [A history of Manchuria]. Tokyo: Kōdansha gendai shinsho, 2008.

Kobayashi Hideo. *Mantetsu chōsabu: 'Ganso shinku tanku' no tanjō to hōkai* [The research department of the South Manchurian Railway Company: The birth and fall of "the original think tank"]. Tokyo: Heibonsha, 2005.

Kobayashi Hideo. "Teion Kenkyūjo o meguru gunji kenkyū" [Military research around the Institute of Low Temperature Science]. *Kokumin no kagaku* [Science of the National Citizens] 1 (March 1955): 19–25.

Koolhaas, Rem, and Hans Ulrich Obrist. *Project Japan: Metabolism Talks . . .* Edited by Kayoko Ota and James Westcott. Cologne: Taschen, 2011.

Koshizawa Akira. *Manshūkoku no shuto keikaku* [Planning the capital city of Manchuria]. Tokyo: Nihon keizai hyōron sha, 1988.

Kotler, Philip. "Atmospherics as a Marketing Tool." *Journal of Retailing* 49, no. 4 (winter 1973–74): 48–64.

Kōyama Ken'ichi. *Miraigaku nyūmon* [Introduction to futurology]. Tokyo: Ushio shinsho, 1967.

Kōyama Ken'ichi. "21 seiki no sekkei: Sousa kanō na mirai" [The Design for the 21st century: The manipulable future] *Ushio* [Tide] 80 (February 1967): 114–48.

Krauss, Rosalind. "Sculpture in the Expanded Field." *October* 8 (spring 1979): 30–44.

Krueger, Myron W. "Responsive Environments." In *The New Media Reader*, edited by Noah Wardrip-Fruin and Nick Monfront, 379–89. Cambridge, MA: MIT Press, 2003.

"'Kurashi kamera' tanjō sutōrī" [An origin story of life camera]. Hitachi Applications, Inc. Accessed June 27, 2018. https://kadenfan.hitachi.co.jp/ra/camera/hamada.html.

Kurokawa Kishō. *Jōhō rettō Nihon no shōrai* [The future of information archipelago Japan]. Tokyo: Dai san bunmei sha, 1972.

Kurokawa Kishō. "Jūtaku no mirai" [The future of housing]. In *Metaborizumu no hassō* [Ideas of Metabolism], 285–87. Tokyo: Hakuba shuppan, 1972.

Kurokawa Kishō. *Metaborizumu no hassō* [Ideas of Metabolism]. Tokyo: Hakuba shuppan, 1972.

Kurokawa Kishō. "Metaborizumu to kyōsei no shisō" [The Metabolist idea of symbiosis]. In Ōtaka and Kawazoe, *Metaborizumu to Metaborisuto tachi* [Metabolism and the Metabolists], 214–42.

Kurokawa Kishō. *Shin kyōsei no shisō* [A renewed idea of symbiosis]. Tokyo: Tokuma shoten, 1996.

Kurokawa Kishō. "Watashi no sumitai megaroporisu" [The megalopolis where I want to live]. In *Metaborizumu no hassō*, 256–58.

Lamarre, Thomas. *The Anime Ecology: A Genealogy of Television, Animation, and Game Media*. Minneapolis: University of Minnesota Press, 2018.

Larkin, Brian. *Signal and Noise: Media, Infrastructure, and Urban Culture in Nigeria*. Durham, NC: Duke University Press, 2000.

Lemke, Thomas. *Biopolitics: An Advanced Introduction*. New York: New York University Press, 2011.

Light, Jennifer S. *From Warfare to Welfare: Defense Intellectuals and Urban Problems in Cold War America*. Baltimore, MD: Johns Hopkins University Press, 2003.

Lin, Zhongjie. *Kenzo Tange and the Metabolist Movement: Urban Utopias of Modern Japan*. London: Routledge, 2010.

Lindgren, Nilo. "Into the Collaboration." In Klüver, Martin, and Rose, *Pavilion*, 3–59.

Livingstone, David N. "Race, Space, and Moral Climatology: Notes toward a Genealogy." *Journal of Historical Geography* 28, no. 2 (2002): 159–80.

Lloyd, Sarah Anne. "Inside the Amazon Spheres: The Plants, the Architecture, and a Transforming City." *Seattle Curbed*. January 30, 2018. https://seattle.curbed.com/2018/1/30/16947838/amazon-spheres-seattle-architecture-photos.

Lo, Andrea. "The Truth behind the Mysterious Holes in Hong Kong's High-Rises." CNN. March 28, 2018. https://www.cnn.com/style/article/hong-kong-skyscrapers-with-holes/index.html.

MacDonald, Scott. *A Critical Cinema 2: Interviews with Independent Filmmakers*. Berkeley: University of California Press, 1992.

Machimura Takashi. *Kaihatsu shugi no kōzō to shinsei* [The structure and disposition of developmentalism]. Tokyo: Ocha no mizu shobō, 2011.

Madeddu, Manuela, and Xiaoqing Zhang. "Harmonious Spaces: The Influence of Feng Shui on Urban Form and Design." *Journal of Urban Design* 22, no. 6 (2017): 709–25.

Mainichi shinbunsha. *1968 nen gurafitii* [Graffiti of 1968]. Tokyo: Mainichi shinbunsha, 2010.

Martin, Reinhold. *The Organizational Complex: Architecture, Media, and Corporate Space*. Cambridge, MA: MIT Press, 2003.

Marutschke, David. *Continuous Improvement Strategies: Japanese Convenience Store Systems*. Basingstoke, UK: Palgrave Macmillan, 2012.

Marvin, Carolyn. *When Old Technologies Were New: Thinking about Electric Com-*

munication in the Late Nineteenth Century. Oxford: Oxford University Press, 1988.

Marx, Karl. *Capital: A Critique of Political Economy.* Edited by Frederick Engels. Translated by Samuel Moore and Edward Aveling. Moscow: Progress. Accessed July 12, 2019. https://www.marxists.org/archive/marx/works/1867-c1/ch27 .htm.

Masco, Joseph. "Bad Weather: On Planetary Crisis." *Social Studies of Science* 40, no. 1 (February 2010): 7–40.

Masuda Yoneji. *Konpyūtopia: Konpyūta ga tsukuru shinjidai* [Computopia: A new era built by computers]. Tokyo: Daiyamondo sha, 1967.

Masuda Yoneji. *The Information Society as Post-Industrial Society.* Tokyo: Institute for the Information Society, 1980.

Matsuda Hiroyuki. *Meiji denshin denwa monogatari: Jōhō tsūshin shakai no 'gen fūkei'* [The tale of telegraphy and telephone in the Meiji era: the "original landscape" of the telecommunication society]. Tokyo: Nihon keizai hyōronsha, 2001.

Matsumoto Toshio. "Cross Talk/Intermedia" program. Tokyo, February 1969.

Mattelart, Armand. *The Invention of Communication.* Translated by Susan Emanuel. Minneapolis: University of Minnesota Press, 1996.

McCormack, Derek P. *Atmospheric Things: On the Allure of Elemental Envelopment.* Durham, NC: Duke University Press, 2019.

McLuhan, Marshall. *Understanding Media: The Extensions of Man.* Cambridge, MA: MIT Press, 1964.

Meadows, Donella H., Dennis L. Meadows, Jørgen Randers, and William W. Behrens III. *The Limits to Growth.* New York: Potomac Associates, 1972.

Medak-Saltzman, Danika. "Settler Colonialism and Phantasmagoria: On Asian, Asian Diaspora, and Indigenous Intersections." *Verge: Studies in Global Asias* 5, no. 1 (spring 2019): 39–46.

Medina, Eden. *Cybernetic Revolutionaries: Technology and Politics in Allende's Chile.* Cambridge, MA: MIT Press, 2011.

Mendieta, Eduardo. "A Letter on Überhumanismus." In *Sloterdijk Now,* edited by Stuart Elden, 58–76. Cambridge: Polity, 2012.

"Milestones." SECOM. Accessed July 16, 2016. http://www.secom.co.jp/english /corporate/vision/history.html.

Miller, Ian Jared. *The Nature of the Beasts: Empire and Exhibition at the Tokyo Imperial Zoo.* Berkeley: University of California Press, 2013.

Miyauchi Takahisa. "Kasōkan no juyō katei ni kansuru minzokugaku teki kenkyū oboegaki" [A folkloric research note on the reception process of house geomancy perspectives]. *Hikaku minzoku kenkyū* [Comparative folklore studies] 3 (March 1993): 214–29.

Mizutani Akihiro. "Tange Kenzō kenkyūshitsu no konpyūta riyō no saihyōka to sono kon'nichi teki igi ni tsuite" [A reevaluation of Tange Lab's use of digital computers and its contemporary significance]. *Nihon kenchiku gakkai kankyō kei ronbun shū* [The Architectural Institute of Japan's collection of research papers on the environment] 81, no. 735 (May 2016): 487–94.

Moon, Whitney. "Environmental Wind-Baggery." *e-flux: architecture*. Accessed July 3, 2019. https://www.e-flux.com/architecture/structural-instability /208703/environmental-wind-baggery/.

Moore, Jason W. "Transcending the Metabolic Rift: A Theory of Crises in the Capitalist World-Ecology. *Journal of Peasant Studies* 1, no. 38 (2011): 1–46.

Morris-Suzuki, Tessa. *Beyond Computopia: Information, Automation and Democracy in Japan*. London: Kegan Paul International, 1988.

Morton, Oliver. *The Planet Remade: How Geoengineering Could Change the World*. Princeton, NJ: Princeton University Press, 2016.

Mosco, Vincent. *To the Cloud: Big Data in a Turbulent World*. Boulder, CO: Paradigm, 2014.

Mukherjee, Rahul. *Radiant Infrastructures: Media, Environment, and Cultures of Uncertainty*. Durham, NC: Duke University Press, 2020.

Musselman, Elizabeth Green. *Nervous Conditions: Science and the Body Politic in Early Industrial Britain*. Albany: State University of New York Press, 2006.

Nakahara Yūsuke. "Shokkaku no fukken" [A revival of tactility]. *SD* 38 (January 1968): 33–36, 48.

Nakajima Naoto, Nishinari Norihisa, Hatsuda Kōsei, Sano Hiroyoshi, and Tsutsumi Takashi. *Toshi keikakuka Ishikawa Hideaki: Toshi kenkyū no kiseki.* [Urban planner Ishikawa Hideaki: A trajectory of urban studies]. Tokyo: Kajima shuppan, 2009.

Nakawada Minami and Atmosphere Ltd. *Expo '70: Kyōgaku Osaka hakurankai no subete* [Expo '70: Everything about the marvelous World's Fair in Osaka]. Tokyo: Daiyamondo sha, 2005.

Nakaya Fujiko. "Kūki to mizu" [Air and water]. Special issue on Expo '70. *Bijutsu techō* [Art notebook] (July 1970): 105–8.

Nakaya Fujiko. "Making of 'Fog' or Low-Hanging Stratus Cloud." In Klüver, Martin, and Rose, *Pavilion*, 207–23.

Nakaya Ukichirō. "Gunji kenkyū to wa nanika" [What is military research?]. *Hokudai kikan* [Hokkaidō University quarterly] (January 1955): 27–28.

Nakaya Ukichirō. "Manshū tsūshin" [Letters from Manchuria]. In *Nakaya Ukichirō kikō shū: Arasuka no hyōga* [A travelogue of Nakaya Ukichirō: Glaciers in Alaska], 41–51. Tokyo: Iwanami bunko, 2002.

Nakaya Ukichirō. *Yuki* [Snow]. Tokyo: Iwanami bunko, 1994.

Nakaya Ukichirō. "Yuki wa shigen de aru" [Snow is a resource]. Accessed August 8, 2019. https://www.aozora.gr.jp/cards/001569/files/57313_59463. html.

Nardi, Bonnie A., and Vicki L. O'Day. *Information Ecologies: Using Technology with Heart*. Cambridge, MA: MIT Press, 1999.

Negroponte, Nicholas. *Soft Architecture Machines*. Cambridge, MA: MIT Press, 1976.

Neves, Joshua. *Underglobalization: Beijing's Media Urbanism and the Chimera of Legitimacy*. Durham, NC: Duke University Press, 2020.

Nguyen, Viet Thanh, and Janet Hoskins. "Introduction: Transpacific Studies; Critical Perspectives on an Emerging Field." In *Transpacific Studies: Framing an Emerging Field*, edited by Janet Hoskins and Viet Thanh Nguyen, 1–38. Honolulu: University of Hawai'i Press, 2014.

Nieboer, Miranda, and Craig William McCormack. "Under Geodesic Skies: A Cultural Perspective on the Former South Pole Dome and Geodesic Domes in Outer Space." *Polar Journal* 7, no. 2 (2017): 351–73.

Nihon Denshi Keisan Kaihatsu Kyōkai [Japan Association for Development of Digital Computers]. *Konpyūta hakusho: MIS to konpyūta ūtiriti no shindōkō* [White Paper on the computer: New directions in MIS and computer utilities]. Tokyo: Nihon denshi keisan kaihatsu kyōkai, 1968.

Nihon Denshin Denwa Kōsha. *Nihon bankokuhaku to Denden kōsha* [Japan's World's Fair and the Nippon Telegraph and Telephone Public Corporation]. Osaka: Nihon Denshin Denwa Kōsha, 1970.

Noguchi Akimasa, Ōtaki Toshiro, Fukuoka Nobusada, Kurimoto Takeshi, Kanno Ayatomo, Kanayama Ken'ichirō, and Sumitomo Hiroshi. "Bankokuhaku dēta tsūshin shisutemu shori puroguram" [The World's Fair's data communication system's processing program]. Special issue on Expo '70. *Hitachi Hyōron* [Hitachi review] (1970): 70–72.

Nomura Takeshi and Ojima Toshio. "Chiiki reidanbō to dōmudo spēsu e no tenbō" [An outlook on regional air-conditioning and domed spaces]. *Shinkenchiku* [New architecture] 45, no. 8 (August 1970): 233–40.

Ojima Toshio. "Banpaku kaijō no jinkō kankyō: Chiiki reibō to sono riyō keikaku" [The World's Fair's artificial environment: Regional air-conditioning and plans for its use]. *Shinkenchiku* 45, no. 8 (August 1970): 284–85.

Ojima Toshio. "Chiiki reibō keikaku" [Plans for regional air-conditioning]. *Kenchiku zasshi* [Architecture magazine] 85, no. 1021 (March 1970): 227–29.

Ojima Toshio. "Jinkō kikō to ningen: Jinrui no han'ei ni machi ukeru kurepasu" [Artificial climate and humans: The pitfalls of humanity's prosperity]. *U.D.C.* 628.8.02 (November 1965): 751–52.

Okazaki Kenjirō. "The Lucid, Unclouded Fog—The Movement of Bright and Swinging Water Particles." In *Kiri no teikō/Resistance of Fog: Nakaya Fujiko ten*, 49–89. Tokyo: Firumu Āto, 2019.

Orville, Howard T. "Weather Made to Order?" *Collier's* magazine, May 28, 1954.

Osakafu keisatsu honbu [Osaka police headquarters], ed. *Nihon bankoku hakuran kai no keisatsu kiroku* [Police records for Japan's World's Fair]. Osaka: Naniwa Insatsu, 1971.

Ōtaka Masato and Kawazoe Noboru, eds. *Metaborizumu to Metaborisuto tachi* [Metabolism and the Metabolists]. Tokyo: Bijutsu shuppansha, 2005.

Ozaki Tetsuya. "Nakaya Fujiko + dNA: MU." *ART iT*. Accessed August 24, 2019. http://www.art-it.asia/u/admin_exrev/HsLPfgloEvCVG10BUwXu/.

Packer, Randall. "The Pepsi Pavilion: Laboratory for Social Experimentation." In *Future Cinema: The Cinematic Imaginary after Film*, edited by Jeffrey Shaw and Peter Weibel, 144–49. Cambridge, MA: MIT Press, 2003.

Papapetros, Spyros, and Julian Rose, eds. *Retracing the Expanded Field: Encounters between Art and Architecture*. Cambridge, MA: MIT Press, 2014.

Parikka, Jussi. "The Alchemic Digital, the Planetary Elemental." In *Subcommunity: Diabolical Togetherness beyond Contemporary Art*, edited by Julieta Aranda, Brian Kuan Wood, and Anton Vidokle, 341–47. *e-flux journal*. London: Verso, 2017.

Parikka, Jussi. *A Geology of Media*. Minneapolis: University of Minnesota Press, 2015.

Parks, Lisa. *Rethinking Media Coverage: Vertical Mediation and the War on Terror*. New York: Routledge, 2018.

Parks, Lisa, and Nicole Starosielski. Introduction to Parks and Starosielski, *Signal Traffic*, 1–28.

Parks, Lisa, and Nicole Starosielski, eds. *Signal Traffic: Critical Studies of Media Infrastructures*. Champaign: University of Illinois Press, 2015.

Peattie, Mark R. "The Japanese Colonial Empire, 1895–1945." In *The Cambridge History of Japan*, vol. 6, *The Twentieth Century*, edited by John Whitney Hall, 217–70. Cambridge: Cambridge University Press, 1988.

Peters, John Durham. *The Marvelous Clouds: Toward a Philosophy of Elemental Media*. Chicago: University of Chicago Press, 2016.

Philippopoulos-Mihalopoulos, Andreas. *Spatial Justice: Body, Lawscape, Atmosphere*. Oxfordshire, UK: Routledge, 2015.

Philippopoulos-Mihalopoulos, Andreas. "Withdrawing from Atmosphere: An Ontology of Air Partitioning and Affective Engineering." *Environment and Planning D: Society and Space* 34, no. 1 (February 2016): 150–67. https://doi.org/10.1177/0263775815600443.

Prichard, Franz. *Residual Futures: The Urban Ecologies of Literary and Visual Media of 1960s and 1970s Japan*. New York: Columbia University Press, 2019.

Pringle, Thomas. "The Ecosystem Is an Apparatus: From Machinic Ecology to the Politics of Resilience." In *Machine*, by Thomas Pringle, Gertrude Koch, and Bernard Stiegler, 49–103. Minneapolis: University of Minnesota Press, 2019.

Rabinow, Paul, ed. *The Foucault Reader*. New York: Pantheon Books, 1984.

Randerson, Janine. *Weather as Medium: Toward a Meteorological Art*. Cambridge, MA: MIT Press, 2018.

Reynolds, Roger. *Cross Talk Intermedia I*. Newsletter for Institute of Current World Affairs, May 10, 1969. Accessed March 18, 2017. http://www.icwa.org/wp-content/uploads/2015/11/PR-20.pdf.

Ritzer, George. *The McDonaldization of Society: An Investigation into the Changing Character of Contemporary Social Life*. Thousand Oaks, CA: Pine Forge Press, 1996.

Rogaski, Ruth. *Hygienic Modernity: Meanings of Health and Disease in Treaty-Port China*. Berkeley: University of California Press, 2004.

Roquet, Paul. *Ambient Media: Japanese Atmospheres of Self*. Minneapolis: University of Minnesota Press, 2016.

Ross, Julian. "Beyond the Frame: Intermedia and Expanded Cinema in 1960–1970s Japan." PhD diss., University of Leeds, 2014.

"Saibanetikusu o megutte" [On cybernetics]. *Shinbun kenkyū* [Newspaper studies] (January 1954): 16–21.

Sakai, Naoki. "Return to the West/Return to the East: Watsuji Tetsuro's Anthropology and Discussions of Authenticity." *boundary 2* 18, no. 3 (autumn 1991): 157–90.

Sas, Miryam. "By Other Hands: Environment and Apparatus in 1960s Intermedia." *The Oxford Handbook of Japanese Cinema*, edited by Miyao Daisuke, 383–415. Oxford: Oxford University Press, 2014.

Sasahara Katsu. *Asada Takashi: Tsukuranai kenchikuka, Nihon hatsu no toshi purannā* [Asada Takashi: Japan's first urban planner and an architect who does not build]. Tokyo: Ohmsha, 2014.

Sawaragi Noi. *Sensō to banpaku* [War and the World's Fair]. Tokyo: Bijutsu shuppansha, 2005.

Schechner, Sara J. *Comets, Popular Culture, and the Birth of Modern Cosmology.* Princeton, NJ: Princeton University Press, 1997.

Scott, Robert. *Kenneth Boulding: A Voice Crying in the Wilderness.* New York: Palgrave Macmillan, 2014.

SECOM home security. Accessed August 4, 2020. https://www.secom.co.jp /homesecurity/goods/idf.html.

Shimazaki, H. T. *Vision in Japanese Entrepreneurship: The Evolution of a Security Enterprise.* London: Routledge, 1992.

Shimoda Hirotsugu. *Tsūshin kakumei to Denden kōsha* [The telecommunication revolution and the Nippon Telegraph and Telephone Public Corporation]. Tokyo: Mainichi shinbunsha, 1981.

Shimokōbe Atsushi, ed. *Jōhōshakai to no taiwa: Mirai Nihon no jōhō nettowaaku* [Dialogues with information society: Information networks for future Japan]. Tokyo: Tōyō Keizai Shinhōsha, 1970.

Siegert, Bernhard. *Cultural Techniques: Grids, Filters, Doors, and Other Articulations of the Real.* Translated by Geoffrey Winthrop-Young. New York: Fordham University Press, 2015.

Siegert, Bernhard. "(Not) in Place: The Grid, or Cultural Techniques of Ruling Spaces." In Siegert, *Cultural Techniques*, 97–120.

Sloterdijk, Peter. *Bubbles, Spheres Volume I: Microspherology.* Translated by Wieland Hoban. Cambridge, MA: MIT Press, 2011.

Sloterdijk, Peter. *Foams, Spheres Volume III: Plural Spherology.* Translated by Wieland Hoban. Cambridge, MA: MIT Press, 2016.

Sloterdijk, Peter. *Globes, Spheres Volume II: Macrospherology.* Translated by Wieland Hoban. Cambridge, MA: MIT Press, 2014.

Sloterdijk, Peter. *In the World Interior of Capital.* Translated by Wieland Hoban. Cambridge: Polity Press, 2013.

Sloterdijk, Peter. *Terror from the Air.* Translated Amy Patton and Steve Corcoran. Cambridge, MA: MIT Press, 2009.

Smil, Vaclav. *Enriching the Earth: Fritz Haber, Carl Bosch, and the Transformation of World Food Production*. Cambridge, MA: MIT Press, 2001.

Somaini, Antonio. "Walter Benjamin's Media Theory: The *Medium* and the *Apparat*." *Grey Room* 62 (January 2016): 6–41.

"Sonic Science: The High-Frequency Hearing Test." *Scientific American*, May 23, 2013. https://www.scientificamerican.com/article/bring-science-home-high -frequency-hearing/.

"The Spheres." Seattle Spheres. Accessed July 16, 2019. https://www.seattle spheres.com/.

Starosielski, Nicole. *Media Hot and Cold*. Durham, NC: Duke University Press, 2021.

Starosielski, Nicole. "Thermocultures of Geological Media." *Cultural Politics* 12, no. 3 (2016): 293–309.

Starosielski, Nicole. *The Undersea Network*. Durham, NC: Duke University Press, 2015.

Steinberg, Marc. "Management's Mediations: The Case of Toyotism." In *Media and Management*, by Rutvica Andrijasevic, Julie Yujie Chen, Melissa Gregg, and Marc Steinberg, 1–30. Minneapolis: University of Minnesota Press, 2021.

Steinberg, Marc. "McLuhan as Prescription Drug: Actionable Theory and Advertising Industries." In Steinberg and Zahlten, *Media Theory in Japan*, 131–50.

Steinberg, Marc. *The Platform Economy: How Japan Transformed the Consumer Internet*. Minneapolis: University of Minnesota Press, 2019.

Steinberg, Marc, and Alexander Zahlten, eds. *Media Theory in Japan*. Durham, NC: Duke University Press, 2017.

Sugiyama Shigeo. *Nakaya Ukichirō: Hito no yaku ni tatsu kenkyū o seyo* [Nakaya Ukichirō: Do the research that helps people]. Tokyo: Mineruva shobō, 2015.

Sumiya, Mikio. *A History of Japanese Trade and Industry Policy*. Oxford: Oxford University Press, 2001.

Suwa Haruo. *Nihon no fūsui* [Japanese feng shui]. Tokyo: Kadokawa sensho, 2018.

Takeda Haruhito. *Nihon no jōhō tsūshin sangyō shi: Futatsu no sekai kara hitotsu no sekai e* [A history of Japan's information and communication industry: From two worlds to a single world]. Tokyo: Yuhikaku, 2011.

Takeuchi, Keiichi. "Japanese Geopolitics in the 1930s and 1940s." In *Geopolitical Traditions: Critical Histories of a Century of Geopolitical Thought*. Edited by David Atkinson and Klaus Dodds. London: Routledge, 2000.

Tanaka Tomohito. *Keibigyō no shakaigaku* [The sociology of the security-guard business]. Tokyo: Akashi shoten, 2009.

Tange Kenzō. *Ippon no enpitsu kara* [From one pencil]. Tokyo: Nihon tosho sentā, 1997.

Tange Kenzō. *Nihon rettō no shōraizō: 21 seiki e no kenchiku* [The future of the Japanese archipelago: Architecture for the 21st century]. Tokyo: Kōdansha, 1966.

Tange Kenzō. "A Plan for Tokyo, 1960: Toward a Structural Reorganization." In *Architecture Culture 1943–1968: A Documentary Anthology*, edited by Joan Ockman, 325–34. New York: Columbia Books of Architecture, 1993.

Tange Kenzō and Kawazoe Noboru. "Nihon bankoku hakurankai no motarasu mono" [What Japan's World's Fair can bring]. *Shin kenchiku* [New architecture] (May 1970): 145–51.

Taniguchi Yūji. "IBM teikoku no sekai senryaku to Nihon" [The world strategies of the IBM empire and Japan]. *Keizai hyōron* [Economic review], June 1971, 174–82.

Team Random. "The General Plan." *Japan Architect* 133 (August 1967): 34.

Terada Kazuhiko and Sakagami Tsutomu. "Jinkō kōu no kenkyū" [Research on aritificial rain]. *Kaishō to kishō* [Oceanic weather and weather] 6, no. 2–4 (December 1954): 1–3.

Terebijon gijutsushi henshū iinkai. *Terebijon gijutsu shi* [A history of television technology]. Tokyo: Terebijon gakkai, 1971.

Thukral, Ruchi. "Sony's Wearable, Pocket-Sized Air Conditioner Is Finally Available for Sale!" *Yanko Design*, July 6, 2020. https://www.yankodesign.com/2020/07/06/sonys-wearable-pocket-sized-air-conditioner-is-finally-available-for-sale/.

Tilton, Mark. *Restrained Trade: Cartels in Japan's Basic Materials Industries*. Ithaca, NY: Cornell University Press, 1996.

Tolon, Kaya. "Future Studies: A New Social Science Rooted in Cold War Strategic Thinking." In *Cold War Social Science: Knowledge Production, Liberal Democracy, and Human Nature*, edited by Mark Solovey and Hamilton Cravens. New York: Palgrave Macmillan, 2012.

Tōno Yoshiaki. "Shokkakuteki to iu koto" [On being tactile]. *SD* 38 (January 1968): 6–8.

Toyokawa Saikaku. "The Core System and Social Scale: Design Methodology at the Tange Laboratory." Translated by Watanabe Hiroshi. In *Kenzō Tange: Architecture for the World*, edited by Seng Kuan and Yukio Lippit. Zurich: Lars Müller and the president and fellows of Harvard College, 2012.

Toyokawa Saikaku. *Gunzō to shite Tange kenkyūshitsu: Sengo Nihon kenchiku toshi shi no meinsutoriimu* [The Tange Lab as a group: The mainstream of postwar Japanese architecture and the history of urban design]. Tokyo: Ohmsha, 2012.

Toyokawa Saikaku. "Kanreichi kyojūkenkyū to nankyoku Shōwa kichi: Asada Takashi no kapuseru kenchikuron" [Research on cold climate housing and the Shōwa Station in Antarctica: Asada Takashi's capsule architecture]. In Hirose et al., *Metaborizumu no mirai toshi ten* [Metabolism: The city of the future], 235–41.

Toyokawa Saikaku. *Tange Kenzō to toshi* [Tange Kenzō and cities]. Tokyo: Kajima shuppan, 2017.

Treinish, Lloyd. "Deep Thunder Now Hyper-Local on a Global Scale." IBM. June 15, 2016. https://www.ibm.com/blogs/research/2016/06/deep-thunder-now-hyper-local-global/.

Tsuchiya Iwao. "Kishō seigyo, Kikō kaizō" [Weather control and climate engineering]. *Kishō kenkyū nōto* [Meteorological research notes] 104 (June 1970): 143–264.

Tsukio Yoshio. "Toshi keikaku no tame no gengo taikei: URTRAN" [A language system for urban planning: URTRAN]. *Computopia* (February 1969): 109–14.

Tuathail, Gearóid Ó. *Critical Geopolitics*. Minneapolis: University of Minnesota Press, 1996.

Turner, Fred. *The Democratic Surround: Multimedia and American Liberalism from World War II to the Psychedelic Sixties*. Berkeley: University of California Press, 2014.

Turner, Fred. *From Counterculture to Cyberculture: Stewart Brand, the Whole Earth Network, and the Rise of Digital Utopianism*. Chicago: University of Chicago Press, 2006.

Umesao Tadao. *Bunmei no seitaishi kan* [An ecological view of the history of civilization]. Tokyo: Chūōkōronsha, 1967.

Umesao Tadao, Katō Hidetoshi, Kawazoe Noboru, Komatsu Sakyō, and Hayashi Yūjirō, eds. *Miraigaku no teishō* [A proposal for futurology]. Tokyo: Nihon seisan honbu, 1967.

Veracini, Lorenzo. *Settler Colonialism: A Theoretical Overview*. London: Palgrave Macmillan, 2010.

Viola, Bill. "Music for Fog Sculpture Event by Fujiko Nakaya, Kawaji Onsen, Japan, 1980." In *Fujiko Nakaya: Fog, Kiri, Brouillard*, 150–55. Paris: Éditions Anarchive, 2012.

Walker, Brett L. *Toxic Archipelago: A History of Industrial Disease in Japan*. Seattle: University of Washington Press, 2010.

Walker, Gabrielle. *An Ocean of Air: A Natural History of the Atmosphere*. London: Bloomsbury, 2007.

Wark, McKenzie. *Molecular Red: Theory for the Anthropocene*. London: Verso, 2015.

Watsuji Tetsurō. *Fūdo: Ningengaku teki kōsatsu* [Climate and culture: Some humanistic reflections]. Tokyo: Iwanami bunko, 1979.

"WDC (howaito dēta sentā) kōsō" [The Structure of the WDC (White Data Center)]. Accessed August 8, 2019. http://www.city.bibai.hokkaido.jp/jyumin/docs/2015090100125/.

Whitehead, Mark. *State, Science and the Skies: Governmentalities of the British Atmosphere*. West Sussex, UK: Wiley-Blackwell, 2009.

Wiener, Norbert. *Cybernetics or Control of Communication in the Animal and the Machine*. New York: John Wiley, 1948.

Wiener, Norbert. *The Human Use of Human Beings: Cybernetics and Society*. Boston: Da Capo Press, 1954.

Wiener, Norbert. Papers. Massachusetts Institute of Technology, Archives and Special Collections, Cambridge, Massachusetts.

Wigley, Mark. "Network Fever." In *New Media, Old Media: A History and Theory Reader*, edited by Wendy Hui Kyong Chun and Thomas Keenan, 375–98. London: Routledge, 2006.

Williamson, Colin. *Hidden in Plain Sight: An Archaeology of Magic and the Cinema*. New Brunswick, NJ: Rutgers University Press, 2015.

Woods, Derek. "Scale Critique for the Anthropocene." *Minnesota Review* 83, no. 1 (2014): 133–42.

Yamamuro Shin'ichi. "Kokumin teikoku: Nihon no keisei to kūkan chi" [The nationalist empire: The formation of Japan and its spatial knowledge]. In *'Teikoku' Nihon no gakuchi: Kūkan keisei to sekai ninshiki* [Imperial Japan's learning: The formation of space and the cognition of the world], edited by Yamamuro Shin'ichi, 20–76. Tokyo: Iwanami shoten, 2006.

Yamamoto Yūzō. *'Dai tōa kyōei ken' keizai shi kenkyū* [A study of the economic history of the Greater East Asia Co-Prosperity Sphere]. Tokyo: Nagoya daigaku shuppankai, 2011.

Yang, Daqing. *Technology of Empire: Telecommunications and Japanese Expansion in Asia, 1883–1945*. Cambridge, MA: Harvard University Asia Center, 2010.

Yatsuka Hajime. "Hon tenrankai no kōsei: 'Metaborizumu nekusasu' to iu 'kindai no chōkoku'" [The trajectory of this exhibit: An overcoming of modernity called the "metabolism nexus"]. In Hirose et al., *Metaborizum no mirai toshi ten*, 10–16.

Yatsuka Hajime. "Kikigatari chōsa: Tange Kenkyūshitsu no āban dezain 1960–70" [An oral history: Tange Lab's urban design 1960–70]. In *Tange Kenzō o kataru: Shoki kara 1970 nendai ni made no kiseki* [Speaking of Tange Kenzō: A trajectory from the early years to the 1970s], edited by Maki Fumihiko and Kamiya Kōji, 176–215. Tokyo: Kajima shuppankai, 2013.

Yatsuka Hajime. *Metaborizumu nekusasu* [Metabolism nexus]. Tokyo: Ohmsha, 2011.

Yatsuka Hajime. *Shisō to shite no Nihon kindai kenchiku* [Modern Japanese architecture as thought]. Tokyo: Iwanami shoten, 2005.

Yoneyama, Lisa. *Hiroshima Traces: Time, Space, and the Dialectics of Memory*. Berkeley: University of California Press, 1999.

Yoneyama, Lisa. "Toward a Decolonial Genealogy of the Transpacific." *American Quarterly* 69, no. 3 (September 2017): 471–82. doi:10.1353/aq.2017.0041.

Yoshimoto Hideyuki. "Denki jigyō to jinkō kōu" [The electric power industry and artificial rain]. *Denryoku* [Electric power] 46, no. 5 (May 1962): 12–21.

Young, Louise. *Japan's Total Empire: Manchuria and the Culture of Wartime Imperialism*. Berkeley: University of California Press, 1998.

Zahlten, Alexander. *The End of Japanese Cinema: Industrial Genres, National Times, and Media Ecologies*. Durham, NC: Duke University Press, 2017.

Zhang, Qiong. "From 'Dragonology' to Meteorology: Aristotelian Natural Philosophy and the Beginning of the Decline of the Dragon in China." *Early Science and Medicine* 14, nos. 1–3 (2009): 340–68.

climatic determinism, 15–16, 88, 174, 182n42

climatic media: artwork and, 26, 42; atmospheric control and, 8–9, 23, 103, 161, 166; computers as, 44, 47; feedback loops and, 165; genealogy and term usage, 2–4, 43, 44, 177n5; greenhouse architecture as, 82, 85, 98, 100, 102; Metabolist architecture as, 21, 105, 117, 129; tear gas and networked surveillance as, 133, 134, 136, 137–38, 161, 163–64; transpacific geopolitical context of, 18, 20, 138, 171

closed-circuit television, 135, 138, 157–58, 161, 211n89

cloud computing: infrastructure of, 2, 19, 25–26, 44, 46–47; networked surveillance and, 157, 161

cloud(s): chamber, 29, 42; formation, 56; intercepting, 35; mimetic replication of, 29–30; projections onto, 27–28

cloud seeding, 20–21, 52, 183n6; to block sunlight, 130, 131; to bring artificial rain, 12, 13, 166, 181n33; for electricity production, 37; military applications, 35–36; Project Cirrus, 34

Club of Rome, 59, 122

cold climate regions, 6, 20, 91; architecture for, 84, 86–87, 98–100; data centers located in, 25–26, 46

Cold War, 3, 4, 35, 69, 135; architectural projects, 84, 86–87, 97, 101; arms race, 136; bunkers/fallout shelters, 46–47, 199n2; computer simulations and, 63–64, 153; future forecasting and, 58, 60, 63, 74; meteorological research and, 55–56; space race, 84, 121; transpacific geopolitics of, 17–18, 49, 51, 55, 74, 161, 175

Columbus, Christopher, 84, 193n7

commodities, 77–78, 104, 172, 179n16; distribution of, 125, 146; waste as, 113, 127

communication systems: biological metaphors for, 94–96; cybernetics and, 138, 140, 144; data, 68, 72–73, 160, 162; interactivity and, 152; organization and, 145

Compton, Karl, 141

computers. *See* digital computers

computer simulations, 55, 59, 63–64, 153, 190n39, 210n72

computopia, 64–66, 68–71, 73

conduct or behavior, 134, 137, 179n15, 206n33, 211n89; atmospheric control and, 2, 8–9

Continental Science Institute (Manchuria), 99, 198n56

control rooms, 134–35; Expo '67 (Montreal), 158–60, 159; Expo '70 (Osaka), 71, 73, 150, 151, 155–56, 156, 158, 208n60; NASA, 150, 155, 208n59

corporate management, 67

cosmologies, 11–12, 13

Cowen, Deborah, 125

crowd control, 19, 64, 157–58, 160–61, 211n94; tear gas usage, 133–34

Crowley, David, 100–101

Crutzen, Paul, 17, 130, 203n60

cryospheric research, 5, 87

cultural atmospherics, 204n1

cultural techniques, 9–12, 77, 83

cybernetics, 15, 19, 59, 163; management, 202n43; as a political technique of control, 144–45, 156, 206n33; responsive environments, 149–56; systems theory and, 14, 85, 94, 124–25, 137; Tange Lab and, 146–49; Wiener's works and reception in Japan, 96, 135, 138, 139–44, 205n19

data centers, 134; air-conditioning and electricity usage, 11, 25, 44, 46–47, 187n1; artificial fog for cooling, 8, 19, 23, 44; cold climate regions for, 25–26

data processing, 67, 160, 208n54

Davis, Heather, 108

DeLoughrey, Elizabeth, 175

digital computers, 11, 22, 35, 79, 151, 157; cybernetic systems and, 14–15; futurology and, 20, 49–50, 59, 63–66; Japanese and US developers, 51, 66–68; weather forecasting and, 10, 51, 52–54, 56–57. *See also* control rooms; networked computing

disaster prevention, 164

domed cities, 12, 19, 21, 85, 103; Arctic, 99–101; Manhattan, 72, 73

Duguet, Anne-Marie, 184n18

houses, 179n16, 193n6; on modernity, 38, 83–84, 168–69

smartphones, 6, 48, 68, 76, 108; apps, 1, 50

smart technologies, 2, 23, 134, 163, 164; air conditioners, 20, 23, 50, 51, 74–75, 78

smart urbanism, 22, 23, 134, 155, 163, 164, 175

smoke and smoke screens, 28–30, 40, 184n18

snow: artificial, 5, 19, 31, 33–34, 46, 198n56; natural, 18, 26, 34, 46

Snow, Ice, and Permafrost Research Establishment (SIPRE), 5, 33

Snow Crystals (1939), 34

social conditioning, 163, 164, 172; air-conditioning and, 2, 8–9, 22, 165, 166, 179n18; tear gas and networked surveillance as, 19, 133–34, 158, 161

soil nutrients, 111–13, 114

solar radiation, 1, 130

space capsules, 21, 121, 122, 124, 127, 155

space colonies, 80, 83–85, 100–103, 199n66

Spaceship Earth, 117, 121, 122, 125, 126, 127

Starosielski, Nicole, 6, 49, 172, 187n1

state, organicist theory of, 88–89, 91–92, 96, 196n20

Steinberg, Marc, 204n14

stratosphere, 21–22, 23, 130–31

sulfur dioxide, 22, 116, 117, 130–31

surveillance cameras, 8, 68, 135, 157–58; Hitachi's, 76. *See also* networked surveillance

sustainable development, 33, 122–24, 126; architecture and, 21, 106, 127, 131

synthetic materials, 28, 99–100, 104, 108. *See also* plastics

systems theory, 58, 122, 147; cybernetics and, 14, 85, 94, 124–25, 137; logistical management and, 126

Taiwan, 91, 115

Tange Kenzō, 59, 85, 109, 195n16, 195n19, 204n13; Arctic City design, 99–100, 102; interest in cybernetics, 96, 138–39, 145; Middle East projects, 128–29; *A Plan for Tokyo, 1960*, 94, 95, 155; use of biological metaphors for urban systems, 94–96; vision of urban planning, 93–94, 145,

197n40, 210n81; wartime design competition, 86, 194n14

Tange Lab, 20–21, 59, 71; avant-garde of, 69; Festival Plaza roof design (Expo '70), 99, 108, 131; imperial roots, 5, 88, 90; Metabolist architects, 14, 85–86, 104–5, 109; national land planning activities, 90; oil economy and financing of, 128–29; proto-capsule housing design, 84, 86–87, 98–99; smart urbanism, 155; studies of information flows, 146–49; use of computer simulations, 64–65, 190n39

Taumoepeau, Latai, 167

tear gas: chemical composition, 135; failures of, 165, 166; networked surveillance and, 22, 23, 161; policing and, 9, 22, 135, 164–65; social conditioning and, 19, 133–34

technocracy, 69–71, 79, 144, 191n62

telecommunication: clouds and, 27; industries, 67, 71, 148–49, 157, 162; infrastructure, 17, 91, 92–93, 97, 125; nervous system comparison, 96, 198n49

telegraphy, 27, 90, 96–97, 198n49

temperature: body, 76, 119; control, 6, 49, 52, 57; Earth's, 22, 130–31; greenhouse, 81; perception of, 73; regulation of, 25; rising, 23

terraforming, 102, 103, 199n66

territorialization, 20–21, 103; atmospheric, 3, 51, 77–78; the future and, 62, 63, 76, 189n36; geopolitics of, 79, 88, 97; Japanese expansion, 33, 54, 62, 85–87, 194n9

thermal manipulation, 6, 49, 187n1

thermostat: "human," 57; planetary, 14, 15, 130; virtual, 1, 49

thermostatic desire, 11, 21, 49, 101, 167; atmospheric control and, 57, 82, 87, 100, 103, 108, 199n66; atmospheric future and, 20, 74, 79, 131, 166; concept, 2

think tanks, 14, 58, 60, 91, 189n30

Toffler, Alvin, 60

Tokyo, 96, 106, 137; layout and design, 94, 95, 153; management of human waste, 112–13, 114